Pattern, Price & Time

Founded in 1807, John Wiley & Sons is the oldest independent publishing company in the United States. With offices in North America, Europe, Australia, and Asia, Wiley is globally committed to developing and marketing print and electronic products and services for our customers' professional and personal knowledge and understanding.

The Wiley Trading series features books by traders who have survived the market's ever changing temperament and have prospered—some by reinventing systems, others by getting back to basics. Whether a novice trader, professional, or somewhere in-between, these books will provide the advice and strategies needed to prosper today and well into the future.

For a list of available titles, please visit our Web site at www.WileyFinance.com.

Pattern, Price & Time

Using Gann Theory in Technical Analysis

Second Edition

JAMES A. HYERCZYK

WILEY

John Wiley & Sons, Inc.

Published by John Wiley & Sons, Inc., Hoboken, New Jersey.
Published simultaneously in Canada.

The Gann charts were produced using Ganntrader 2.1; copyright © 1996 by Peter A. Pich. Release: 2.113, SN: 35182. Gannsoft Publishing Company, 509-548-5990.

Microsoft Excel is a registered trademark of Microsoft Corporation.

Navigator Software is a registered trademark of Genesis Financial Data Services.

TradeStation is registered trademarks of Omega Research Inc.

For general information on our other products and services or for technical support, please contact our Customer Care Department within the United States at (800) 762-2974, outside the United States at (317) 572-3993 or fax (317) 572-4002.

Wiley also publishes its books in a variety of electronic formats. Some content that appears in print may not be available in electronic books. For more information about Wiley products, visit our web site at www.wiley.com.

Library of Congress Cataloging-in-Publication Data:

Hyerczyk, James A.
  Pattern, price & time : using Gann theory in technical analysis / James A. Hyerczyk. – 2nd ed.
    p. cm. – (Wiley trading series)
  Includes index.
  ISBN 978-0-470-43202-0 (cloth)
  1. Speculation. 2. Gann, William D., b. 1878. I. Title. II. Title: Pattern, price, and time. III. Series.
  HG6015.H94 2009
  332.64′5–dc22

                                     2008048191

ISBN-13 978-0-470-43202-0

10 9 8 7 6 5 4 3 2

Contents

Preface

I'm sure you've all heard the expression, "The more things change, the more they remain the same." This is true when it comes to technical analysis. Although there have been advances in technology since the first edition of *Pattern, Price & Time* was published in 1998, the markets are still creating patterns, making percentage retracements, or hitting cycle lows just as they were in 1998 and even before then.

With each new software program there seems to be another way to analyze and trade the markets with some new oscillator or indicator in an attempt by the trader to gain an edge. Unfortunately, this theme of smoothing out valuable information like the Open, High, Low, and Close has, in my opinion, created more difficult trading conditions. Today, despite all the new technical analysis tools and equations, the definitions of an uptrend—higher tops and higher bottoms—and of a downtrend—lower tops and lower bottoms—have remained unchanged for decades. Today, while traders remain fascinated with smoothing out data in an effort to get the edge, the art of analysis of the simple basic data has been cast aside.

As I wrote in the first edition of *Pattern, Price & Time*, my intention is not to write about W. D. Gann, but instead to write a book about what I consider to be the major themes of Gann's work: pattern, price, and time. In addition, I wanted to write a book that can be used by the analyst and trader who can apply Gann's basic rules to the markets without having to learn astrology or buy Gann wheels and plastic overlays. I wanted to write a book that would introduce a trader to techniques that would allow a trader to take basic data that is available every day and through study, experimentation, and practice create sound market analysis.

My experience in the futures business has shown me that too often traders become hooked on either pattern, price, or time in their analysis. They tend to weight their analysis one way without an equal balance. The most common mistakes are systems built around time to enter and price to exit, or price to enter and time to exit. In addition, traders who use pattern often enter or exit at poor prices or with poor timing. These observations provided further evidence that a combination of all three methods is necessary for success in the marketplace. It is on this premise that I have based my book.

As I outlined this edition of the book, I decided to maintain my original objective to write about the simplest approaches that would demonstrate how each of Gann's methods worked individually, and how each method worked in combination. In *Pattern, Price & Time*, 2nd edition, I even decided to include other popular pattern, price, and time indicators to show how they can be incorporated with Gann's basic premise of balancing price and time.

After a brief introduction as to why I choose to write about pattern, price, and time, I introduce W. D. Gann and his theory. I follow this up with information on the importance of having correct data and charts. This is followed by descriptions of the key elements of technical analysis: pattern, price, and time. In the pattern chapters, I discuss trend indicators and chart formations. In the price chapters, percentage retracements and Gann angles are detailed, followed by a chapter on combining pattern and price. Finally, concepts of time analysis finish the core analysis techniques. The last chapter demonstrates the effects of combining pattern, price, and time into an analysis and trading tool.

After the last book was published, I received criticism that I was holding back on Gann's secrets. This could not be further from the truth. I stated in the book that teaching financial astrology was beyond the scope of this book and could take years to learn and apply. I stated it was not my intention to write or teach financial astrology. I can say that if you understand the basics of this book then learn financial astrology, you will have an edge over those who only know astrology because, after all, astrology is a time indicator. Remember that although Gann said that time was most important in identifying changes in trend, price and time and money management are just as important when trading. In order to appease those who feel I am keeping secrets, I will publish a few surprises in this book that will point those who want to study the metaphysical elements of Gann analysis in the right direction. This includes what I believe is the source of his Law of Vibration and a list of books that he recommended. In an effort to provide the reader with more automation I've attached a link to the TradeStation code for my trend indicator at www.wiley.com/hyerczyk. This will allow the reader to create swing charts in the same manner as W. D. Gann.

In conclusion, this book is intended to be educational and informative. It is by no means intended to replace the books and courses written by W. D. Gann. At times the book may seem repetitive, especially in the chapters about the trend indicator. This is done intentionally because I wanted to emphasize, just as Gann did in his books, that the analyst must study, experiment, and practice these techniques over and over. If anything, this book should be used by the novice as an introduction to the subjects of pattern, price, and time. It should be required reading before computerized analysis is attempted. It is very important to learn how pattern, price, and time techniques work before using computerized trading indicators. This book will provide a good base for the analyst who wants to use more sophisticated technical analysis techniques. The expert trader could also use this book to enhance his or her analysis or trading abilities. While Gann analysis concepts are discussed in this book, it is not intended to be a book solely on Gann analysis as many original ideas and techniques are introduced throughout the text. Gann, for example, left no record on how to trade stock indices, Treasury bonds, or Forex markets. Although at times limited by page size in this book, I believe pattern, price, and time analysis is presented in a detailed but clear manner. I hope that you find the ideas in the book as useful as I have.

James A. Hyerczyk
Palos Park, Illinois
September 2008

Acknowledgments

I would like to thank my wife, Mary Colleen, and my daughters Amy, Kelly, and Erin for giving me the time and the space to pursue my passion for technical analysis. Each of you has a special place in my heart, and I love you all very much.

Pattern, Price & Time

CHAPTER 1

Why Pattern, Price, and Time?

D espite the proliferation of trading analysis programs claiming to have "new" indicators and "new" ways to analyze the markets, I've come to the conclusion that there really is not anything new under the sun and that all of these discoveries can be placed into the categories of pattern, price, and time.

Ever since the early days of trading up until today, traders have been trying to create ways to manipulate data in an effort to find an edge over everyone else. Today's sophisticated programs have the ability to smooth data and create sophisticated formulas to make the market's basic data appear to show anything the programs want to find. Some programs create moving averages, while others try to break down the markets into oscillators that move between 0 and 100. All of these new ways to look at data may be fine for some, provided that they understand how these numbers are created, and the programs create rules on how to use them, but I find working with the original Open, High, Low, and Close data to be most beneficial. In addition, while I acknowledge that using computer-generated oscillators or indicators may speed up the process of analyzing a market, I have found that all of these smoothing tools will eventually collapse to or agree with my simple analysis of the markets using the Open, High, Low, and Close.

This book, although it is concerned with the technical analysis approaches to trading Forex, futures, and equities, should not be considered the definitive answer to making tremendous amounts of money in trading. Instead it should be used as a guideline to give the trader an edge as to what is actually taking place in the marketplace. My application of pattern, price, and time analysis allows me to see and understand what is happening in the markets. It does not hide anything in complicated formulas or computer number crunching. Although this is a personal preference, I feel that the analyst who understands how pattern, price, and time work independently and in unison with each other creates an edge to trading the markets that computerized analysis cannot.

Throughout the book the reader will see the phrase "study and experiment." This is because the reader is encouraged to learn as much as he can about the movements of the markets, the characteristics of these movements, and how to make informed trading decisions once this knowledge is applied.

The basic premise behind pattern, price, or time analysis is that these three factors have not changed in the 100 or more years since Charles Dow unleashed his Dow Theory to the world. In fact, if you want to go back even further, take a look at Candlestick analysis which is said to have its roots back to the 1700s. This very popular analysis tool is a study of pattern with basic Open, High, Low, and Close the major elements. Despite the proliferation of today's "new" trading analysis tools and trading systems as a result of the personal computer and trading software, trading tools used today can nevertheless still be categorized as pattern, price, or time.

Today's pattern studies include stochastic indicators, relative strength indicators, overbought/oversold indicators, moving average crossovers, and Candlesticks. Price is categorized as moving averages, daily pivots, and retracements. Finally, time is used today in the form of seasonality, cycles, and time of day studies.

Hang around a trading room long enough, and you will often hear, "I had the right price, but was a little early" or "I've got a cycle low due at 11:00, I just don't know where the market will stop." These are the types of problems that can be created by using only price, or only time, or only a pattern. In this book I want to show the trader that there is a way to bring the factors of pattern, price, and time together in an effort to improve trading results.

When studying the history of technical analysis I came across several valid methodologies to analyze and trade the markets, but I found that these methods were weighted toward only one of the three main components of pattern, price, and time. This created problems for me because although at times one of these factors had control of the market, I found I did not have control of the trade. This frustration caused me to study the disciplines of Elliott and Dow, but I found personal issues with each. One relied too much on the forecast and prevented me from changing my mind while in a trade. My ego became too connected to the forecast, and I often failed to make necessary adjustments to the trade. The other analysis technique took too long to develop. I also tried to work with point and figure charts, and although I understood how to use the formations, I still felt time was necessary to help me become a better trader. When Candlestick analysis became readily available on the computer, I tried to use it, but found some of the patterns occurred too frequently and at random places on the chart, so I sensed that price and time would be necessary to improve this sort of analysis.

All of this study and experimentation of these other analysis disciplines led me back to the pattern, price, and time analysis of W. D. Gann. I chose Gann Theory as my primary source of analysis because throughout his works he wrote about the balance of price and time. This became very important to me because my work needed balance. I knew from my analysis and trading that I could not just rely on pattern, or price, or time independently. I knew that although I could use his techniques independently, I could improve

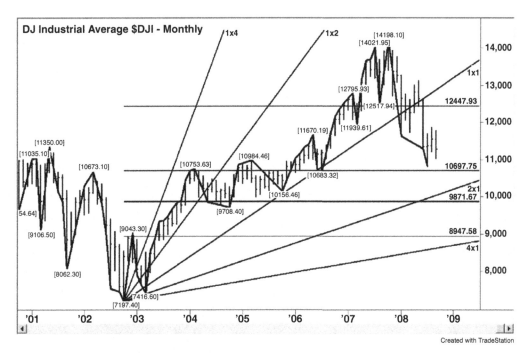

FIGURE 1.1 Gann Format Monthly Dow Jones Chart
Copyright © TradeStation.

my analysis and trading by finding a balance between his two or three key elements of pattern, price, and time (Figure 1.1).

In summary, the purpose of this book is to inform the trader of the analysis tools that are available just using the Open, High, Low, and Close. The other purpose is to teach the trader to categorize his trading tools into pattern, price, and time techniques and to apply combinations of the three to improve his analysis and trading. Finally, in an effort to jump-start the reader's study and experimentation of pattern, price, and time, I have chosen to highlight the analysis and trading techniques of W. D. Gann because he was one of the first to speak of the balance of price and time.

CHAPTER 2

Who Was W. D. Gann?

I f not the first technical market analyst, W. D. Gann was certainly among the more successful. Creating and publicizing a new approach to analyzing markets, Gann claimed that he had set a world's record in leverage and accuracy more than once, that he had developed trading strategies for speculators, and that he could predict market moves to exact price levels.

William Delbert Gann was born on a cotton ranch on June 6, 1878, in Lufkin, Texas. He displayed a strong aptitude in mathematics during his early years, completed a high school education, and started trading in 1902 at the age of 24. By his own admission, Gann's early trading was based on "hope, fear and greed," all of which he later realized were not compatible with a successful trading strategy.

After losing significant sums of money, Gann began to observe that markets followed mathematical laws and certain time cycles. He was particularly interested in the connection between price and time, a relationship he referred to as the "square" of price and time. He began studying this interaction diligently, even traveling to England, India, and Egypt to research mathematical theory and historical prices.

In developing his theories, Gann was undoubtedly one of the most industrious technical analysts. He made thousands of charts displaying daily, weekly, monthly, and yearly prices for a wide variety of stocks and commodities. He was an avid researcher, occasionally charting a price back hundreds of years. At a time when most market analysis was strictly fundamental, Gann's revolutionary theories relied on natural laws of mathematics, time cycles, and his unshakable conviction that past market activity predicted future activity.

Gann moved to New York City in 1908. He opened brokerage offices at 18 Broadway and began testing his theories and techniques in the market. Within a year it was clear to others that Gann's success was based on more than just luck. A December 1909 article in *The Ticker and Investment Digest* explained that "... Mr. Gann has developed an entirely new idea as to the principles governing stock market movements" (reprinted in the W. D. Gann Commodities Course [Pomeroy, WA: Lambert-Gann Publishing, 178]).

In this article, Gann asserted that most traders enter the market without any knowledge or study, and that most eventually lose money. He explained that he noticed a cyclic recurrence in the rise and fall of stocks and commodities, and decided to study and apply natural laws to trading strategy. Gann indicated that months of studying at the British Museum in London revealed what he called the "Law of Vibration." This law determines the exact points to which a stock would rise or fall, and predicts the effect well before the Street is aware of either the cause or the effect. Beyond this vague explanation, Gann was reticent about his strategies and unwilling to explain his theories in any detail.

Although past success is not an indication of future results, Gann's trading was extremely successful, at least to a point. An analysis of his trading record over 25 market days revealed that Gann made 286 trades, 264 of which were profitable. His success rate of 92.31 percent turned an initial investment of $450 into $37,000. A colleague of Gann's said, "I once saw him take $130.00 and in less than one month run it up to over $12,000.00. He can compound money faster than any man I ever met." It is not surprising that the press concluded ". . . such performances as these. . . . are unparalleled in the history of the street" (Gann Course, 180). Although Gann's theories were apparently profitable at times, he was equally subject to the potentially substantial risk of loss that is inherent in commodities futures trading.

Gann issued annual market predictions of major moves and exact support and resistance levels (Figure 2.1). Newspapers around the country kept track of his predictions for 1921, 1922, and 1923, substantiating his accuracy. In January 1929, he issued an annual forecast that read:

> *September—One of the sharpest declines of the year is indicated. There will be a loss of confidence by investors and the public will try to get out after it is too late. . . . A "Black Friday" is indicated and a panicky decline in stocks with only small rallies.*
>
> *Truth of the Stock Tape* (reprint Pomeroy, WA: Lambert-Gann
> Publishing, 1976, 36).

His facility in analysis and prediction extended to areas other than the market. He predicted the exact date of the Kaiser's abdication, the end of World War I, and the elections of presidents Wilson and Harding. Gann also predicted the occurrence of World War II 13 years in advance and described the stealth bomber 61 years before its invention.

Gann's original reticence about his success later turned into an almost religious fervor to share his knowledge. He had begun writing during his trading career, starting with *Truth of the Stock Tape*, written in 1923 (originally published by Financial Guardian Publishing Co.; reprinted by Lambert-Gann Publishing Co.). This book was intended to help traders analyze market activity using a standard stock tape. In 1927, he wrote *The Tunnel Thru the Air: Or, Looking Back from 1940* (reprint Pomeroy, WA: Lambert-Gann Publishing Co., 1976). This seemingly autobiographical novel provides

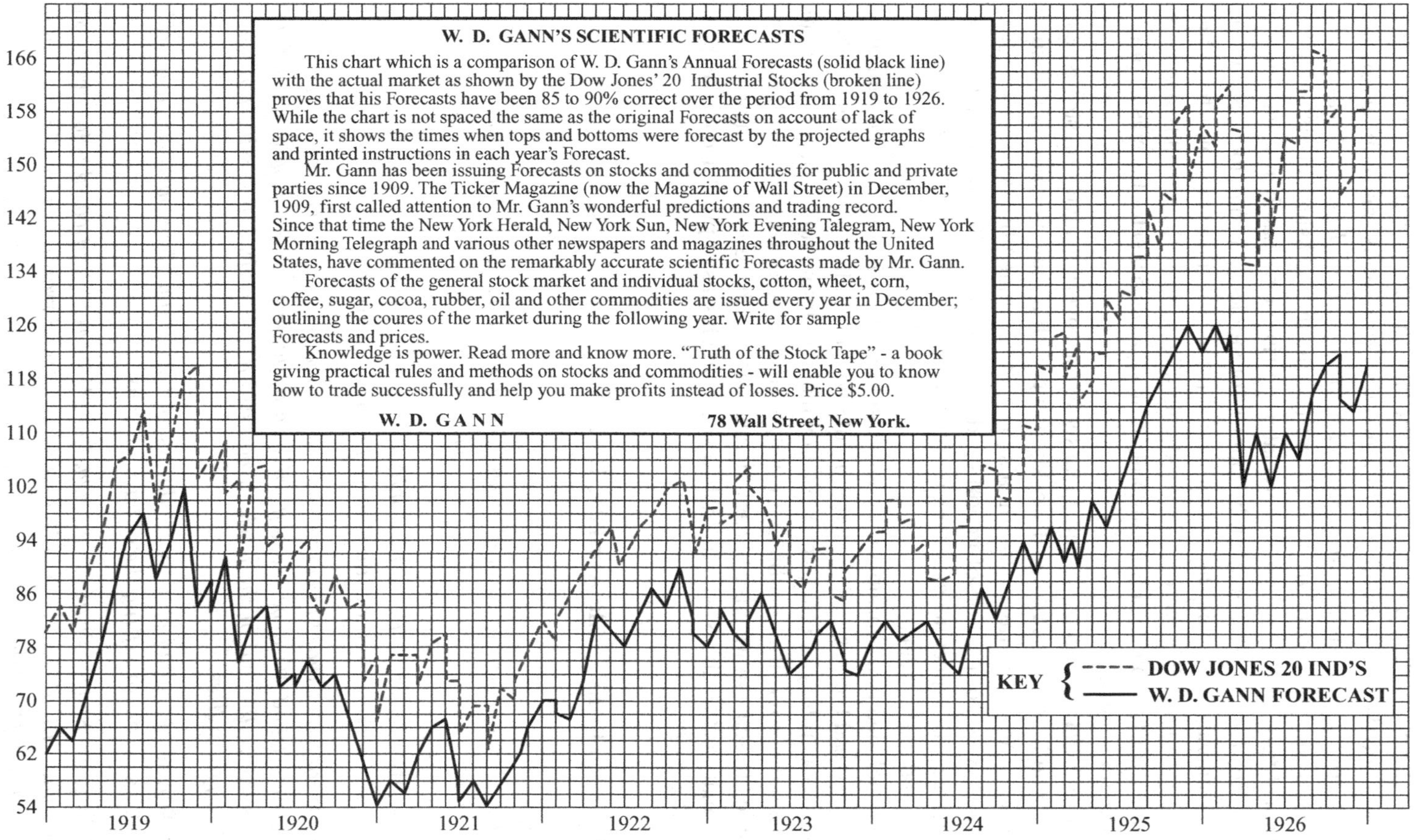
W. D. GANN'S SCIENTIFIC FORECASTS
This chart which is a comparison of W. D. Gann's Annual Forecasts (solid black line) with the actual market as shown by the Dow Jones' 20 Industrial Stocks (broken line) proves that his Forecasts have been 85 to 90% correct over the period from 1919 to 1926. While the chart is not spaced the same as the original Forecasts on account of lack of space, it shows the times when tops and bottoms were forecast by the projected graphs and printed instructions in each year's Forecast.
Mr. Gann has been issuing Forecasts on stocks and commodities for public and private parties since 1909. The Ticker Magazine (now the Magazine of Wall Street) in December, 1909, first called attention to Mr. Gann's wonderful predictions and trading record. Since that time the New York Herald, New York Sun, New York Evening Talegram, New York Morning Telegraph and various other newspapers and magazines throughout the United States, have commented on the remarkably accurate scientific Forecasts made by Mr. Gann.
Forecasts of the general stock market and individual stocks, cotton, wheet, corn, coffee, sugar, cocoa, rubber, oil and other commodities are issued every year in December; outlining the coures of the market during the following year. Write for sample Forecasts and prices.
Knowledge is power. Read more and know more. "Truth of the Stock Tape" - a book giving practical rules and methods on stocks and commodities - will enable you to know how to trade successfully and help you make profits instead of losses. Price $5.00.
W. D. GANN
78 Wall Street, New York.
166
158
150
142
134
126
118
110
102
94
86
78
70
62
54
1919
1920
1921
1922
1923
1924
1925
1926
KEY
DOW JONES 20 IND'S
W. D. GANN FORECAST

FIGURE 2.1 W.D. Gann's Scientific Forecasts 1919–1926

insight into Gann's trading theories and his morals. (It also includes his predictions of World War II and the stealth bomber.) He went on to write books and courses explaining his new discoveries, including *New Stock Trend Indicator, How to Make Profits in Commodities,* and *45 Years in Wall Street* (originally published in 1936, 1942, and 1949, respectively; all three books were later reprinted by Lambert-Gann Publishing Co., 1976). He also created home study courses for stocks and commodities and taught weekend seminars to explain the use of special price and time calculator tools he had invented. These materials were considered valuable enough that in 1932 people were paying $1,500 for his home study commodity course, and $5,000 for his master price and time calculator seminar.

In the late 1940s Gann published a market letter covering advice on stocks, cotton, and grain. The letter was produced weekly along with a daily version published three days a week. The letter was written in a style that combined fundamentals with chart points. There was no mention of important dates or time cycles, but it included comments such as "We expect heavy selling during the next few days and much lower prices before the end of the week."

I have included two reprints of the letter in this chapter. Because the reprints may be difficult to read I have typed the letter in full. When I studied these letters I looked for references to astrology or other timing phenomena but found none. This does not mean that Gann did not use it in his timing; it may just mean that Gann was a businessman who wanted to sell a newsletter to earn income. He may have saved his advanced price and time analysis for clients who had taken personal classes or purchased his expensive courses (Figure 2.2).

COMMODITY LETTER: April 21, 1947

Wheat
All the Grain markets showed weakness today and from Secretary Anderson's statement today, it was evident that the Government realizes that there are going to be plenty surplus commodities later and that prices will have to come down and parities lowered. The market will not wait for the Government to do something to get prices down but will decline and discount future developments.

We are confident that the market has seen final highs and is now starting on the long down-trend. We expect heavy selling during the next few days and much lower prices before the end of the week. If you are not already short, sell short without waiting for rallies.

May Wheat—*Is showing more weakness and breaking 250 could decline quickly to 240–238. We favor selling the distant options.*

July Wheat—*Short sale at the market. Very little rally indicated before big decline takes place. Breaking 218 will indicate lower and breaking 215 will be a signal for very much lower prices.*

Supply and Demand Letter

RISING PRICES   FALLING PRICES

W.D.GANN & SON, INC. · INVESTMENT ADVISERS · 82 WALL STREET, NEW YORK 5, N.Y.

The information contained herein is the editor's personal opinion, and while we believe it to be correct, we do not guarantee it.

COMMODITY LETTER   April 21, 1947

WHEAT   All the Grain markets showed weakness today and from Secretary Anderson's statement today, it was evident that the Government realizes that there are going to be plenty surplus commodities later and that prices will have to come down and parities lowered.   The market will not wait for the Government to do something to get prices down but will decline and discount future developments.

We are confident that the market has seen final highs and is now starting on the long down-trend. We expect heavy selling during the next few days and much lower prices before the end of the week. If you are not already short, sell short without waiting for rallies.

May Wheat – Is showing more weakness and breaking 250 could decline quickly to 240-238. We favor selling the distant options.

July Wheat – Short sale at the market. Very little rally indicated before big decline takes place. Breaking 218 will indicate lower and breaking 215 will be a signal for very much lower prices.

Sept. Wheat – Short sale at the market. Breaking 213 will indicate lower and breaking 210 will indicate 205-203.

CORN   Sold off Saturday and was weak and lower again today. It is getting into position for a fast decline as support levels have been broken. If you are short, stay short. If not, sell at the market.

July Corn – Breaking 163½ indicates 156-155.

Sept. Corn – Breaking 152 could decline quickly to 145-144.

OATS   Buyers are withdrawing from the market and offerings are increasing. Today's high prices are not likely to be exceeded before a decline to much lower levels.

July Oats – Breaking 78 indicates 72 or lower.

Sept. Oats – Breaking support at 72 will indicate 68 or lower.

EGGS   The market was weak on Saturday with prices recording the greatest decline for several months. There was very little rally today and the market closed weak. The buying has been overdone and the market is in a position for a sharp decline. We advise staying short.

October Eggs – Not likely to cross 49¢ and breaking 4785 indicates 4550-4500.

COTTON   The market rallied on Saturday and had a further rally early today, and the distant options sold off about 50 points while the old crop options held up, and closed strong. We advise short sales of October and December. These options are not likely to rally to today's highest before going much lower. The weather is improving and planting is making good progress. Price cutting is going on in the textile industry, and the old crop options are much too high but might hold up a while longer while hedge selling depresses the new crop options. We consider this a real opportunity to go short of October and December.

Oct. Cotton – Breaking 2940 will indicate lower and breaking 2900 indicates 2800 or lower.

Dec. Cotton – Breaking 2860 indicates lower and breaking 2800 will be in a very weak position and could decline fast.

W. D. GANN & SON, Inc.

FIGURE 2.2   Supply and Demand Letter, April 21, 1947

Sept. Wheat—*Short sale at the market. Breaking 213 will indicate lower and breaking 210 will indicate 205–203.*

Corn

Sold off Saturday and was weak and lower again today. It is getting into position for a fast decline as support levels have been broken. If you are short, stay short. If not, sell at the market.

July Corn—*Breaking 163$^1/_2$ indicates 156–155.*

Sept. Corn—*Breaking 152 could decline quickly to 145–144.*

Oats

Buyers are withdrawing from the market and offerings are increasing. Today's high prices are not likely to be exceeded before a decline to much lower levels.

July Oats—*Breaking 78 indicates 72 or lower.*

Sept. Oats—*Breaking support at 72 will indicate 68 or lower.*

Eggs

The market was weak on Saturday with prices recording the greatest decline for several months. There was very little rally today and the market closed weak. The buying has been overdone and the market is in a position for a sharp decline. We advise staying short.

October Eggs—*Not likely to cross 49 cents and breaking 4785 indicates 4550–4500.*

Cotton

The market rallied on Saturday and had a further rally early today and the distant options sold off about 50 points while the old crop options held up, and closed strong. We advise short sales of October and December. These options are not likely to rally to today's highest before going much lower. The weather is improving and planting is making good progress. Price cutting is going on in the textile industry, and the old crop options are much too high but might hold up a while longer while hedge selling depresses the new crop options. We consider this a real opportunity to go short of October and December.

Oct. Cotton—*Breaking 2940 will indicate lower and breaking 2900 indicates 2800 or lower.*

Dec. Cotton—*Breaking 2860 indicates lower and breaking 2800 will be in a very weak position and could decline fast.*

W.D. Gann & Son, Inc.

Gann also published a weekly market letter. In this letter he provided more information on support and resistance for the reader as well as buy/sell recommendations and stop loss suggestions (Figure 2.3).

COMMODITY LETTER: January 26, 1948

Grain

All grains declined near the close today in anticipation of a bearish Government report on stocks of grain in trade channels. This report was not foreshadowed by prior reports from the Southwest to the effect that elevator stocks had about been "cleaned out" by Government purchases. It is too early to say for sure, but if today's action was caused by factors other than the Government report there is substantial evidence that the end of the long bull market in grains is not far off. And, if May wheat is unable to close above $298^1/_2$ very shortly, we expect lower prices for all grains. Corn behaved the best. It was followed by oats and wheat, which were cleaned out yesterday, in that order.

We recommend short sales of May wheat on rallies with a stop that will reverse your position it closes above $298^1/_2$.

May Wheat—*Will meet resistance on rallies at $296^1/_4$–$8^1/_2$, $300^1/_4$–2 and 305–07. Watch the market closely at these resistance points for indications of a change in trend. After such points have been penetrated on the way up, they become support points on subsequent declines. Move stops up under them after they have been penetrated as protection against a reversal of trend.*

Will meet support on declines at $293–^1/_2$, $289^1/_2$–$90^1/_2$ and $286^1/_2$–8. Watch the market closely at these support points for indications of a change in trend. After such points have been penetrated on the way down, they become resistance points on subsequent rallies. When short, move stops down over them after they have been penetrated as protection against a reversal of trend.

July Wheat—*Will meet resistance on rallies at 264–$5^1/_2$, $267^1/_2$–$9^1/_2$, and 272–4. Will meet support on declines at $260^1/_2$–2, $257^1/_2$–9, and $253^3/_4$–5. Closing below $253^3/_4$ indicates lower. See* May Wheat *for comment on use of support and resistance points.*

May Corn—*Will meet resistance on rallies at 268–9 and $269^3/_4$–$71^3/_4$. Will meet support on declines at $264^1/_4$–5, 262–3, $258^1/_2$–60. Closing below $258^1/_2$ indicates lower. See* May Wheat *for comment on use of support and resistance points.*

July Corn—*Will meet resistance on rallies at 256–7 and $258^1/_2$–$60^1/_4$. Will receive support on declines at $251^1/_2$–$2^1/_4$ and $248^1/_2$–50. Closing below $248^1/_2$ indicates lower. See* May Wheat *for comment on use of support and resistance points.*

Supply and Demand Letter

RISING PRICES   FALLING PRICES

W.D. GANN RESEARCH, INC. · INVESTMENT ADVISERS · 82 WALL STREET, NEW YORK 5, N.Y.

COMMODITY LETTER   January 23, 1948

Advice for the Week Beginning January 26, 1948

GRAIN   All grains declined near the close today in anticipation of a bearish Government report
on stocks of grain in trade channels. This report was not foreshadowed by prior reports
from the Southwest to the effect that elevator stocks had about been "cleaned out" by Government
purchases. It is too early to say for sure, but if today's action was caused by factors other than
the Government report there is substantial evidence that the end of the long bull market in grains
is not far off. And, if May wheat is unable to close above 298½ very shortly, we expect lower prices
for all grains. Corn behaved the best. It was followed by oats and wheat, which were cleaned out
yesterday, in that order.

We recommend short sales of May wheat on rallies with a stop that will reverse your position if it closes above 298½.

May Wheat - Will meet resistance on rallies at 296½-8½, 300½-2 and 306-7. Watch the market
closely at these resistance points for indications of a change in trend. After such points have been
penetrated on the way up, they become support points on subsequent declines. Move stops up under them
after they have been penetrated as protection against a reversal of trend.

Will meet support on declines at 293-½, 289½-90½ and 286½-8. Watch the market closely at
these support points for indications of a change in trend. After such points have been penetrated
on the way down, they become resistance points on subsequent rallies. When short, move stops down
over them after they have been penetrated as protection against a reversal of trend.

July Wheat - Will meet resistance on rallies at 264-5½, 267½-9½, and 272-4. Will meet
support on declines at 280½-2, 267½-9 and 253½-5. Closing below 253½ indicates lower. See May
wheat for comment on use of support and resistance points.

May Corn - Will meet resistance on rallies at 268-9 and 269½-71½. Will meet support on
declines at 264½-5, 262-3 and 258½-60. Closing below 258½ indicates lower. See May wheat for comment
on use of support and resistance points.

July Corn - Will meet resistance on rallies at 256-7 and 258½-60½. Will receive support on
declines at 251½-2½ and 248½-50. Closing below 248½ indicates lower. See May wheat for comment on
use of support and resistance points.

May Oats - Will meet resistance on rallies at 128 and 129-¾. Will receive support on declines at 126-½, 124½-5, 122-3 and 119½-20. See May Wheat for comment on use of support and resistance points.

July Oats - Will meet resistance on rallies at 105½-6½ and 108-10½. Will receive support
on declines at 103¾-4½, 102-½, 101 and 99¼-100. See May wheat for comment on use of support and
resistance points.

EGGS   After an early rally, January eggs went off the board low and weak. Egg futures rallied and
closed fairly firm.

October Eggs - New purchases should be confined to reactions to 4990-5020. Protect long
commitments with a stop that will take you out if they break 4940 or close below 4970. Closing below 4970 indicates 4920-30, and perhaps lower. Closing above 5095 is first indication of higher
prices. Closing above 5125 indicates 5240-5300, and perhaps higher.

COTTON   Rallied yesterday in response to General Marshal's testimony. However, the rally in the
spot market was very feeble (26 points), and it lost all of this today. Spot cotton closed
in New York tonight at 3552, or about 85 points over March.

The trend of cotton is down and short sales on rallies are advised.

March Cotton - Crossing 3500 indicates 3510-30, a selling zone with a stop that will take
you out if it crosses 3570 or closes above 3540. Breaking 3415 indicates 3340-75. Closing below
3340 indicates lower.

May Cotton - Crossing 3500 indicates 3510-35, a selling zone /with a stop that will take you out if it
crosses 3560, or closes above 3540. Breaking 3425 indicates 3390-3400, and possibly 3380-70. Closing below 3370 indicates lower.

BEST TRADE - Sell Cotton on Rally as advised.

W. D. GANN RESEARCH, INC.

FIGURE 2.3 Supply and Demand Letter, January 23, 1948

May Oats - *Will meet resistance on rallies at 128 and 129–³/₄. Will receive support on declines at 126–¹/₂, 124¹/₂–5, 122–3, 119¹/₂–20. See* May Wheat *for comment on use of support and resistance points.*

July Oats—*Will meet resistance on rallies at 105 1/2–6 1/2 and 108–10 1/2. Will receive support on declines at 103³/₄–4 1/2, 102–1/2, 101 and 99 1/2–100. See May Wheat for comment on use of support and resistance points.*

Eggs
After an early rally, January eggs went off the board low and weak. Egg futures rallied and closed fairly firm.

October Eggs—*New purchases should be confined to reactions to 4990–5020. Protect long commitments with a stop that will take you out if they break 4940 or close below 4970. Closing below 4970 indicates 4920–30, and perhaps lower. Closing above 5095 is first indication of higher prices. Closing above 5125 indicates 5240–5300 and perhaps higher.*

Cotton
Rallied yesterday in response to General Marshal's testimony. However, the rally in the spot market was very feeble (26 points), and it lost all of this today. Spot cotton closed in New York tonight at 3552, or about 85 points over March.

The trend of cotton is down and short sales on rallies are advised.

March Cotton—*Crossing 3500 indicates 3510–30, a selling zone with a stop that will take you out if it crosses 3570 or closes above 3540. Breaking 3425 indicates 3390–3400, and possibly 3330–70. Closing below 3370 indicates lower.*

Best Trade
Sell Cotton on Rally as advised.

W.D. Gann Research, Inc.

As you can see from these samples, Gann was all about the trend, support, resistance, and a target. First he identified the trend, then he found prices that would accelerate the move in the direction of the trend and a price that would change the trend. Note in the first letter he signed it W.D. Gann & Son, Inc. and in the second letter W.D. Gann Research, Inc. At some time between 1947 and 1948 he is said to have had a falling out with his son John. Some Gann biographers cite his work ethic and intensity as too much to handle by his son. Others claim his son quit when Gann married a woman many years his junior.

Gann continued to refine his techniques and teach them to others until his death on June 14, 1955. From notes and papers, some of which were dated just two weeks before he died, it is evident that Gann was continuing his pursuit of a perfect trading system.

For example, there is written evidence that he was developing a three-dimensional chart that incorporated price, time, and volume, and how they applied to the market.

Since his death, rumors of a $50,000,000 fortune have circulated throughout the futures and stock industries. However, this figure is unsubstantiated by the material that was left after his death. Also, brokerage statements indicate that he traded an account with a balance in excess of $2,000,000, and his will, filed in Miami, indicates a figure considerably below $50,000,000.

I have never seen any of Gann's actual account statements other than reprinted trade confirmations in one of this courses, nor have I seen his tax returns. I have searched in various places and spoken with individuals who may have known how much money he made in the markets, but these people cannot prove the accuracy of his personal trading profits. Throughout his books and courses he did mention being successful, but never any mention of taking out as much as $50,000,000 from the markets. I can say this with conviction, the first mention of Gann's $50,000,000 fortune that I have seen is from a May 1982 *Commodities Magazine* article by Mr. Billy Jones, the man who purchased Gann's original material, books and courses from Ed Lambert. In the article one sentence was written about the $50,000,000 fortune. The sentence said "Over the next half century, Gann would take over $50 million in profits out of the markets—and keep most of it." This one sentence spawned a generation of Gann analysts and newsletter writers who still advertise today anything from "Gann made $50 million in the markets" to "Gann took $50 million from the markets from 1929 to 1932." This sentence by Billy Jones could be interpreted in many ways. Gann, for instance, may have had $50 million in profits and $49 million in losses. It is also possible since he traded a long time that he took out $1,000,000 or more per year for 50 years. No one will ever know without documentation so I consider this a moot point and irrelevant to the book. Since this amount cannot be proved, I choose not to believe it or write about how he may have accomplished it.

Most of the evidence of Gann's trading success is found in the numerous articles by newspaper writers who witnessed and verified his short-term trading activity. These articles, which have been reprinted in many of his books, highlight his trading successes in terms of both accuracy and trading results. Since Gann was a great promoter of his trading books and courses, only his successes are highlighted. Although his losing streaks and major losses are never cited, Gann always warned about the danger of trading without stop loss orders.

Following Gann's work in chronological order shows that he experienced losses when he first started to trade. In addition to trading losses, Gann also lost money in bank and brokerage firm failures. These events probably played a major part in his desire to succeed in the market. Like many traders today, Gann initially derived income from selling his advisory service and his books while simultaneously trading. His obituary lists him as an author and a stockbroker; as his popularity and success grew, however, it is probably safe to assume that he turned more of his attention to trading.

As he got older, his health began to fail, which made writing and lecturing very difficult. During this time he sold his publishing rights to Ed Lambert and formed Lambert-Gann Publishing. Based on this business deal, he was able to maintain some income by reprinting his books and courses, but, in my opinion, he focused more attention on deriving an income from the market. In May 1954, he stated "I am nearing my 76th birthday and am writing this new course of instructions, not to make money (for I have more income than I can spend) . . ." (Gann Course, 1).

Based on the physical evidence left behind and the substantiated articles highlighting his trading activity, Gann did trade the markets successfully but did not amass the huge fortune alleged by rumor.

CHAPTER 3

Gann Theory in a Nutshell

G ann Theory can be described as the study of pattern, price, and time relationships and how these relationships affect the market. Gann Theory looks at pattern, price, and time as the key important elements in forecasting the future movement of the market. While each element has its own characteristics, each also has a unique, overlapping quality.

The focus of Gann Theory is to find the interlocking relationship between these three primary indicators of changes in trend and market direction. In other words, in certain instances a pattern has a large influence on the market, while at other times price and time exert their dominance. It is the balance of these three elements, especially price and time, that creates the best trading opportunities that can lead to more success in the market. Gann Theory helps the trader to determine the best combinations of pattern, price, and time to initiate successful trades. While trades can be triggered by each element individually, a trader who weights his signal too much toward one of these elements may experience a large number of losses, whereas a trader who is patient enough to wait for a proper balancing of pattern, price, and time may experience more success.

Pattern study consists of the proper construction of minor, intermediate, and main trend-indicator swing charts and closing-price reversal patterns. Price study consists of Gann angle analysis and percentage retracements. Time study looks at swing timing, cycle timing, and historical dates. The combination of these three time factors helps the trader decide when and where to buy or sell. In this book, I describe techniques that help the trader determine how to discover these elements through proper chart construction and how they are related in trading activity.

While there is much material available *about* Gann Theory, very little of it explains *how* to put the Gann tools to practical use in a trading system. I used to think that this sort of material was valuable until I placed a stop according to some huge astrophysical law. In other words, information about the origins of cycles and price and time relationships is very interesting, but if it cannot be converted to practical use in a trading system then I consider it essentially useless. Research that reveals that a sixty-year cycle bottom is due in 2009 plus or minus two years does not help you trade soybeans profitably today. This is why you have to focus your attention on the market and what pattern, price, and time are telling you at the present.

It is my intention to focus you on the portions of Gann Theory that can be used to create a profitable trading system. My studies of Gann's original work show that he primarily used swing charts, Gann angle clusters, and cycle counts from former tops and bottoms. There also is evidence that he used astrology to initiate some trades. This latter topic is not discussed in great detail, however, as it involves a great deal of background research before it can be utilized. Since it does fall under the concept of time, which is a key element of Gann analysis, I do discuss some simple examples of how Gann applied financial astrology to the markets. In addition, Gann created and used a series of master price and time charts, which he used to determine current and future support and resistance points.

Many of his writings contain rules for trading hypothetical examples. The only evidence I found of an actual trade recommendation was in his *Master Egg Course*. This information, however, became the basis for my research, as it made clear to me what was important and what was not in developing a Gann-based trading system. Each paragraph highlighted how Gann combined pattern, price, and time into a trading strategy. In the following paragraph,[*] he speaks of his use of the Master Chart (Figure 3.1).

Example: May 3, 1949, October Eggs high 5025. This was on the timing of 168, which is 14 years, and 169 is the square of 13. Note that the price of 5010 hits 7/16 point of the circle at 5010, which would make this a resistance and selling level based on the Master Square Chart. See notes and time periods on the right hand of this Master Chart.

This example concerns his use of support and resistance angles:

I wired Chicago last night that October Eggs was a sure sale today. The reasons were as follows: Based on the angles on the daily high and low chart, the angle of 4 × 1, which moves 2$^1/_2$ points per day from the first top at 4760 made December 6, 1948, crossed at 5020. The 45 degree angle moving up from the low of 4685 on March 16, 1949, crossed at 5020. The angle of 67$^1/_2$ degrees, which moves up 20 points per day from the low of 4785 on April 18, crossed at 5020 and the angle moving up from 4735 on February 14 crossed at 5005, making 4 important angles coming out at this high point. A sure point for great resistance because the time from the starting of the option was over 6 months. The time from the first

---

[*]All quotations in this chapter about the *Master Egg Course* are from the W. D. Gann Commodities Course, and are reprinted with permission per Nikki Jones of Lambert-Gann Publishing Co., Inc., Box O, Pomeroy, Washington 99347.

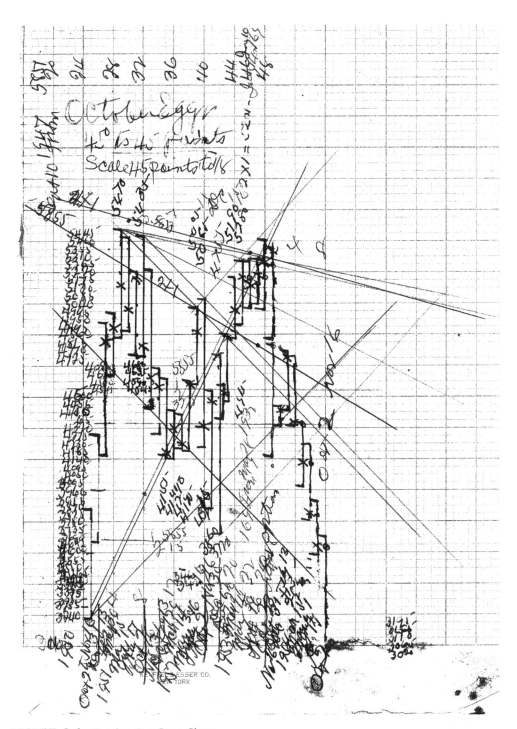

FIGURE 3.1 October Egg Gann Chart

important top on December 6, 1948, was close to 5 months and the angle from this top called the top exactly.

In the next example, Gann speaks of the importance of a price scale:

Since receiving 1 letter stating that the contracts for Eggs were changed on February 1 and that 1 point now equals $1.44, I did some experimenting to adjust angles to the money value because that is very important. I wanted to get something that would work to an angle of $11^1/_4$ angle and by multiplying 144×8 it gave 1152 or $11.52 profit on 8 points. This would give an angle 5×4 or about 39 degrees, moving up at the rate of 8 points per day, instead of the 45 degree angle which moves 10 points per day.

A discussion of the swing chart and angles appears in the following paragraph:

Years of this research and experience have proved that the first advance from which a reaction runs more than 3 days will set an angle for an important top later. This rule works on weekly and monthly charts also. After there is a second or third top and when there is a greater decline from the third top, an angle from that bottom must call bottoms and tops of the next advance. You will note that on the greatest decline from January 24 to February 8, the price declined to the angle from the extreme low of 4485, and the angle of 2×1 from the third top called the second and also the last bottom at 4560. From this low of 4560 we start the angle moving up at the rate of 8 points per day. It calls the low for March 2, next it called the top at 4850 on March 30 from which a 2-day reaction followed, and finally on May 3 this angle in green crossed the first top angle at 5020, on May 3, 1949.

In the next paragraph, Gann combines a percentage retracement point, the swing chart, and angles:

The market closed at the halfway [point of] the range of the day on May 3. May 4 was signal day. The opening was at 50 cents; the high was 5005; the low for the day was 4980; the market closed at 4985. This was the first day since April 18 that the market had broken the low of the previous day and closed under. The total time from 4560 to 5025 was 58 market days in view of the fact that the option is over 6 months old a greater reaction can be expected. The 45 degree angle from the last low of 4795 is the most important one to watch for support and a secondary rally. The decline should run at least 5 days with not more than 1 day rally.

He then interprets the data obtained from the swing chart. Other reasons for the top on May 3 were as follows:

First move up from 4485 to 4760—total gain 275 points.
First move down 215 points.

Second move up from 4560 to 4850—total gain 290 points.
Second move down 4850 to 4775—loss 75 points.
Third move up 4775 to 5025—total gain 250 points. This was 25 points less than the first gain and 40 points less than the second gain up.

In this paragraph, Gann discusses the importance of timing using the swing chart:

The greatest time period from January 24 to February 8 was 11 market days. And the last advance from April 18 was 11 market days; therefore, when the market declines more than 11 days, it will overbalance the greatest time period. When it declines more than 75 points it will overbalance the last price declines or space reversal, and indicate lower prices.

The next four paragraphs use the Master Chart (Figure 3.2) to interpret the market. Also, time and price are discussed in geometric terms.

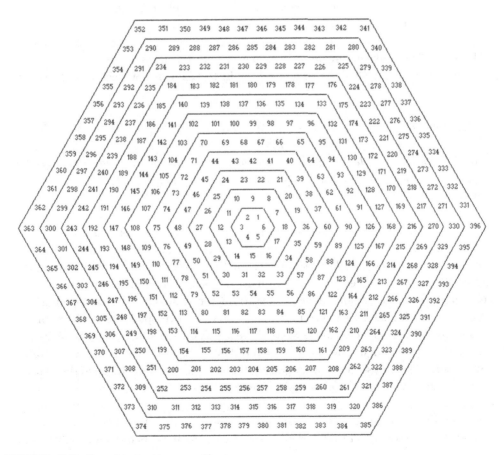

FIGURE 3.2 Gann Master Hexagon Chart

Study the Master Chart against previous tops and bottoms and you will see how it confirms the geometrical angles on other charts.

Example: 5010 is opposite 180 degrees from 60 cents, 4890 is on a 45 degree angle from 1050, the extreme low price. 4950 is 180 degrees from 45 cents. From 30 cents, which is half of 60, the 45 degree angle crosses at 48 cents. This is why the market made 3 bottoms around 48 cents on April 13 to 18. The Master Chart shows the same resistance levels and by using the time period with it you will learn the basic mathematical and geometrical law for market movement.

By going over back records and carefully studying all the important tops and bottoms you will see the working of the law.

Since the fluctuation of Eggs on the minimum of 5 points now equals $7.20 which is 2 circles of 360 degrees, $1/_2$ of this is 360 and makes an angle moving at the rate of $2^1/_2$ points per day very important. The fluctuations will now work better to the circle of 360 degrees. In a few days I will send you another Master Chart showing each 15 degree angle and the resistance levels which will help you to determine resistance and turning points.

Finally, after analyzing swing charts, percentage retracements, support and resistance angles, and the Master Chart, he is able to reach a conclusion and executes the trade.

Example: The range in fluctuations and the life of the present option of October Eggs is 4485 low and 5025 high, making a range of 540 points. Subtract from 540 and we have the balance of 180. This means that the market had advanced $1^1/_2$ circles or cycles and was at a 180 degree angle on May 3, 1949. The writer sold October Eggs at 5015 on May 3, 1949.

Although this trade failed to live up to its expectations, I was more interested in the thought process that led to determining the entry level. Studying Gann's first-person account, I discovered the trading techniques that he considered important in determining a trade. When Gann started trading seriously, he used a combination of swing charts, percentage retracements, and angles to determine price support, and swing charts and anniversary (cycle) dates to determine timing. Later, he developed master charts of price and time to trade. This technique is beyond the scope of this introductory book because the more simple techniques need to be mastered before they can be used successfully. In addition, specific analysis tools are required that are only available through the Lambert-Gann Publishing Company. Additionally, a deep understanding of cycles and their causes is required.

Generally speaking, however, Gann used a combination of pattern, price, and time to generate his trades. As I said earlier, these are the main parts of Gann analysis that I consider important in developing a trading system. Therefore, although Gann demonstrated an interest and proficiency in many other areas dealing with price and time analysis, pattern, price, and time are the major themes of this book.

THE BASIS OF GANN THEORY: THE LAW OF VIBRATION

During an interview Gann once revealed that the secret to his trading was understanding the vibration of a commodity. The "Law of Vibration," as he called it, explains the cause of the periodic recurrence of the rise and fall in commodities. The following excerpts are from an article Gann wrote that covers this topic in greater detail.

I soon began to note the periodical recurrence of the rise and fall in stocks and commodities. This led me to conclude that natural law was the basis of market movements. After exhaustive researches and investigations of the known sciences, I discovered that the Law of Vibration enables me to accurately determine the exact points to which stocks or commodities should rise and fall within a given time. The working out of this law determines the cause and predicts the effect long before the Street is aware of either. Most speculators can testify to the fact that it is looking at the effect and ignoring the cause that has produced their losses.

It is impossible here to give an adequate idea of the Law of Vibration as I apply it to the markets, however, the layman may be able to grasp some of the principles when I state that the Law of Vibration is the fundamental law upon which wireless telegraphy, wireless telephone and phonographs are based. Without the existence of this law the above inventions would have been impossible.

In going over the history of markets and the great mass of related statistics, it soon becomes apparent that certain laws govern the changes and variations in the value of stocks and there exists a periodic or cyclic law, which is at the back of all these movements. Observation has shown that there are regular periods of intense activity on the Exchange followed by periods of inactivity. Mr. Henry Hall, in his recent book, devoted much space to "Cycles of Prosperity and Depression" which he found recurring at regular intervals of time. The law which I have applied will not only give these long cycles or swings, but the daily and even hourly movements of stocks. By knowing the exact vibration of each individual stock I am able to determine at what point each will receive support and at what point the greatest resistance is to be met.

Those in close touch with the markets have noticed the phenomena of ebb and flow, or rise and fall in the value of stocks. At certain times a stock becomes intensely active, large transactions being made in it; at other times this same stock will become practically stationary or inactive with a very small volume of sales. I have found that the Law of Vibration governs and controls these conditions. I have also found that certain phases of this law govern the rise in a stock and entirely different rules operate on the decline.

I have found that in the stock itself exists its harmonic or inharmonic relationship to the driving power or force behind it. The secret of all its activity is therefore apparent. By my method I can determine the vibration of each stock and by also taking certain time values into consideration I can in the majority of cases tell exactly what the stock will do under given conditions.

The power to determine the trend of the market is due to my knowledge of the characteristics of each individual stock and a certain grouping of different stocks under their proper rates of vibration. Stocks are like electrons, atoms, and molecules, which hold persistently to their own individuality in response to the fundamental Law of Vibration. Science teaches "that an original impulse of any kind finally resolves itself into periodic or rhythmical motion," also, "just as the pendulum returns again in its swing, just as the moon returns in its orbit, just as the advancing year ever brings the rose to spring, so do the properties of the elements periodically recur as the weight of the atoms rises."

From my extensive investigations, studies and applied tests, I find that not only do the various stocks vibrate, but that the driving forces controlling the stocks are also in the state of vibration. These vibratory forces can only be known by the movements they generate on the stocks and their values in the market. Since all great swings or movements of the market are cyclic they act in accordance with the periodic law.

If we wish to avert failure in speculation we must deal with causes. Everything in existence is based on exact proportion and perfect relationship. There is no chance in nature, because mathematical principles of the highest order lie at the foundation of all things. Faraday said: "There is nothing in the Universe but mathematical points of force."

Through the Law of Vibration every stock in the market moves in its own distinctive sphere of activities, as to intensity, volume and direction; all the essential qualities of its evolution are characterized in its own rate of vibration. Stocks, like atoms, are really centers of energies, therefore they are controlled mathematically. Stocks create their own field of action and power; power to attract and repel, which in principle explains why certain stocks at times lead the market and "turn dead" at other times. Thus to speculate scientifically it is absolutely necessary to follow natural law.

After years of patient study I have proven to my entire satisfaction as well as demonstrated to others that vibration explains every possible phase and condition of the market.

Reprint The W. D. Gann Technical Review, *1, no. 11*
(November 12, 1982): 1.

This information helps us to understand a little more about the type of research W. D. Gann did to develop his analysis technique. The article should be read as background material, as it is beyond the scope of the material that is covered in this book. In this book I accept Gann's basis for market movement and that the markets are being influenced by the Law of Vibration. I do not wish to explain how to prove the existence of the Law of Vibration, but find it more useful to write about how to use the techniques Gann used to trade the market. For example, I have assumed that cycles and vibrations exist and, at this point, do not intend to prove either their existence or the existence of their influence on the movement of stock and commodity prices.

The Origin of the Law of Vibration

I have often seen it printed that Gann "discovered" the Law of Vibration. This statement may be misleading because based on my research it was "discovered" years before his interview in *Ticker Digest* in 1909. I believe the proper way to present this information is to give Gann credit for applying it to stock and equity markets.

While doing research on the Law of Vibration I came across two publications which were published prior to the publication of the *Ticker Digest* article. The first book was titled *The New Knowledge: A Popular Account of the New Physics and the New Chemistry in Their Relation to the New Theory of Matter* by R. K. Duncan (A. S. Barnes & Company, 1905). On page 23 of this book I found a curiously familiar sentence: "... just as the advancing year ever brings the rose of spring, so do the properties of the elements periodically recur as the weights of the atoms rise...."

The sentence looked familiar because it was directly quoted in Gann's Law of Vibration interview with *Ticker Digest* in 1909. I was completely stunned by the connection between the article and the book and at first dismissed it as coincidence until I read more excerpts from the book. Another intriguing sentence in the book caused me to think that this was no coincidence and that W. D. Gann had read this book in order to formulate his Law of Vibration. From the book I read the following, "It will also be seen that the numbers of analogous elements generally differ, either by 7 or by some multiple of 7; in other words, members of the same group stand to each other in the same relation as the extremities of one or more octaves in music." This reference to the number 7 and to the octaves in music made me think about Gann even more since in his course he wrote about the number 7 and the scale, rhythm, harmony, and period of the markets.

While continuing my research on the Law of Vibration, I also found the following excerpt in the *New England Medical Gazette* from September 1909, "Briefly and technically, the law states the 'properties of an element are a periodic function of its atomic weight.'" This statement formulates an extraordinary fact. To quote Duncan again, it means no more nor less than this: "If you know the weight of an atom of the element you may know, if you like, the properties, for they are fixed. Just as the pendulum returns again in its swing, just as the moon returns in its orbit, just as the advancing year ever brings the rose of the spring, so do the properties of the elements periodically recur as the weights of the atoms rise."

Since I saw this quote appear twice in textbooks and once in Gann's Law of Vibration interview, I had to conclude that the basis of Gann's Law of Vibration was not planetary in nature as some have believed, but may actually have something to do with the vibration of the atomic weights of the elements. Since making this discovery I have found more books that link to the Law of Vibration article.

Mathematics

Gann was a rare mathematician. He was a student of numbers, number theory, and the progression of numbers. He often said his analysis theory was based on natural law and mathematics.

Since time progresses as the earth turns on its axis, and time is measured by numbers and progressions of numbers, and since prices in their movement upward and downward are measured in numbers, we can understand why Gann had an intense interest in numbers, number theory, and mathematics. And remember . . . he did not have a personal computer, or even a handheld or desktop calculator—just a pencil.

Gann said his trading method was based on natural and mathematical law. For years he refused to reveal any part of this method. The method was based on natural law, but the theory behind it was based on mathematics. Since price and time are denoted in mathematical terms (numbers), his system involved numbers and number progressions. He simply said that he had researched far back into history and even went to India for old pre-Hindu records and philosophies as well as the ancient archives of the pre-Hindu period.

As we study Gann's works, we begin to see that some numbers took a dominant place in his trading method. The square of numbers was an important issue with him, namely: 16, 25, 36, 49, 64, 121, and 144. He thought that markets moved in patterns sensitive to the price movement of these squares in terms of both price and time. For example, a rally in a specific market may have a tendency to find resistance 64 cents or 64 days from a bottom. Similarly, a decline in a market may find support 144 dollars or weeks from a top. This technique was combined with others that he developed, and it became a major part of his analysis tools (Figure 3.3).

Key Numbers

At this point, some of you may be discounting Gann's methods because of their relative obscurity, but I would ask you to suspend disbelief. Gann found several numbers significant for a variety of reasons, some religious or spiritual, some historical, and some

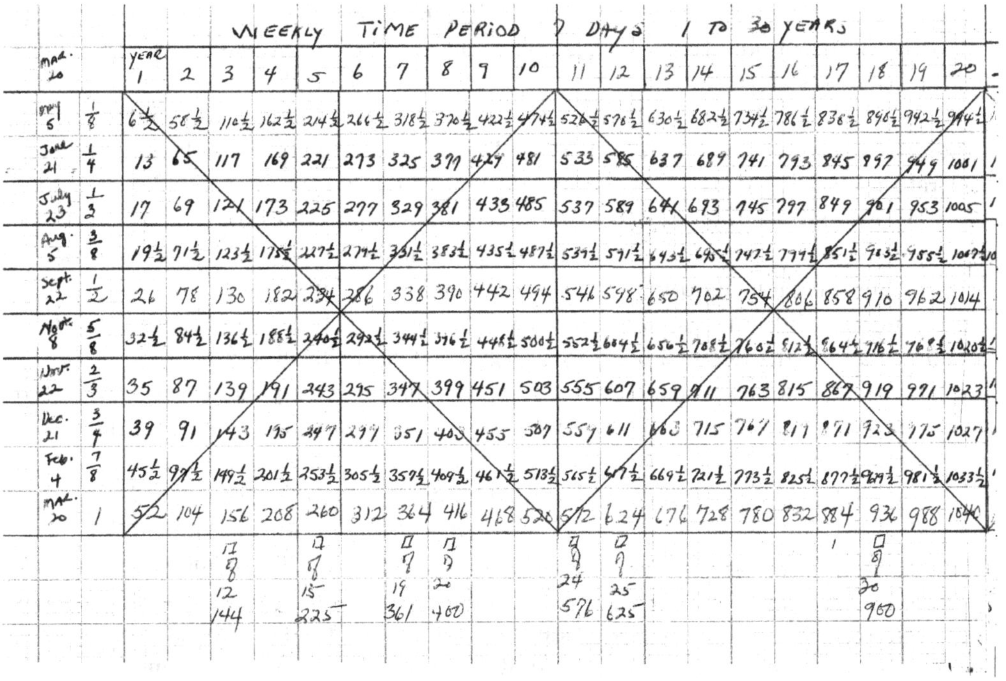

			WEEKLY	TIME	PERIOD	7	DAYS	1	TO	30	YEARS									
Mar. 20	year	1	2	3	4	5	6	7	8	9	10	11	12	13	14	15	16	17	18	19	20
Apr. 5	1/8	6½	58½	110½	162½	214½	266½	318½	370½	422½	474½	526½	576½	630½	682½	734½	786½	838½	896½	942½	994½
June 21	1/4	13	65	117	169	221	273	325	377	429	481	533	585	637	689	741	793	845	897	949	1001
July 23	1/3	17	69	121	173	225	277	329	381	433	485	537	589	641	693	745	797	849	901	953	1005
Aug. 5	3/8	19½	71½	123½	175½	227½	274½	331½	383½	435½	487½	539½	591½	643½	695½	747½	799½	851½	903½	955½	1007½
Sept. 22	1/2	26	78	130	182	234	286	338	390	442	494	546	598	650	702	754	806	858	910	962	1014
Nov. 8	5/8	32½	84½	136½	188½	240½	292½	344½	396½	448½	500½	552½	604½	656½	708½	760½	812½	864½	916½	968½	1020½
Nov. 22	2/3	35	87	139	191	243	295	347	399	451	503	555	607	659	711	763	815	867	919	971	1023
Dec. 21	3/4	39	91	143	195	247	299	351	403	455	507	559	611	663	715	767	811	871	923	975	1027
Feb. 4	7/8	45½	97½	149½	201½	253½	305½	357½	409½	461½	513½	565½	617½	669½	721½	773½	825½	877½	929½	981½	1033½
Mar. 20	1	52	104	156	208	260	312	364	416	468	520	572	624	676	728	780	832	884	936	988	1040

7/8 12 144   15 225   19 361   20 400   24 576   25 625   30 900

FIGURE 3.3 Gann Weekly Time Period Chart

psychological. Whether or not his belief was reasonable or based on provable fact is largely irrelevant here—he used them as the basis for his trading, and they can work if incorporated properly into a technical trading system.

Gann researched numbers and cycles in many unique ways. Much of his research focused on the specific meaning of a number and how it relates to market movement. His research included the study of early Egyptian writings as well as cycle information. He also did extensive research of the cycles highlighted in the Bible. Records indicate that the early Egyptians considered the number seven to be the symbol of both earthly and eternal life. It is thought of as a number symbolizing a complete cycle, for seven is denoted as the number of time and rhythm. This information was used by Gann to develop a seven-day-cycle theory for short-term market moves.

Gann deemed $3\frac{1}{2}$ important, as it is half of 7, and in the Bible it occurs several times—for example, in the Book of Revelation, where the woman was sent into the wilderness for $3\frac{1}{2}$ years; during Daniel's vision of 42 months ($3\frac{1}{2}$ years); when the Christ child was hidden in Egypt for $3\frac{1}{2}$ years; and during Jesus' public ministry, which lasted for exactly $3\frac{1}{2}$ years. Gann used this information to study and research the $3\frac{1}{2}$ -day, -week, -month, and -year cycle, and applied the knowledge he gained to trade the market.

Gann also considered the number nine important, as it occurs in the nine beatitudes recorded in Matthew's Gospel, and he believed that nine corresponds with the number of stages of a disciple's advance to a higher life. The number 12 was important to Gann, as it denoted space for him. He found it recurring in the 12 tribes of Israel, the 12 disciples, and the 12 houses of the Zodiac.

Other important Gann numbers are derived as follows: One year is 365 days, as this is the time it takes the sun to enter a hemisphere, move to the opposite hemisphere, and then return to the starting point. The movement of the sun produces definite seasons, affects crops and weather, and therefore has a dominant effect on our lives. For this reason the 30-day or sun cycle has dominance. Besides what has already been said about the number seven, it is important because of its link to the lunar cycle.

The number 144 was also important to Gann, whether because of there being 1,440 minutes in a day (the decimal point is disregarded), it is 40% of a circle ($360° \times 0.40 = 144°$), or because it is the square of 12. Numbers that occur repeatedly in the different sciences—such as mathematics, geometry, physics—cycles, and other natural studies were very important to Gann.

After studying mathematics and researching number patterns, Gann had to find a practical use for his newly acquired knowledge. Armed with this information Gann turned to the stock and commodity markets. After applying his strong background in mathematics to these markets, he concluded that markets adhere to mathematical law. From this conclusion he was able to develop his trading theory. This theory basically stated that market movement is governed by the forces of pattern, price, and time.

PATTERN

In Gann Theory, pattern is defined as the study of market swings. Swing charts (Figure 3.4) determine trend changes. For example, a trend changes to up when the market crosses swing tops, and it changes to down when the market crosses swing bottoms. The trader can also gain information from swing charts about the size and duration of market movements. This is how price, which is size, and time, which is duration, are linked to a pattern. In addition, the trader can learn about specific characteristics of a market by analyzing the patterns formed by the swing charts. For example, the charts delineate a market's tendency to form double tops and bottoms, signal tops and bottoms, and the tendency to balance previous moves.

PRICE

In Gann Theory, price analysis consists of swing-chart price targets, angles, and percentage retracement points.

Swing-Chart Price Targets

After constructing a swing chart, the trader creates important price information that can be used to forecast future tops and bottoms. These prices can be referred to as *price*

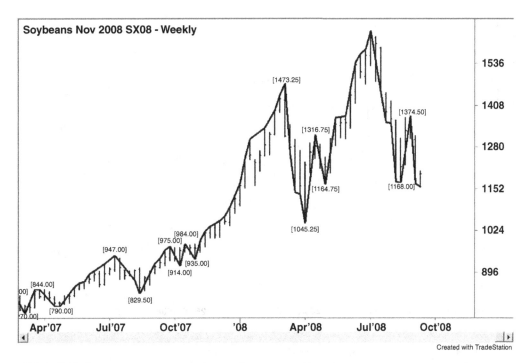

FIGURE 3.4 2008 Weekly November Soybean Swing Chart
Copyright © TradeStation.

balance points. For example; if the swing chart shows the market has had a recent tendency to rally 7–10 cents before forming a top, then from the next bottom, the forecast will be for a subsequent 7–10 day rally. Conversely, if the market has shown a tendency to break 10–12 points from a top, then following the next top, the trader can forecast a break of 10–12 cents. If the swings equal previous swings, then the market is balanced.

Angles

Geometric angles are another important part of the Gann trading method (Figure 3.5). The markets are geometric in design and function, so it follows that they will follow geometric laws when charted. Gann insisted on the use of the proper scale for each market when charting, to maintain a harmonic relationship. He therefore chose a price scale that was in agreement with a geometric design or formula. He mainly relied on a 45-degree angle to divide a chart into important price and time zones. This angle is usually referred to as the "1 × 1" angle, because it represents one unit of price with one unit of time. He also used other proportional geometric angles to divide price and time. These angles are known as 1 × 2 and 2 × 1 angles because they represent one unit of price with two units of time and two units of price with one unit of time, respectively. All of the angles are important because they indicate support and resistance. They also have predictive value for future direction and price activity—all of which is necessary to know in order to forecast where the market can be in the future and when it is likely to be there.

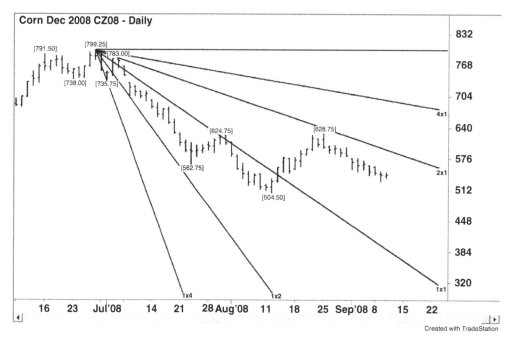

FIGURE 3.5 2008 Daily December Corn Gann Angle Chart
Copyright © TradeStation.

Percentage Retracement Points

Just as Gann angles offer the trader price levels that move with time, percentage retracement points (Figure 3.6) provide support and resistance that remain fixed as long as a market remains in a price range. Gann is commonly acknowledged to have formulated the percentage retracement rule, which states that most price moves will correct to 50 percent. Other percentage divisions are 25 percent and 75 percent, with the 50 percent level occurring the most frequently.

Gann believed traders would become successful if they used price indicators such as swing-chart balance points, angles, and percentage retracement points to find support and resistance. In essence, however, the combination of the two price indicators provide the trader with the best support and resistance with which to work. For example, while the uptrending 1 × 1 angle from a major bottom and a 50 percent price level provide strong support individually, the point where these two cross provides the trader with the strongest support on the chart.

TIME

According to Gann, time had the strongest influence on the market because when time is up, the trend changes. Gann used swing charts, anniversary dates, cycles, and the square of price to measure time.

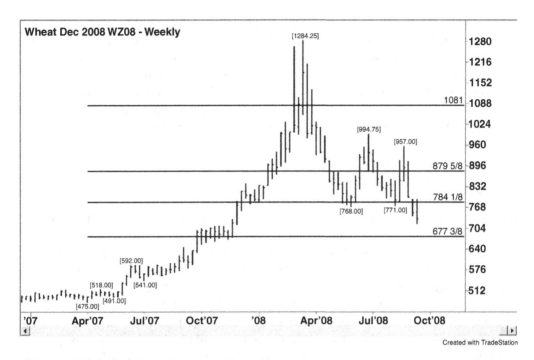

FIGURE 3.6 2008 Weekly December Wheat Gann Retracement Chart
Copyright © TradeStation.

Swing-Chart Timing

A properly constructed swing chart is expected to yield valuable information about the duration of price swings. This information is used to project both the duration of future up moves from a current bottom and the duration of future down moves from current tops. The basic premise behind swing-chart timing is that market patterns repeat; this is why it is necessary to keep records of past rallies and breaks. As a swing bottom or top is being formed, the trader must utilize the information from previous swings to project the minimum and maximum duration of the currently developing swing. The basic premise is that price swings balance time with previous price swings. However, in strong up moves the duration of a rally is greater than the duration of a break, and subsequent upswings are equal to or greater than previous up moves. Conversely, in strong down moves the duration of a break is greater than the duration of a rally, and subsequent downswings are equal to or greater than previous down moves.

Anniversary Dates

Among the timing tools Gann used is a concept he referred to as "anniversary dates." This term refers to the historical dates the market made major tops and bottoms. The information collected in effect reflects the seasonality of the market because often an anniversary date repeats in the future. A cluster of anniversary dates indicates the strong tendency of a market to post a major top and bottom each year at the same time. For example, in order to predict future tops and bottoms in wheat, Gann claimed to have studied prices back to the twelfth century, noting not only the prices, but the dates of the highs and lows. The dates and time spans between these anniversary dates—top to top, top to bottom, bottom to bottom, and bottom to top—were fundamental factors in this thinking. The information he learned from the research was very important to his analysis, and these dates gave obvious clues to another of his approaches to the market: time cycles.

Cycles

As mentioned earlier, Gann tried to build analysis tools that were geometric in design. When looking at anniversary dates he saw a series of one-year cycles. In geometric terms, the one-year cycle represented a circle or 360 degrees. Building on the geometric relationship of the market, Gann also considered the quarterly divisions of the year to be important timing periods. These quarterly divisions are the 90-day cycle, the 180-day cycle, and the 270-day cycle. In using the one-year cycle and the divisions of this cycle, you will find a date where a number of these cycles line up (preferably three or more) on a single point in time in the future. A date where a number of cycles line up is called a *time cluster*. This time cluster is used to predict major tops and bottoms. Time cycles are a major part of Gann analysis and should be combined with price indicators to develop a valid market forecast.

SQUARING THE PRICE RANGE WITH TIME

The squaring of price and time was one of the most important and valuable discoveries that Gann ever made. In his trading course he stated "if you stick strictly to the rule, and always watch when price is squared by time, or when time and price come together, you will be able to forecast the important changes in trend with greater accuracy."

The squaring of price with time means an equal number of points up or down, balancing an equal number of time periods—either days, weeks, or months. Gann suggested traders square the range, low prices, and high prices.

Squaring the Range

When Gann angles are drawn inside a range, the angles provide the trader with a graphical representation of the squaring of the range. For example, if a market has a range of 100 and the scale is 1 point, a Gann angle moving up from the bottom of the range at 1 point per time period will reach the top of the range in 100 time periods. A top, bottom, or change in trend is expected during the time period when this occurs. This cycle repeats as long as the market remains inside the range.

Squaring a Low

Squaring a low means an equal amount of time has passed since the low was formed. This occurs when a Gann angle moving up from a bottom reaches the time period equal to the low. For example, if the low price is 100 and the scale is 1, then at the end of 100 time periods an uptrending Gann angle will reach the square of itself. Watch for a top, bottom, or change in trend at this point. The market will continue to square the low as long as the low holds.

A graphical representation of squaring a low price can be seen on a chart Gann called a *zero-angle chart*. This chart starts an uptrending angle from price 0 at the time the low occurred and brings it up at one unit per time period. When this angle reaches the original low price, a top, bottom, or change in trend is expected.

Squaring a High

Squaring a high means an equal amount of time has passed since the high was formed. This occurs when a Gann angle moving down from a top reaches the time period equal to the high. For example, if the high price is 500 and the scale is 5, then at the end of 100 time periods a downtrending Gann angle will reach the square of itself. Watch for a top, bottom, or change in trend at this point. The market will continue to square the high as long as the high holds.

A graphical representation of squaring a high price can be seen on a zero-angle chart. This chart starts an uptrending angle from price 0 at the time the high occurred and brings it up at one unit per time period. When this angle reaches the original high price, a top, bottom, or change in trend is expected.

Time analysis in Gann Theory requires the trader to study market swings, anniversary dates, cycles, and the squaring of price and time to help determine future top, bottom, and change in trend points.

While the previous time studies require the trader to derive the data from actual charts, the basis of much of this analysis is drawn from Gann's fundamental studies of financial astrology and his proprietary master charts. In the next section a brief discussion of the complexity of these two techniques is presented.

ADVANCED PRICE AND TIME TECHNIQUES

Natural Cycles and Financial Astrology

While this book covers the most conventional methods of time analysis, another important tool Gann used to analyze time was the study of natural cycles (Figure 3.7). A natural cycle is a cycle that cannot be altered by humans. For example, although a 28-day cycle in a market can be discovered through analysis of historical price action, a naturally occurring 14-day cycle is the moon cycle. While one cycle may be changed or altered as more data becomes available, the moon cycle cannot change. Since the moon cycle follows a

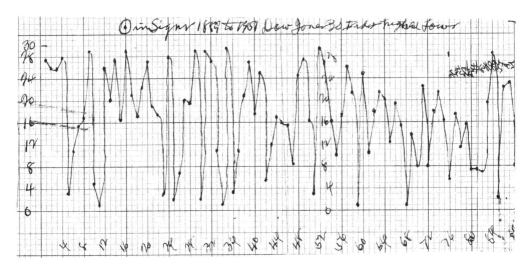

FIGURE 3.7 Gann Sun in Signs 1889 to 1951 Dow Jones 30 Index High and Low Chart

natural law, its position can be predicted well into the future. To Gann the division of time by the natural cycles of the moon, the sun, and the planets was very important. For example, his 30-day cycle was based on the sun cycle, and the 12-year and 84-year cycles were based on Jupiter and Uranus cycles, respectively.

The study of natural cycles, their origins, and their influences on the markets led Gann to develop a trading system based on financial astrology. Financial astrology is the study of how planets and their phenomena affect commodity and stock markets. The financial astrologer believes planetary influences are the cause of bull and bear markets.

Gann was often quoted as saying that there was nothing mysterious about his methods of prediction. He also claimed, in effect, that if he had the appropriate data, he could use geometry and algebra along with the theory of cycles to predict when a certain event would happen. This is ultimately the language of the astrologer. Also note that in much of his work Gann used the term *cycle* as did the Greeks (to the Greeks the word "cycle" meant circle, again an astrological term). Astrologers use math, geometry, and algebra to find the locations of the planets and the moon, study past effects when the planets were in certain positions relative to each other, the sun, and the earth, and then use their calculations to make their forecasts.

For years Gann made charts predicting the future of prices, a year in advance (his annual forecasts), and financial astrology was apparently the method he used in making these forecasts. Included in them were the exact price, the time of the day, as well as the day and month.

The fundamental principle behind financial astrology is that the planets' orbits, rulerships, groups of planets, and the sun and moon have an effect on the minds and actions of people and events, and in particular, these planetary effects affect the cycles and prices of stocks and commodities (Figure 3.8). That in sum is the meaning of financial astrology. While you may wish to reserve judgment on this matter, the fact remains that Gann was

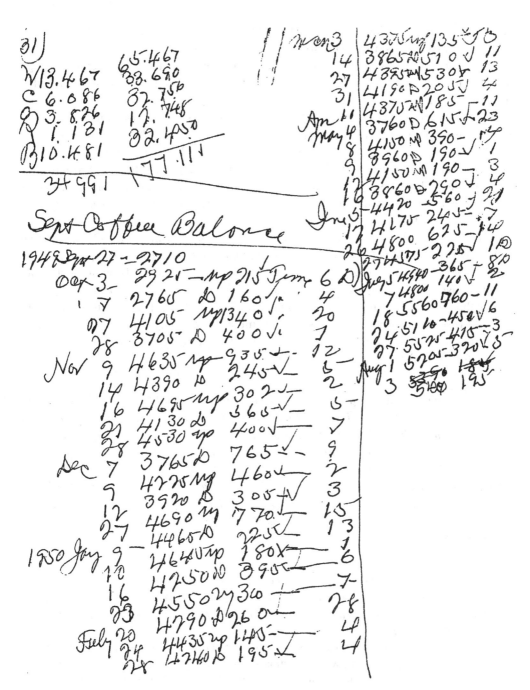

FIGURE 3.8 Gann Astrological September Coffee Balance Calculations

expert at financial astrology, that he was totally committed to it, and that he used it as a means of improving his trades (Figure 3.9).

He was careful not to publish anything whatsoever on his use of financial astrology because he knew such a revelation would receive bad press and harm status and his brokerage and advisory business.

Gann certainly broke new ground in financial astrology. Most astrologers are capable of using the longitude readings or time periods only. However, he was able to convert longitude to price, and was thereby able to generate a methodology for support and resistance levels. This was a new advance in financial astrology, and helps to explain how he could allegedly make calls within one-eighth of a point on stocks for highs and lows. You can begin to see how he was able to make long-range predictions, as well as minute-to-minute forecasts.

Finally, the study of, but not necessarily the belief in, astrology played a major role in the development of Gann's forecasting technique. Rather than try to explain how he used astrology, the following is an excerpt from a rare item that explains in great detail how he converted astrological analysis into price and time analysis and a trading system. Rather than write in his normal veiled language, in which astrological references were replaced with market terms, Gann used terms unique to astrology.

In the first paragraph Gann explains how to convert degrees of the planets to price to find support and resistance (Figure 3.10):

> ... 67 (cents), add 90 gives 157 or 7 degrees Virgo. Add 135 gives 202 or 22 degrees Libra. Add 120 gives 127 or 7 degrees Leo. Add 180 gives 247 or 7 degrees Sagittarius. Add 225 gives 292 or 22 degrees Capricorn. Add 240 gives 307 or 7 degrees Aquarius. Add 270 gives 337 or 7 degrees Pisces. Add 315 gives 382 or 22 degrees Aries. Add 360 gives 427 or 7 degrees Gemini. Add $271^1/_4$ gives $438^1/_4$. High on May Beans was $436^3/_4$. After that high the next extreme low was $201^1/_2$. Note that 67 plus 125 gives 202, and that one-half of 405 is $202^1/_2$, and 180 plus $22^1/_2$ is $202^1/_2$, which are the mathematical reasons why May Soy Beans made bottom at $201^1/_2$.

> All of the above price levels can be measured in Time Periods of days, weeks and months, and when the time periods come out at these prices, it is important for a change in trend, especially if confirmed by the geometrical angles from highs and lows (Figure 3.11).
>
> From a missive on Gann letterhead with the title, "Soy Beans: Price Resistance Levels," which originally came with the W. D. Gann Commodities Course, but which was left out of later reprints of the course.

Here, Gann created support and resistance levels using the longitude of the position of the sun. In the next excerpt, Gann used the longitude of the major planets to create support and resistance levels.

AUTHOR OF
TRUTH OF THE STOCK TAPE
WALL STREET STOCK SELECTOR
NEW STOCK TREND DETECTOR
HOW TO MAKE PROFITS IN COMMODITIES

W. D. GANN
820 S. W. 26TH ROAD
MIAMI 45, FLORIDA

- 2 -

ASTROLOGICAL, Continued

The Astrological Ready Reckoner and Students Assistant --Sepharial	1.00
Your Stars and Destiny --Paul Councel	1.00
Manual of Astrology --Sepharial	2.50
Text-Book of Astrology --A. J. Pearce (Old Rare)	3.00
The Witness of the Stars--Bullinger	1.00
Solar Biology --Butler	3.00
Cosmic Symbolish --Sepharial	3.00
Popular Astronomy --Flammarion and Gore	1.00
Eclipses in Theory and Practice --Sepharial	1.00
Sun Spots and Weather --W. T. Foster	.50
Popular Astrology for Everybody -- Fredrick Hathaway	.50

SCIENTIFIC AND MISCELLANEOUS

The Candle of Vision --A. E.	.50
The Path to Wisdom -- Richard Lynch	.50
The Doctor Prescribes Colors --Edward Podolsky, M.D.	1.00
Cosmic Causation in Geophysics --Paul Councel	1.00
The Master Key of Festiny --Gregorius	1.00
Evolution and Reincarnation --Essie M. Ducquan	1.00
Miracle of the Ages --Worht Smith	.50
The Kybalion --Three Initiates	3.00
Sixth and Seventh BOOKS OF MOSES -	.50
Mysteries Unveiled --William A. Redding	1.00
Pax Tecum or Peace and Relaxation through Technique and Truth, Henry C sper	.50
Faith as a Constructive Force --Swami Paramananda	1.00
Oracles of Nostradamus --Chas A. Ward	2.00
The Scikle -- William W. Walter (Cost $25.00)	10.00
Lessons in Truth --H. Emilie Cady	1.50
Secret -- Wesley W. Stout	.50
Open the Door --Wilfred Brandon	2.00
The Proofs of Astral Influence on Man -- Paul Choismrd	1.00
Spiritual Radio --Archbishop Du Vernet	.50
Yoga System of Study -- (Occult Chemistry) --Yoga Hari Rama	1.00
The Law of Psychic Phenomena --Hudson	1.00
Power of Will --Frank Channing Haddock, M.S. Ph. D.	2.00
Oahspe --Dr. John Ballou Newbrough (Cost $10.00 Price now...	5.00
Philosophy of Natural Magic --Henry Cornelius Agrippa (Rare)	2.00
The World Book of the Ages from Adam to the Millennium --H. J. Kerns	1.00
Bible Mystery and Bible Meaning --T. Troward	2.00
God-Man. The Word Made Flesh --Carey -Perry	2.00
Tertium Arganum --P. D. Ouspensky (Cost $10.00) Price ...	5.00
The Chemistry and Wonders of the Human Body --Dr. Geroge W. Carey	1.00
The Wrold's Greatest Thought Discovery --Mack Stauffer	1.00
The Goal of Creation --Ed,imd Shaftesbury	1.00

FIGURE 3.9 Gann List of Astrological and Scientific Books

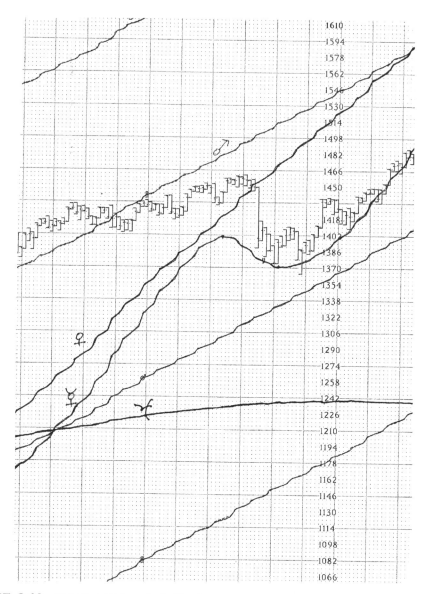

FIGURE 3.10 Gann Format Longitude Chart

Active Angles and Degrees

   By live or active angles is meant Prices and Time Periods where the Longitude of the major planets are or where the squares, triangles, oppositions are to these planets.

   The averages of the six major planets Heliocentric and Geocentric are the most powerful points for Time and Price Resistance (Figure 3.11). Also the Geocentric

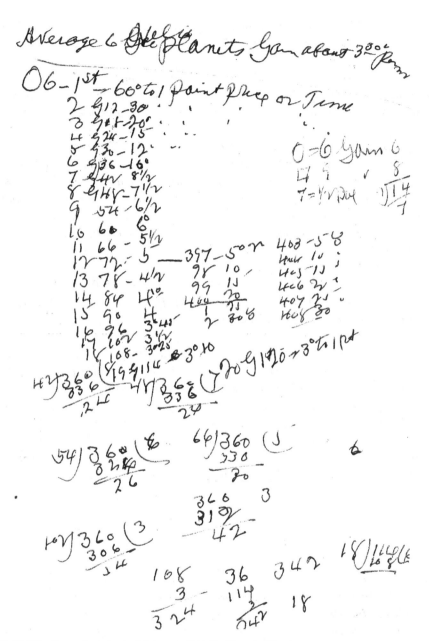

FIGURE 3.11 Gann Astrological Average 6 Helio Planets Chart

and Heliocentric average of the five major planets with Mars left out, is of great importance and should be watched.

You should also calculate the averages of eight planets which move around the Sun as this is the first most important odd square. The square of "1" is one, and "1" is the Sun. 8 added to "1" gives 9, the square of 3 and completes the first important odd square, which is important for Time and Price.

Examples of live, active angles: At the present writing, January 18, 1954, Saturn Geocentric is 8 to 9 degrees Scorpio. Add the square or 90 degrees gives 8 to 9 degrees Aquarius and equals the price 308–309, for May Beans.

The planet Jupiter is at 21 degrees Gemini, which is 81 degrees in longitude from "0" the square of 9. Subtract 135 degrees from Jupiter gives 306 or 6 degrees Aquarius. This is why Soy Beans have met resistance so many times between 306 and $311^{1}/_{4}$. The Price Resistance levels come out strong around these degrees and prices and the Geometrical angles come out on daily, weekly and monthly, but the Power of Saturn and Jupiter aspects, working out Time to these Price Resistance Levels, is what halts the advance in Soy Beans.

Example: December 2, 1953, May Soybeans high $311^{1}/_{4}$. This equaled 18 degrees 45' in Pisces, close square or 90 degrees of Jupiter, 135 degrees to Saturn and 180 degrees of the averages, and 120 degrees of Uranus.

300 price equals 30 degrees Virgo. 302 equals 30 degrees Libra. 304 equals 30 degrees Scorpio. On January 18, 1954, the planet Saturn Geocentric is 8 degrees 30 hours Scorpio, and 15 degrees Scorpio gives a price of 303, therefore when May Beans decline to 302, they will be below the body or longitude of Saturn and will indicate lower. At the same time, using the Earth's revolution of $365^{1}/_{4}$ days to move around the Sun, a price of $308^{1}/_{2}$ is 90 degrees or square to Saturn. As long as the price is below $308^{1}/_{2}$ it is within the square and in position to go lower. But by the 24th revolution, when the price breaks below 304, it is in the bear sign of Scorpio, a fixed sign and will indicate lower prices.

Study and analyze all options of all commodities in the same way as we have analyzed May Beans. Remember, when these Resistance Points are met you must give the market time to show that it is making tops or bottoms and getting ready to make a change in trend. Do not guess, wait until you get a definite indication buy or sell against these resistance levels and place a stop loss order. Having before you all the information outlined above, you would certainly have gone short of May Soy Beans on December 2, 1953 and cover your shorts on December 17 at 296 because the price was down to the 45 degree angle from 44 on the Monthly high and low chart.

To a trained astrologer and experienced trader, these excerpts reveal an important link between pattern, price, and time. In addition, they also show that although using financial astrology can be a useful trading tool, a trader should not abandon conventional charting techniques, as both aspects have to be used together. For example, knowledge of astrology is necessary to interpret and convert the degrees of the planets, but knowledge of technical analysis techniques is still needed to build charts, interpret tops and bottoms, find support and resistance, and place stop orders. All of this information may seem complicated to follow, but remember the overwhelming theme in each paragraph is pattern, price, and time.

The Master Charts

Researching and trading required a tremendous amount of time, especially since Gann had to chart everything by hand. At the same time, he sensed the need to simplify his

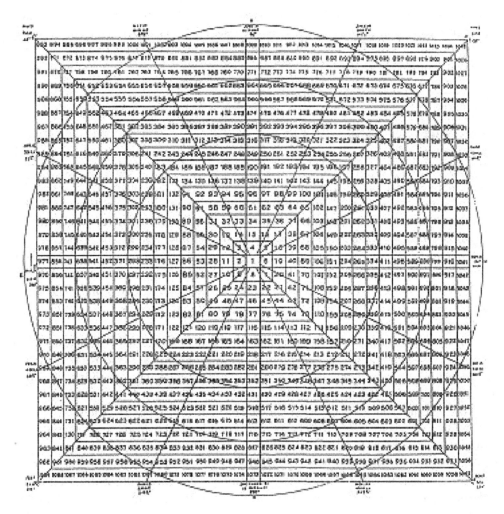

FIGURE 3.12 Gann Price and Time Chart for Grains

analysis by developing a pattern, price, and time chart that was universal and permanent. This became the motivating force behind the design and invention of the master charts.

Over the years Gann developed a number of master charts, including the Square of Nine, the Square of Four, and the Master 360 Degree Chart. These charts incorporated the best features of his price and time techniques, and provided him with a quick and easy way to forecast a market. The master charts can best be described as permanent charts in the form of circles, squares, and spirals, which represent natural angles and permanent resistance points for either price, time, or volume. Although it is claimed that he used these charts exclusively to trade late in his career, the *Master Egg Course* example demonstrates how he used his master charts in conjunction with his conventional bar charts.

It should be noted that these charts probably represent Gann's life work, and should therefore not be used until the more conventional Gann analysis tools are mastered. Since deep study and research are necessary to learn how to use the master charts, a proper background in Gann analysis is necessary. This is why I consider the master charts beyond the scope of this book. In addition, the master charts are only available in his trading course.

GANN THEORY AND ITS APPLICATION TO TRADING

Gann theory is based on the principle that price and time must balance. Markets are constantly in a position of change and subject to movement, sometimes with great volatility. Gann Theory states that there is order to this movement. By using the proper tools to analyze this movement, an accurate forecast for future direction can be made.

Finding the balancing points is necessary to predict future prices and movement. Gann developed a number of methods to help determine these balance points. The first method uses patterns created by swing charts to find the balance points. The second method uses angles and the squaring of price and time to find the balance points. The third method uses time.

While the perfect market remains balanced all the time, it also proves to be uninteresting, because major moves occur when price is ahead of time or time is ahead of price. The proper use of the various Gann analysis tools will help you to determine when these major moves are most likely to occur.

Now that the theory has been explained, how can it be applied to trading?

The first step is to create the charts that properly demonstrate the concepts of pattern, price, and time analysis. The second step is to create swing charts or trend indicator charts that provide the trader with a way to analyze the size and duration of the rallies and breaks. The third step is to use the information derived from the swing chart to forecast future price and time targets. In addition to forecasting, this chart is also used to determine the trend of the market.

After the pattern has been analyzed in the form of the swing chart, the trader moves to the fourth step, which is the creation of Gann angle charts. Using the tops and bottoms discovered with the swing chart, the trader draws properly scaled geometric angles up from bottoms and down from tops. Since these angles move at uniform rates of speed, the trader uses the angles as support or resistance, and attempts to forecast the future direction and price potential of the market.

Percentage retracement levels are also created using the information derived from the swing charts. Each paired top and bottom on the swing chart forms a range. Inside of each range are the percentage retracement levels, the strongest being the 50 percent price level. The fifth step is to draw the percentage retracement level inside of each range. At this point the trader can judge the strength or weakness of the market by relating the current market price with the percentage levels. For example, a strong market will be trading above the 50 percent price and a weak market will be trading below the 50 percent price.

Time studies are then applied to the market in the sixth step. Traders should use historical charts to search for anniversary dates and cycles that could indicate the dates of future tops and bottoms. The swing chart is used to forecast the future dates of tops and bottoms based on the duration of previous rallies and breaks. Gann angle charts are used to predict when the market will be squaring price and time. Now the percentage retracement chart indicates the major time divisions of the current range, with 50 percent in time being the most important.

In the seventh step, the information obtained from the pattern, price, and time charts is combined to create a trading strategy. This is the most important step because it demonstrates where the three charts are linked. For example, the swing chart tells the trader when the trend changes. If the trend changes to up, the trader uses the previous rallies to forecast how far and how long the rally can be expected to last. The Gann angles drawn from the swing chart bottom show the trader uptrending support that is moving at a uniform rate of speed. In addition, the Gann angle chart shows the trader the time that will be required to reach the swing chart objective based on the speed of the Gann angle. The 50 percent price level acts as support when the market is above it, and as resistance when it is below it. The strongest point on the chart will occur at the intersection of the uptrending Gann angle and the 50 percent price. Finally, time indicators are used to prove to the trader that the upside target is possible because anniversary dates and cycles can verify the existence of similar market movement in the past.

Combining pattern, price, and time, the trader creates a trading strategy. This trading strategy is based on the principle of price and time balancing at certain points on the chart. The three methods of analysis draw this information out of the chart. Without the proper application of the three analysis tools, valuable information would be lost to the trader. This is the essence of Gann Theory, which states that there is order to the market if the proper tools are used to read the charts.

CHAPTER 4

Chart Basics

Throughout this book, many references will be made to charts, and it will become clear to the reader that certain charts are more important than others. It is my intention to make you aware of as many different types of charts as space allows because traders find some charts easier to "read" than others. Such preferences are mainly psychological, probably based on an individual's thought process. These charts use the data generated by the market action and are not created by oscillators or averages, which sometimes smooth out the important price activity taking place in the market. As stated, our primary theme is pattern, price, and time. Each time a chart is created or analyzed, references are created that highlight these three main points. Some traders pick out the key information contained in the swing charts, others find angle charts easier to use, while a small percentage is able to use the information produced by a combination of the two types of charts. Finally, even if you find this type of analysis too difficult to grasp, you should be aware that these types of charts are absolutely necessary in technical analysis.

Charts are the tools of the Forex, futures, and equity market analyst. Just like the doctor who relies on special instruments to perform complex medical procedures, the lawyer, who relies on law books and court precedents, and the architect, who uses form and structure to create magnificent buildings, the chartist must have the necessary instruments to correctly analyze, forecast, and trade the Forex, futures, and equities markets.

GANN-FORMAT CHARTS

The main charts to be used for technical analysis should contain the following data: the open, the high, the low, and the close. The charts can be simple bar or Gann-style that feature a vertical line for the range with a hook to the left on the high, a hook to the left on the low, a dot to the left of the range for the opening, and a dash to left of the range for the close (Figure 4.1). Both charts contain the same data, but since much of charting is perception, some chartists may prefer one look over the other.

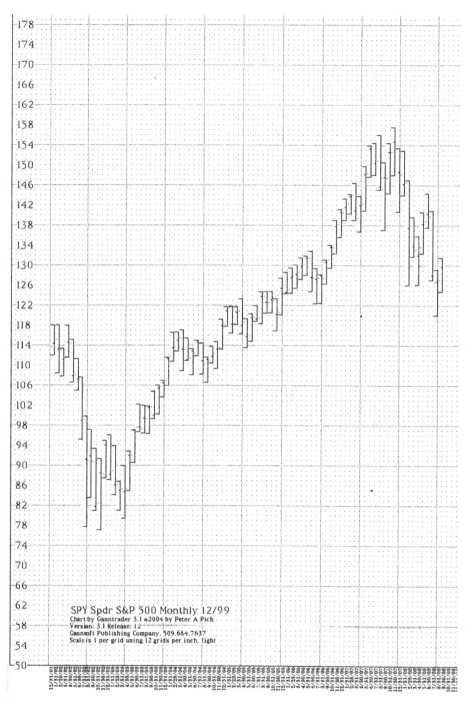

FIGURE 4.1 Gann Format Chart

Scale

The scale of the chart is important in price and time charting because of the sensitivity of the price movement per time period. Price and time or Gann-format charts need to have a one-to-one scale or an equal number of squares in the grid up and to the right. For example, Gann preferred 8 grid and 12 grid to the inch chart paper. This gives the market a square look that is necessary when drawing Gann angles from tops and bottoms. A line drawn diagonally from one corner to the next corner on this type of chart cuts the square exactly in half and produces a true 45-degree angle.

If you do not have the Ganntrader 2 program or have no desire to make your charts by hand, then you will have to use charts created by other charting software. These types of charts often cause problems for Gann analysts because they are created to fit a rectangular screen shape. When using programs such as Genesis Financial Technologies Trade Navigator or TradeStation, it is important for the analyst to adjust the scale of the chart on the screen to the proper price and time scale of the market being analyzed. Make sure your charting program gives you the opportunity to adjust the point value. Do not place angles set by degrees on your chart unless you are sure the x and y axes are at equally spaced intervals. This means that one unit on the x-axis must be the same distance as one unit on the y-axis. For example, a soybean chart should be charted at 1 cent per day or a Treasury bond should be charted at $4/32$ per day. Although Gann angles drawn from tops and bottoms on a square chart produce 45-degree angles, simply drawing a 45-degree angle from tops or bottoms on an improperly scaled chart does not produce angles at the same points as on a properly scaled chart, which means the market is not likely to follow the up- and downtrending angles. When this occurs, the trader loses the ability to accurately forecast future price movement as well as support and resistance.

Observe the details on Gann's October Egg Chart (Figure 4.2). This chart is a Gann angle chart. Notice on the chart that he identified price levels on the left of the chart moving up and down and time along the bottom of the chart moving left to right. Gann also indicated on the chart the scale of the Gann angles which is 45 degrees equals 45 points. Notice also that after the first range was made Gann identified the 50 percent price and other retracement levels on the chart. Finally, observe the turning points in this market. Just like today's markets the October Egg market turned where two or more angles crossed and even accelerated to the downside when two or more angles were penetrated. These are good examples of what is meant by a price cluster. At the top, the downtrending angle provided resistance while the penetration of the uptrending angle helped accelerate the move to the downside.

Size

A small chart tends to cloud the chart pattern, as all of the major support and resistance points are compressed into a compact area (Figure 4.3). Although many chart programs have the ability to focus on identifiable points on the chart, there are usually too many

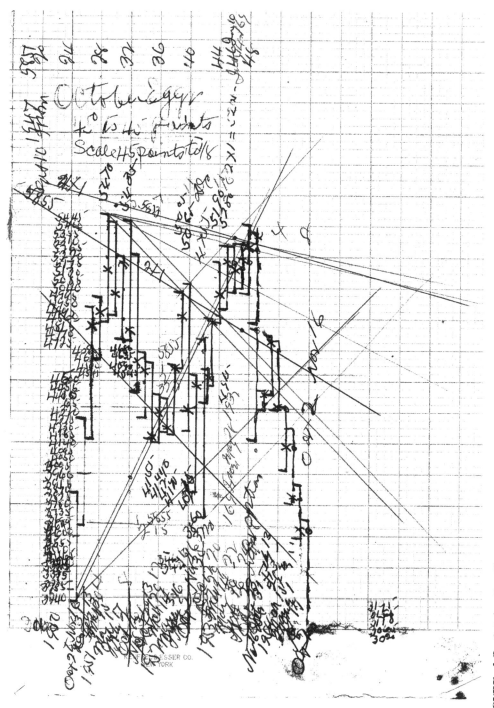

FIGURE 4.2 October Egg Chart

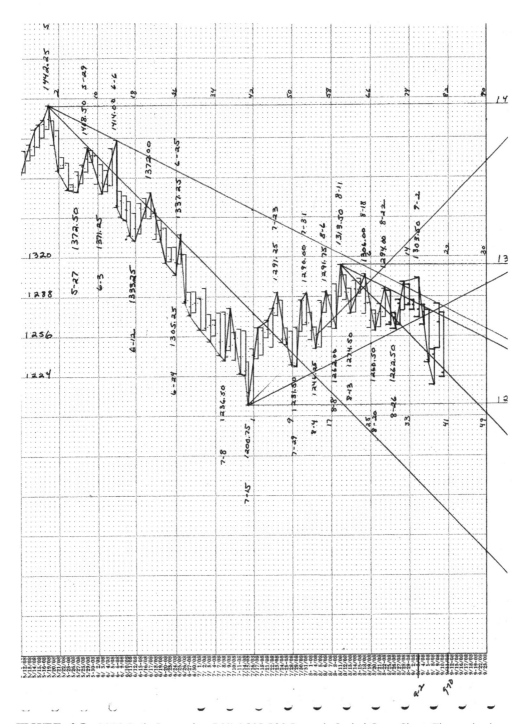

FIGURE 4.3 2008 Daily September E-Mini S&P 500 Properly Scaled Gann Chart. The angles have a mathematical relationship to the market

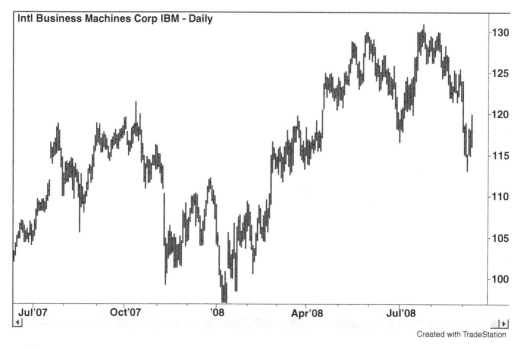

FIGURE 4.4 Compressed bars make this chart difficult to analyze using Gann techniques. Copyright © TradeStation.

steps in the process. This is one of the reasons why charting on paper and off the computer is the best way to chart a market using Gann-based price and time analysis. Although it takes time to manually update markets each day, week, or month, the benefits derived by having the ability to give the chart predictive value by drawing support and resistance into the future outweighs by far the time used to update the chart manually (Figure 4.4).

A large chart is therefore a must. All of the relevant angles must be visible on the chart, not just the nearby angles. This is because angles drawn from historical tops and bottoms often have an effect on current market conditions. Also, simply charting nearby angles can distort the support and resistance levels because the analyst will not be able to note clusters of support and resistance angles. If all of the relevant angles cannot be seen, the analyst may mistakenly perceive chart points as weak support or resistance when they are actually strong points.

PROPER CHART CONSTRUCTION

When making long-term charts the analyst should be aware of variations in the chart format. Gann insisted on the proper construction of the long-term chart. For example, he recommended combining same-contract months as opposed to the very popular nearby market continuation chart. Thus, when the 2008 November Soybean Chart expired, the analyst would begin to chart the 2009 November Soybean Chart on the same long-term chart, and so on with future contracts. This is different from combining near-term charts such as November Soybeans with January Soybeans with March Soybeans and so on.

The reason for long-term charting is to maintain the mathematical relationships of the tops and bottoms of the same-contract months. Furthermore, it avoids the mixing of old-crop and new-crop commodity contracts, which often produced large gaps in the chart. Although large gaps also appear in same-contract continuation charts, the market usually begins trading at or near important reference points unique to the specific contract, such as the 50 percent price of the all-time range. Major tops and bottoms, which may not have shown up in the deferred contracts, may have occurred in nearby contracts. By charting the market same-contract month to same-contract month instead of nearby to nearby, historical tops and bottoms unique to a specific contract can more easily be compared, as also can cycles and trading swings.

At this point I differ somewhat with Gann's charting style. My research suggests that this type of charting is fine for long-term observation of the market, but not necessarily for short-term trading. This is because the majority of the trading public will be focusing on the price action of the current active contract. Furthermore, during Gann's trading days, data were sparse, and most of the time the contract traded for only three to six months. Today a trader is able to create Gann-format charts of over two years for most contracts before the contract becomes actively traded. Valuable information can be lost if these data are combined with data from a previous time period. Research shows that creating monthly, weekly, and daily charts of a contract from its first trading day can yield valuable information in regard to cycle timing as well as the main trend and major support and resistance levels. My research strongly suggests that a specific-year contract be charted from the first day of trading if the data are available for at least 12 months. For example, creating a monthly, weekly, or daily chart of the 2009 November Soybeans from the first trading day in November 2009 can at times provide more precise and relevant data in terms of both price and time than can combining the 2008 November Soybean Chart with the 2009 November Soybean Chart.

I am not advocating abandoning Gann's style of combining same-contract month with same-contract month. The trader should continue to do this in order to find historical tops and bottoms as well as major cycle and seasonal dates. In order to produce more precise information for trading, however, it is strongly recommended that the chartist use all of the price and time information available from the currently traded active contract. Additional support for this conclusion can be found by analyzing and trading the 2009 November Soybean contract while the 2008 November Soybean contract is most active.

If you were trading the 2009 November Soybean contract, why would you need to know what the 2008 November Soybean contract was doing? Because all of the information you would need to trade is contained on the 2009 November Soybean chart. Gann was not wrong in recommending the same-contract roll because during his day the contract years did not overlap as they do today.

Remember, continue to build same-contract continuation charts for observation for major tops and bottoms and cycles, but use the currently active contract from the first trading day to trigger trading opportunities.

The continuation method is not recommended for markets that do not have an "old crop" or a "new crop," for example, foreign currencies, stock indices, precious metals, and financial instruments. The rollover from one month of a financial contract to the next month does not have as great an impact on the chart pattern as does a rollover from old-crop cotton to new-crop cotton. This is not to suggest you not chart the same-contract to same-contract for the financials. This type of contract may still be used to identify major tops and bottoms that are contract specific. For trading purposes, however, the long-term charting of the current active contract is highly recommended.

One other difficulty of contract-to-contract long-term charting is the rollover. These charts can be rolled on the first notice day or the last trading date or somewhere in between. Often markets get quite active during the delivery month. This activity can lead to high volatility, which can run a market sharply higher or lower. The spike moves that can be produced can distort the chart picture.

Although Gann had good intentions when he suggested rolling over same-contract month to same-contract month, conditions have changed since he was trading. His technique was not wrong, because valuable information can be obtained from the chart style he suggested, but this style is not functional in today's trading markets. Gann encouraged traders to research and experiment, and often changed his techniques to fit changes in contract specifications and market activity. In order to keep up with conditions that exist today, the trader must be flexible in her analysis. The chartist is therefore strongly encouraged to use all of the data that are available for each contract. Based on current market conditions, the trader should build monthly, weekly, and daily charts with the most actively traded contract from the first day of trading along with Gann continuation charts.

Price and Time Charting Requirements

Price and time charting also requires the analyst to chart the market on all of the days the futures contract traded (Figure 4.5). Therefore, no spaces are left for holidays or weekends. This is because each day has a specific point value, so allowing space for nontrading days can distort the future value of the angle. For example, if today is January 5, a Gann angle drawn from a bottom a few days before Thanksgiving on an improperly spaced chart will give value to holidays such as Thanksgiving, Christmas, and New Year's Day. If the value of the grid is 2 cents per day, the angle will then be off by as much as 6 cents on January 5. By being off this much, a trader may inadvertently buy a market that is 6 cents too high. The main rule to follow is to chart the market on an open trading day and skip the days when the particular exchange is closed from trading. During the early life of a contract, there may only be one price for the open, high, low, and close. On these days, simply mark the close on the proper day (Figure 4.6).

A calendar day chart has a different look from a market day chart. It also distorts the future value of the angles as it will include the value of the nontrade days.

FIGURE 4.5   2008 Daily December Cotton Market Days Chart

FIGURE 4.6 2008 Daily December Cotton Calendar Days Chart

Pit and Electronic Combinations and 24-Hour Trading

Traders have more price data in different formats available to them today than ever before. In addition, traders now have the opportunity to trade 24 hours per day, thereby eliminating trading gaps caused by after-hours news. Although these two developments have revolutionized trading, they have caused some issues for the analyst and trader. The main issues concern pit versus electronic trading and day-session trading versus 24-hour trading.

In staying with the rule to use as much data as possible, it is highly recommended to use a combination of pit and electronic data as well as 24-hour charts. If one chooses to use pit data, then it is important that the analyst not combine it from time to time with 24-hour data. The key is to maintain consistency in the data that you use This is in keeping with Gann's requirement to maintain the mathematical relationships between tops and bottoms of similar contracts. Furthermore, the trend in the industry is toward the elimination of pit-trading so this issue may be eliminated within a few years.

As mentioned earlier, consistency in charting is the key to proper analysis. Combining the day session and overnight trading open, high, low, and close on a chart made up primarily of day-session-only ranges will yield improperly constructed ranges, percentage retracement points, swing charts, and Gann angles. If an ambitious chartist creates a full-day chart and a day-session-only chart, he must designate the difference between the two charts. Although the day-session range may at times be the same as the 24-hour range, it is very important not to mix the two time periods.

Traders should pay particular attention to what appear to be gap openings on day-session charts. They should know whether the opening is a true gap or just a gap caused by choosing one chart over the other. This will often make a difference in trading results because traders have a tendency to fade gap openings. A good analyst must be able to distinguish between a true gap opening, and a continuation of an overnight move.

The Importance of Using Clean Data

Good analysts have to be aware of many factors, but the most important is working with clean data. During the course of the trading day bad ticks can occur, which alter chart formations. Sometimes a high or low for the day is different from the high or low on the intraday chart. Other times, connections go down, and data are missing. The analyst has to be aware that these things occur, and they must be handled quickly and properly.

One of the most common problems is with the settlement. Most data vendors claim to use the exchange settlement as their settlement. This should be checked from time to time to verify its accuracy. The settlement is the most important price of the day. If the settlement is incorrect, then signals that relay on this price will be incorrect, causing missed trading opportunities or overtrading. The charts are sometimes wrong, too. Some charts are set to pick up the last price traded. Often this is not the settlement for the day. When back-testing trading systems make sure the data used in the test will be the same used in live trading. Traders often discard well-thought-out trading systems because a bad price here or there caused a losing trade by triggering an entry that should not have existed or by missing a signal on a potentially winning trade.

Major highs and lows should also be verified because Gann angles will be drawn from these prices, and over time these Gann angles will be at incorrect prices on the chart, causing problems with support, resistance, and timing. Furthermore, incorrect highs and lows will cause percentage retracement prices to be miscalculated. Traders will encounter problems with bad percentage retracement prices because they will either buy or sell too early or be waiting for a price that never existed.

Intraday Charting Techniques

An intraday chart poses a similar time-period problem. The chartist must designate an intraday chart "full session" or "day session." Incorrectly charting the intraday full session and day-session will yield improperly constructed ranges, percentage retracement points, swing charts, and Gann angles. If the chartist chooses full session only, then she must connect the data properly when combining the overnight session with the day session. There should be no spaces on the charts for periods when thinly traded markets did not post a price during overnight action when the market was open. This is in keeping with the rule that each grid has a point value when the market is required to be open. On days when the trading session ends early, such as the day before a holiday in the financial markets, the chartist must end the chart when the market stops trading for the day and begin the chart on the very next bar when trading resumes. The basic idea is to avoid leaving holes in the intraday chart unless the data are unavailable because they are corrupted or, in the case of computer charts, off-line at the time of retrieval.

CHARTING PROGRAMS

As mentioned before, the larger the chart, the better. A program such as Ganntrader 2 can produce very large Gann-format charts. This program reads CSI (Commodity Systems, Inc.) data and can easily create charts with or without Gann techniques applied to the body of the chart. Chartists using this program have the option of creating either charts with full details already applied at printing time or bare Gann-format charts. Charts printed with full analysis techniques applied are fine for observation of the market, but at some point the charts will have to be re-created each time a bar changes. These charts can also be created with plenty of room to update. When using programs such as Genesis Financial Technologies Trade Navigator, or TradeStation, the chartist has the ability to save the angles on the chart for future use. These chart programs are also able to update the angles as the market trades into the future. A large chart enables the chartist to see all of the relevant information and also allows for the ability to draw Gann angles, percentage retracement points, and tops and bottoms into the future. This is one of the major benefits of these three programs. The ability to extend all of the important analysis tools into the future, makes it possible to forecast future market activity.

At this point the chartist should note that the programs mentioned for creating Gann charts and Gann analysis tools simply place the information on the charts where instructed. For example, Ganntrader 2 has the ability to draw angles from charts once the desired top or bottom is identified. There are functions that allow for the automatic generation of swing charts and Gann angles, but at some point these points must be filtered to make the data obtained relevant to the current market conditions.

In addition, Trade Navigator and TradeStation simply draw Gann angles from the places on the chart where the user tells them to begin drawing. These points are not predetermined by the program. It is therefore necessary to have a strong background in Gann Theory if these programs are to be utilized to their full extent.

These programs provide the analyst with quick snapshots of the market with Gann techniques applied, but they cannot replace the need to study and practice Gann Theory on charts generated manually.

TYPES OF CHARTS

Yearly and quarterly charts can be constructed primarily to show major long-term tops, bottoms, and percentage retracement points for the purpose of long-term forecasting. Trading using these charts is not recommended because the trend changes take too long to develop. Instead these charts should be used to identify the beginning or ending of major trends or cycles with the short-term charts used to pinpoint entries and exits. Gann incorporated a top-down approach to trading. In other words, he started his analysis with the big picture charts then made a more precise trade entry with the smaller time period charts, even using tape reading at times for entry. Since most of this book is dedicated to developing trading techniques and strategies, I chose to focus on the monthly, weekly, and daily charts for developing a trading system (Figure 4.7).

Monthly Charts

The monthly chart (Figure 4.8) is an important chart to observe if the database contains at least five years of data. Gann-style charts are highly recommended, however, individual charts may be used when there is at least two years worth of data. This is especially true with Crude Oil and Eurodollar charts, which trade for almost five years. Study and experimentation is necessary to determine the relevance of each chart. The monthly chart consists of the open, high, low, and close of each month of the year. With this chart the trader can observe the major tops, bottoms, and percentage retracement points. In addition, traders can note the dates of tops and bottoms in order to track the long-term cyclical and seasonal movement of a market. The monthly chart identifies the major tops and bottoms on the weekly and daily charts as well as smoothing out the swings. Using this chart, the trader will have an excellent opportunity to track the size and duration of the swings of the market from top-to-bottom, bottom-to-top, top-to-top, and bottom-to-bottom. Finally, traders can see where and how major moves begin and end.

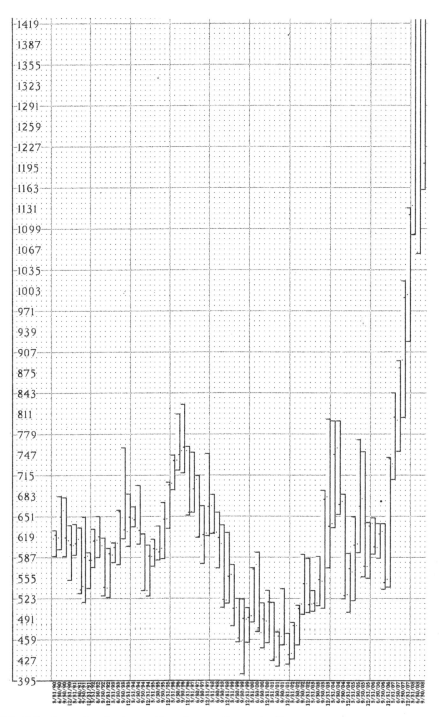

FIGURE 4.7   November Soybeans Gann Format Quarterly Chart

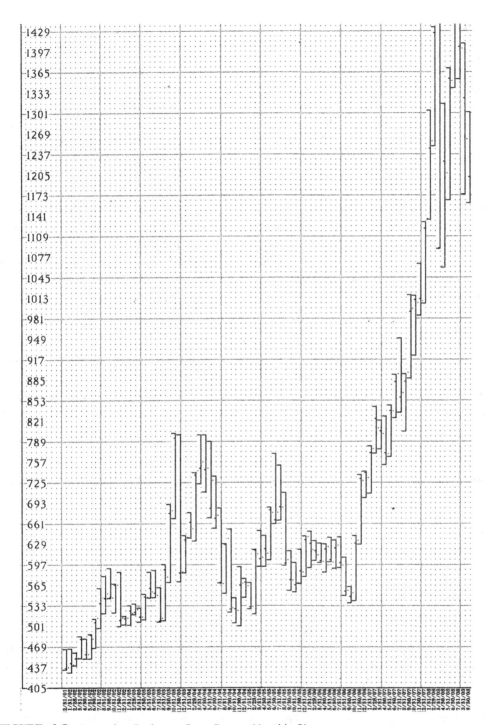

FIGURE 4.8 November Soybeans Gann Format Monthly Chart

Weekly Charts

The weekly chart (Figure 4.9) is an important chart to observe if the database contains at least two years of data. This amount of data is especially important if analyzing an individual contract. There are two options available to the analyst: a Gann format weekly chart or an individual contract, provided that this contract has at least two years of data. This will allow the trader to identify developing long-term trends well before the contract becomes the most actively traded. In addition, if the trader is in a long-term position, the trader will not have to worry about rollover issues. The weekly chart consists of the open, high, low, and close on a weekly basis. With this chart the trader can observe the major tops, bottoms, and percentage retracement points. In addition, traders can note the dates of tops and bottoms in order to track the intermediate cyclical and seasonal movement of a market. The weekly chart smoothes out the swings and emphasizes the major tops and bottoms on the daily chart. Using this chart, the trader will have an excellent opportunity to track the size and duration of the swings of the market from top-to-bottom, bottom-to-top, top-to-top, and bottom-to-bottom. Finally, traders can see where and how major moves begin and end.

Daily Charts

The daily chart is an important chart to observe if the database contains at least one year of data. It is recommended to begin tracking a contract when it comes on board, but at least six months before expiration if possible. Watching a contract from its first day of trading allows the trader to observe the size and duration of swings and the important Gann angles. The daily chart consists of the open, high, low, and close. With this chart the trader can observe the major tops, bottoms, and percentage retracement points. In addition, traders can note the dates of tops and bottoms in order to track the short-term cyclical and seasonal movement of a market. The daily chart is also used to identify the major tops and bottoms on the intraday charts and to smooth out the multiple swings. Using this chart, the trader will have a great opportunity to track the size and duration of the swings of the market from top-to-bottom, bottom-to-top, top-to-top, and bottom-to-bottom. Finally, traders can see where and how major moves begin and end.

Intraday Charts

It is recommended for intraday charts to begin with a weekly swing top or weekly swing bottom. At a minimum, a daily chart main top or main bottom should be the starting point. This is important because it will allow the trader to participate in a move at the beginning or end when the best trading opportunity exists. The swing tops and bottoms on the daily chart are the major tops and bottoms on an intraday chart. In order to maintain a clear intraday chart, at a minimum, identify the major tops and bottoms from the daily chart on the intraday chart. This helps the trader because he will know at all times where the market is trading on an intraday basis in reference to the daily chart's major support and resistance levels.

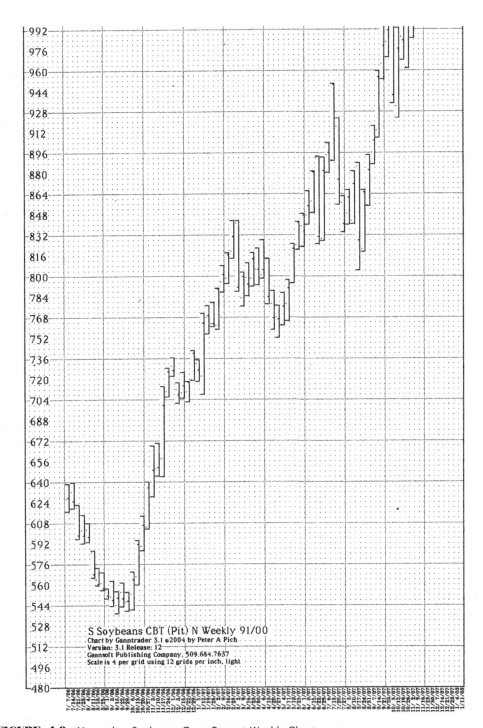

FIGURE 4.9 November Soybeans Gann Format Weekly Chart

Horizontal, Diagonal, and Vertical Charts

The basis of Gann Theory is the interlocking relationships between pattern, price, and time. At certain times a pattern may be most influential to the market. At other times price and time wield the biggest influence. These points may be a time cycle or a Gann angle. It is the balance of these three factors, however, that creates the best trading opportunities that can lead to more success in the market. Using the proper tools can help an analyst determine the best combinations of pattern, price, and time.

Throughout his writings, W.D. Gann implied that in order to learn the markets you must study its horizontal, diagonal, and vertical movements. Horizontal movements are tops and retracement prices. Diagonal movements refer to Gann angles. Finally, vertical movements are time. Learning how to combine pattern, price, and time into something useful is really the goal of the analyst.

The three main concepts can be categorized this way:

Pattern: Horizontal indicators, trend indicators or swing charts, chart formations, swing tops and bottoms, and percentage retracements.
Price: Diagonal indicators, Gann angles, and planetary longitude.
Time: Swing chart counts, cycle timing, seasonals, historical dates, square dates, and astrological phenomena.

The Trend Indicator or Swing Charts

After observing the trading pattern of a market, the analyst has to work on the chart to produce useful information. The first chart the analyst must construct is the trend indicator or swing chart (Figure 4.10). All other charts are based on the information created and observed on this chart. The swing chart, which follows the up and down movements of the market, can be created for all time periods—that is, monthly, weekly, daily, and intraday. This is because all markets make swings and all markets have trends. The swing chart is necessary because when properly constructed it provides the trader with valuable price and time information that can be useful in forecasting future price movement, cycle tops and bottoms, and for building mechanical trading systems.

Swings can be created in terms of both price and time. The most popular forms of swing charting are the one-time-period or minor-swing chart, the two-time-period or intermediate swing chart, and the three-time-period or main-trend swing chart. Some analysts also refer to the daily chart as the minor-trend chart, the weekly as the intermediate-trend chart, and the monthly as the main-trend chart. Either way, all charts make swings, and all swings can be traced and marked on a chart regardless of the time period charted.

After studying market movement according to the three swing charts, the trader will begin to learn the characteristics of a market. These characteristics include which markets have a tendency to make double or triple tops and bottoms, which markets have a tendency to post signal tops (closing price reversal tops) or signal bottoms (closing price reversal bottoms), and which markets can be pyramided. In addition to the support and

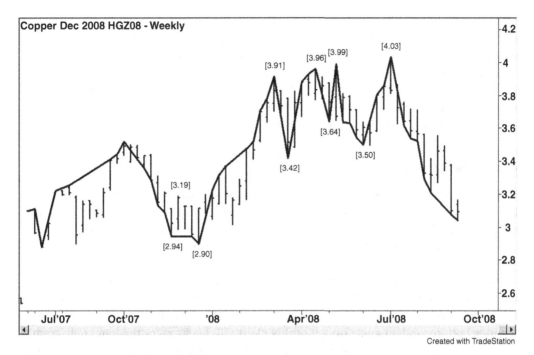

FIGURE 4.10 2008 December Weekly Copper 2-Bar Swing Chart
Copyright © TradeStation.

resistance (price information) that are contained on the swing chart, the trader will also find time information readily available. This time information includes anniversary dates (cycle dates), length of swings up and down, and the seasonality of the market. It is important to derive all of the pattern, price, and time information the market is offering, so a properly constructed swing chart must be maintained at all times.

Besides the pattern, price, and time information that appear on the swing chart, the trader must know that this information is what the author refers to as "horizontal and vertical" information. The horizontal information are the tops and bottoms. This is because a line drawn into the future from these tops and bottoms is always horizontal. These lines move out to infinity. On the other hand, time is always expressed as a vertical line on the chart, and traces the dates of important tops and bottoms into the future. The points at which these lines cross are important support, resistance, and timing zones into infinity.

Percentage Retracement Charts

Another chart to be observed and constructed is the percentage retracement chart. This chart is also constructed from the swing chart. The swing chart tops and bottoms form ranges. Inside these ranges are percentage retracement points such as 33 percent, 50 percent, and 67 percent. These points represent potentially important support and resistance prices. Some traders prefer to use eighths and tenths to divide the market while others prefer Elliott Wave retracements with a Fibonacci retracement. When these percentage retracement points are combined with former tops and bottoms and angles, they create very strong impact points that can turn a market or change a trend.

The range created by a top and bottom also forms important timing points such as the end of the range and the percentage retracement points of time inside the range. The combination of the strong price and time points forms a tool that is useful in predicting and easily identifying support and resistance points.

Gann-Angle Charts

Inside the horizontal and vertical zones the market also moves diagonally. These diagonal lines or angles represent both price and time and create patterns that have to be judged to determine the strength and direction of the market. Because of the price and time nature of these angles, they have predictive value, which gives the trader the ability to forecast future price movement (Figure 4.11).

The angles are drawn from tops and bottoms (Figure 4.12). Each angle drawn from a top or bottom carries the characteristics of that top or bottom. For example, an angle drawn from a three-day main bottom will have more strength than an angle drawn from a minor bottom, and an angle on a monthly chart will be stronger than an angle from a weekly or daily chart. This is another reason why the major tops and bottoms have to

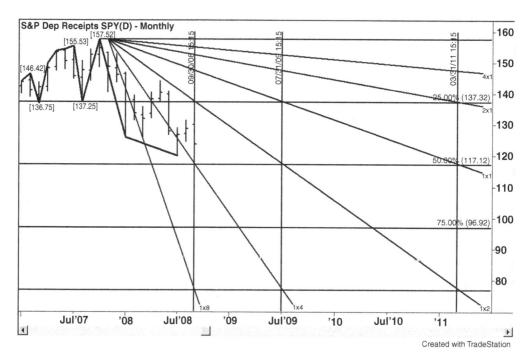

FIGURE 4.11 Monthly SPY Square of the Range Chart
Copyright © TradeStation.

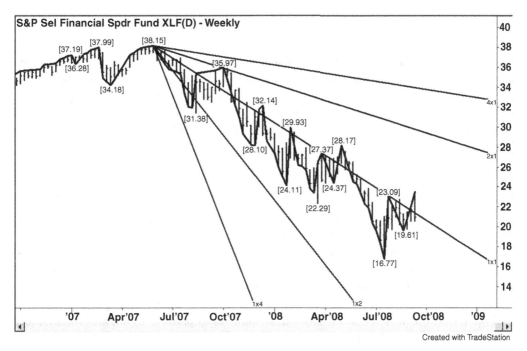

FIGURE 4.12 Weekly XLF Gann Angle Chart
Copyright © TradeStation.

be identified properly on the swing charts. Missing or failing to update just one swing top or bottom can have future ramifications. This is because the past, present, and future all exist on the angle at the same time: they are drawn from the past, we know where they are currently, and can extend them into the future. This is in keeping with Gann's statement from his Master Egg Course that was quoted earlier:

> *Years of this research and experience have proved that the first advance from which a reaction runs more than 3 days will set an angle for an important top later. This rule works on weekly and monthly charts also. After there is a second or third top and when there is a decline from the third top, an angle from that top must call bottoms and tops of the next advance.*

In order to have a properly constructed angle chart, the chartist must know the correct scale for each market traded. Without the correct scale, price and time will be incorrect and predictive information will be lost. Finally, the crossing of two or more independently determined support and resistance points must be noted, as these price levels become the strongest support and resistance zones on the chart. These support and resistance points can come from the same chart, for example, the daily main trend-indicator chart with angles, or they can be combinations of time periods such as support angles from the monthly and daily charts.

Time Charts

On a separate chart or on a working chart, the analyst must mark time. Time is identified by vertical lines or arrows. Time can consist of divisions of the circle counts (that is, 30, 60, 90, 120 days), anniversary dates of major tops and bottoms (5-year top), beginning and ending seasonal dates, Fibonacci counts, or astrological dates (conjunctions, squares, oppositions). Sometimes marking on a chart the dates of major economic releases or central bank meetings can help identify trend objectives.

SUMMARY

Price and time data come in two forms: (1) tabular data and (2) visual data. The first type is the raw data that are contained in computer files, which list the date, open, high, low, close, volume, and open interest. Anyone with a computer is most familiar with this type of data. The second is a graph representation of these tabular data. The three main elements of tabular and graphic data are price, time, and volume. The main topics in this book are price and time and the combination of the two, which forms pattern. Volume and open interest, which can be major determinants of pattern, trend, and trading, are not discussed in great detail in this book.

Traders are encouraged to study and experiment with the massive amount of data available. It is important to be consistent with the data being used, particularly when it comes to deciding whether to use 24-hour charts or day-session-only charts. Good analysts should try to use all of the available data to make a sound analysis of market conditions. This may mean making a decision to chart combinations of pit/electronic trading activity. Accuracy in data is important. Confirm that the data are clean and error-free before they become an issue. Candlestick patterns to Gann angles can be incorrectly identified if open, high, low, and settlement data are posted in error.

Price can be charted in various increments: Euros/Dollar, Dollars/Bushel, or Dollars/Ounce, to name a few. When it comes to price and time analysis, the price scale used on a chart is most important because the trader must have control of the chart, and using the correct price scale per grid helps the chartist accomplish this task. Studying the market movement on a chart can help the chartist determine quite accurately which price scale to use. An incorrect price scale will make a trade use incorrect support and resistance points as well as force the chartist to mistime the market while looking for specific price and time matchups. It cannot be overemphasized how important it is to properly scale a chart.

Time is another important factor that must be considered when constructing charts. The chartist must give herself an opportunity to observe the market in as many time periods as possible. These time periods should range from long-term (yearly) to short-term (five minutes). Creating charts in various time periods can help the trader to understand the nature of the market being analyzed. This can then help her determine when the market will turn with reasonable accuracy.

A properly constructed chart consists of price and time factors that, when combined, produce easily identifiable patterns that can help a person trade with reasonable accuracy. In addition, successful trade-system design and money-management techniques are better applied when the trader is working with a consistently designed chart. Records are necessary in a well-run business, and without them, the business will fail. Charts are records that must be designed and maintained properly or the trader will fail. Care should be taken to create usable charts. The past must be studied to determine the future, and the charts are the records of past market action. Just as markets take time to develop, the chartist must take time to develop the necessary charts to study the development of bull or bear markets. In order to move on and learn some of the finer points of pattern, price, and time analysis, the trader must make a commitment to maintaining first-rate charts.

From the simple bar chart the trader can create the swing chart that identifies the trend, tops, and bottoms. The swing chart also creates patterns that the trader can use to identify when and how a trend is likely to begin or end. In addition, the swing chart offers the trader a chance to discover the important timing points of the current contract that can be used for future trading, and it records the horizontal support and resistance points in a market (Figure 4.13). Angle charts created from the swing charts show diagonal movement in a market and carry the characteristics of the bottom or top from which the

FIGURE 4.13 2008 December Cocoa Percentage Retracement Chart
Copyright © TradeStation.

angle was drawn. In other words, the stronger the original top or bottom, the stronger the angle from which it was drawn. Each set of swings forms a range, inside of which are percentage retracement points. The combination of the horizontal and diagonal points form impact points that can turn a market or change a trend. These points can be created by the various analysis tools or by combining time periods. Time can also be combined in the same manner to provide the trader with key cycle dates. Finally, combining pattern, price, and time can become the basis for the development of a trading system.

CHAPTER 5

Pattern: Trend Indicator Charts

T rend indicator charts also known as swing charts are used to identify the tops and bottoms in the market for any time period. In order to avoid confusion about whether we are speaking exclusively of the monthly, weekly, daily, or intraday charts, we will call each trading time period a bar.

The trend indicator chart follows the up and down movements of the market. Basically, from a low price each time the market makes a higher-high than the previous bar, a trend line moves up to the new high. This action makes the low price a bottom. From a high price each time the market makes a lower-low than the previous bar the trend line moves down from the high to the new low. This action makes the high price a top. The combination of a trend line from a bottom and a trend line from a top forms a swing. This is important information, because when stop placement is discussed, traders will be told to place stops under swing bottoms, not under lows, and over swing tops, not over highs. Learn and know the difference between a low and a swing bottom, and a high and a swing top.

Once the first swing is formed, the trader can anticipate a change in the trend. If the swing chart begins from the first trading month, week, or day, and the trend line moves up to a new high, this does not mean that the trend has turned up. Conversely, if the first move is down, this does not mean the trend is down. The only way for the trend to turn up is to cross a top, and the only way for the trend to turn down is to cross a bottom. In addition, if the trend is up and the market makes a swing down that does not take out the previous swing bottom, this is a correction. If the trend is down and the market makes a swing up that does not take out the previous swing top, this is also a correction. A market is composed of two types of up and down moves. The swing chart draws attention to these types of moves by identifying trending up moves and correcting up moves, as well as trending down moves and correcting down moves.

In summary, when implementing the swing chart, the analyst is merely following the up and down movements of the market. The intersection of an established downtrending line with a new uptrending line is a swing bottom. The intersection of an established uptrending line with a new downtrending line is a swing top. The combination of swing tops and bottoms forms the trend indicator chart. The crossing of a swing top changes the trend to up. The penetration of a trend bottom changes the trend to down. The market is composed of uptrends, downtrends, and trend corrections.

MINOR TREND INDICATOR

While studying Forex, equity, and commodity market charts, the trader will inevitably discover the small fluctuations of the market. These small fluctuations collectively make up the minor trend. Although they are minor in nature, these trends provide useful information the trader can use to determine what the minor trend of a market is and when it will change.

The fascination with the minor trend makes this indicator quite popular, as traders envision vast profits seemingly available from capturing the minor swings of the market. Unfortunately, traders who attempt to make a quick buck at trading the minor trend find the situation to be the opposite because of the numerous false signals and prohibitive costs of doing business. Although it is necessary to construct this chart to become aware of the role the minor trend plays in the intermediate- and long-term trends, it is not recommended to be the sole source of trend information.

Traders accustomed to a gambling mentality can find themselves in a situation where they are hooked on the pure emotion of trading the minor swings, the greed stemming from capturing the "whole move," and the fear of missing out on the "big move." The trader who relies exclusively on the minor swings of the market is likely to develop doubts in his trading ability, and most often will abandon or fade his system after a series of losses or missed moves. This loss of confidence can have major ramifications on the future of his trading, as there will always be doubt lurking in his head as he develops more sophisticated systems.

The pitfalls of trading exclusively with the minor trend have to be addressed, not to discourage the use of the minor trend as an indicator of future market movement, but to make the trader aware of the part the minor trend has in creating successful trading tools. At this time it should be noted that the minor trend should be used to learn more about the intermediate and main trends. This is its most beneficial use unless the trader is forced because of her career decision to trade the minor trend on an intraday or day-to-day basis. While it can be shown that more money is made over the long run by trading the major market swings, those who can afford the risk, have low trading costs, instantaneous access to the market, and the time to develop an optimized trading system can have positive results.

Trading the minor trend is a full-time job. The trader has to maintain a properly constructed chart at all times. This is because a major move can occur at any time, and the trader has to be ready. Those who find success at trading the minor trend are those who can control risk and are willing to take a series of losses in exchange for a few trades whose profits are far greater than the losses. Traders who cannot handle the prospect of having more losing trades than winning trades, who have a closed mind and the inability to accept changes in trend quickly should avoid trading the minor trend.

Given the noted pitfalls of using the minor trend as the sole indicator of future market direction, the reader invariably asks: "Why the minor trend indicator chart?" Following the proper construction of this chart, the trader will have before him a chart depicting each minor top and minor bottom and the date each one occurred. In addition, the trader will also be able to determine when minor trend changes have taken place and the duration of the swings in terms of price and time.

Minor Trend Definition

Since the minor swing chart can be used to identify the minor tops and bottoms for any time period, in order to avoid confusion about whether we are speaking exclusively of the monthly, weekly, daily, or intraday charts, we call each trading time period a bar.

The minor swing chart, or one-bar chart, follows the one-bar movements of the market. From a low price each time the market makes a higher-high than the previous bar, a minor trend line moves up from the recent low to the new high. This action makes the previous low price a minor bottom (Figure 5.1). From a high price each time the market

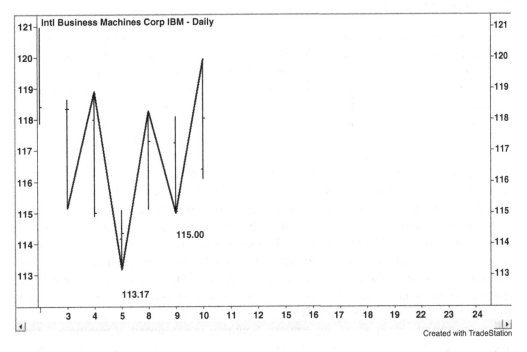

FIGURE 5.1 Minor Bottoms at 113.17 and 115.00. A low price becomes a minor bottom when the market posts a higher-high.
Copyright © TradeStation.

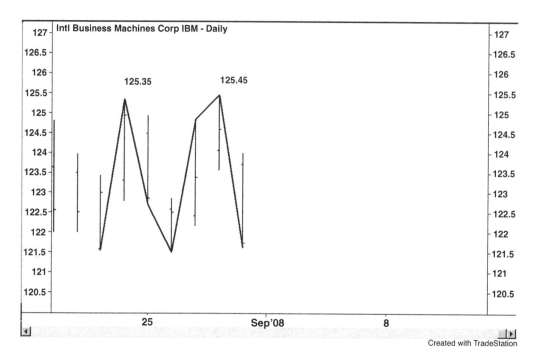

FIGURE 5.2 Minor Tops at 125.35 and 125.45. A high price becomes a minor top when the market posts a lower-low.
Copyright © TradeStation.

makes a lower-low than the previous bar, a minor trend line moves down from the recent high to the new low. This action makes the previous high price a minor top (Figure 5.2). The combination of a minor trend line from a bottom and a minor trend line from a top forms a minor swing. This is important information, because when stop placement is discussed, traders will be told to place stops under minor swing bottoms, not under lows, and over minor swing tops, not over highs. Learn and know the difference between a low and a minor swing bottom, and a high and a minor swing top. This will help you take losses faster and stay in moves longer.

Once the first minor swing is formed, the trader can anticipate a change in the minor trend (Figure 5.3). If the minor swing chart begins from the first trading month, week, or day, and the minor trend line moves up to a new high, this does not mean that the minor trend has turned up. Conversely, if the first move is down, this does not mean the minor trend is down. The only way for the minor trend to turn up is to cross a minor top (Figure 5.4), and the only way for the minor trend to turn down is to cross a minor bottom. In addition, if the minor trend is up and the market makes a minor swing down that does not take out the previous minor swing bottom, this is a correction. If the minor trend is down and the market makes a minor swing up that does not take out the previous minor swing top, this is also a correction. A market is composed of two types of up and down moves. The minor swing chart draws attention to these types of moves by identifying trending up moves and correcting up moves, as well as trending down moves and correcting down moves.

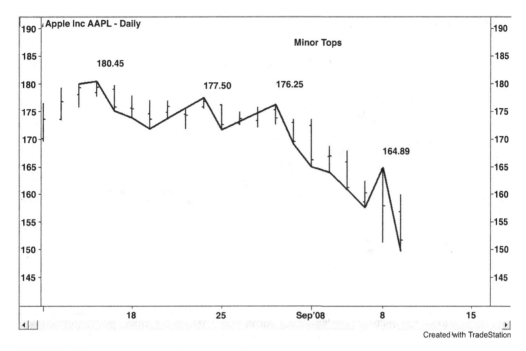

FIGURE 5.3 Minor Trend Indicator Bars from a High Price. Minor tops are formed by the 1-bar swings of the market. From a high, the minor trend line moves down to the lower-low. Copyright © TradeStation.

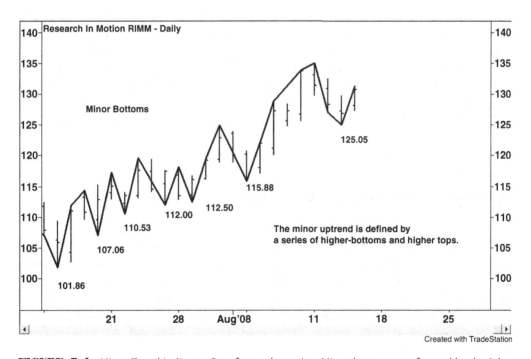

FIGURE 5.4 Minor Trend Indicator Bars from a low price. Minor bottoms are formed by the 1-bar up swings of the market. From a low, the minor trend line moves up to the higher-high. Copyright © TradeStation.

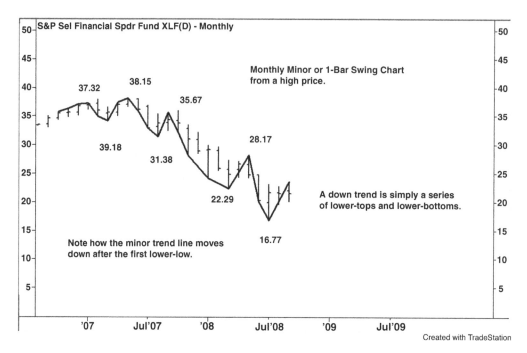

FIGURE 5.5 Monthly Minor Trend Indicator Chart from a High Price
Copyright © TradeStation.

In summary, when implementing the minor swing chart (Figure 5.5), the analyst is merely following the one-bar up and down movements of the market. The intersection of an established downtrending line with a new uptrending line is a minor swing bottom. The intersection of an established uptrending line with a new downtrending line is a minor swing top. The combination of minor swing tops and bottoms forms the minor trend indicator chart. The crossing of a minor swing top changes the minor trend to up. The penetration of a minor trend bottom changes the minor trend to down. The market is composed of uptrends, downtrends, and corrections (Figure 5.6).

INTERMEDIATE TREND INDICATOR

After studying the minor swing chart and learning some of its disadvantages, the analyst may naturally be drawn to the intermediate swing chart (Figure 5.7). After being made aware of the exigencies relating to the minor trend chart, the trader may feel that trading the intermediate swing chart offers a better opportunity to trade successfully. In addition, the intermediate trend chart offers the trader more "true" changes in trend and is less likely to whipsaw. Finally, the cost of trading is decreased considerably because fewer signals are generated by the intermediate trend chart as compared to the minor trend chart.

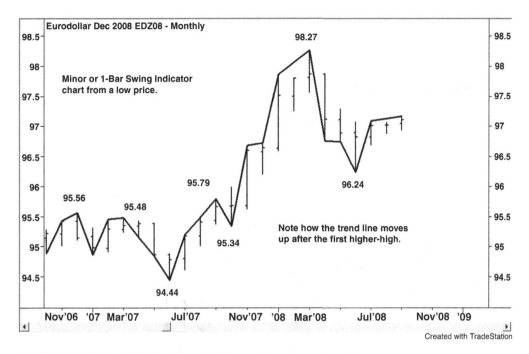

FIGURE 5.6 Monthly Minor Trend Indicator Chart from a Low Price
Copyright © TradeStation.

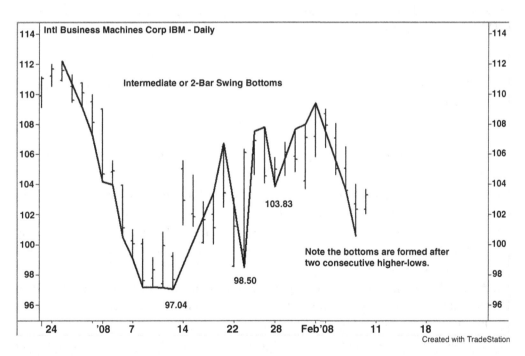

FIGURE 5.7 Intermediate or 2-bar Swing Bottoms at 97.04, 98.50 and 103.83
Copyright © TradeStation.

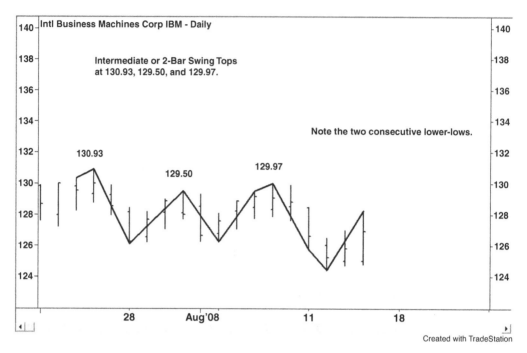

FIGURE 5.8 Intermediate or 2-bar Swing Tops at 130.93, 129.50 and 129.97
Copyright © TradeStation.

Following are some of the major benefits of trading using the intermediate swing chart (Figure 5.8):

1. Intermediate trend opportunities occur less frequently than minor trend opportunities. This keeps the cost of trading to a minimum.
2. Trading less frequently than the minor trend indicator makes the trader less likely to be whipsawed and also makes the possibility of a long series of losses less likely.
3. Intermediate trend trading opportunities develop more slowly and more predictably than minor trend opportunities. This gives the trader time to watch the formation and to make adjustments when necessary.
4. Although the same technique is required to create the intermediate trend chart, and the minor trend chart, the amount of time devoted can be less especially if the market is currently in a steep uptrend or downtrend.
5. The mental exhaustion caused by frequently changing direction, overtrading, and taking a series of losses is not as common for the intermediate trend trader as it is for the minor trend trader.

6. Study of the minor trend chart is helpful in determining upcoming trend changes on the intermediate trend chart. Additionally, study of the intermediate trend chart is helpful in determining trend changes in the main trend chart.

After learning the disadvantages of the minor trend chart and learning some of the advantages of the intermediate trend chart, the trader often chooses the intermediate trend chart as her sole source of trend data and information. Following the proper construction of this chart, the trader will have before her a chart depicting each intermediate top and intermediate bottom and the date on which each of them occurred. In addition, she will be able to determine when intermediate trend changes have taken place and the duration of the intermediate swings in terms of price and time. From this information a simple trading system can be developed.

Intermediate Trend Definition

The intermediate swing chart can be used to identify the intermediate tops (Figure 5.9) and bottoms (Figure 5.10) for any time period. In order to avoid confusion about whether we are speaking exclusively of the monthly, weekly, daily, or intraday charts, we will refer to each trading time period as a bar.

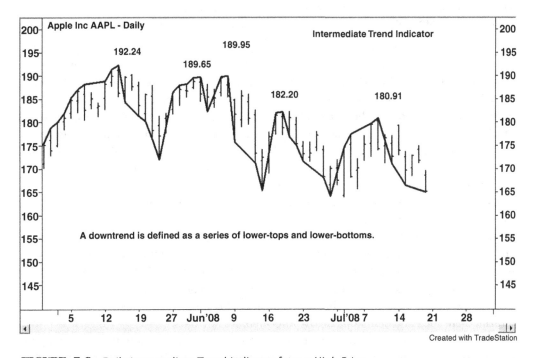

FIGURE 5.9 Daily Intermediate Trend Indicator from a High Price
Copyright © TradeStation.

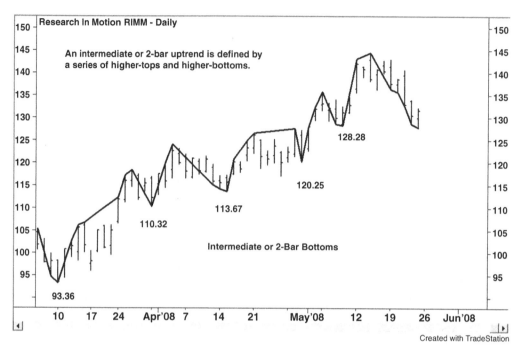

FIGURE 5.10 Daily Intermediate Trend Indicator from a Low Price
Copyright © TradeStation.

The intermediate swing chart, or two-bar chart, follows the two-bar movements of the market (Figure 5.11). From a low price each time the market makes a higher-high than the previous bar for two consecutive time periods, an intermediate trend line moves up from the low two bars back to the new high. This action makes the low price from two bars back an intermediate bottom. From a high price each time the market makes a lower-low than the previous bar for two consecutive time periods, an intermediate trend line moves down from the high two bars back to the new low. This action makes the high price from two bars back an intermediate top. The combination of an intermediate trend line from an intermediate bottom and an intermediate trend line from an intermediate top forms an intermediate swing.

It is important that the trader distinguish between a low and an intermediate bottom and a high and an intermediate top. Too often the trader is tempted to buy with a stop placed under the previous day's low or short with a stop placed above the previous day's high. This stop placement is incorrect and most likely to be caught. Although this matter will be discussed later in the chapter, it is important that buy stops be placed above intermediate tops and sell stops below intermediate bottoms.

Once the first intermediate swing is formed, the trader can anticipate a change in the intermediate trend. If the intermediate swing chart begins from the first trading month, week, or day, and the intermediate trend line moves up to a new high, this

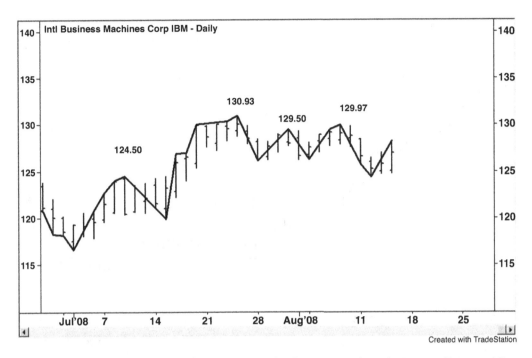

FIGURE 5.11 Daily Intermediate or 2-Bar Trend Indicator. Note how the intermediate trend line moves down after two consecutive lower-lows.
Copyright © TradeStation.

does not mean that the intermediate trend has turned up. Conversely, if the first move is down, this does not mean the intermediate trend is down. The only way for the intermediate trend to turn up is to cross an intermediate top, and the only way for the intermediate trend to turn down is to cross an intermediate bottom. In addition, if the intermediate trend is up and the market makes an intermediate swing down that does not take out the previous intermediate swing bottom, this is a correction. If the intermediate trend is down and the market makes an intermediate swing up that does not take out the previous intermediate swing top, this is also a correction. A market is composed of two types of up and down moves. The intermediate swing chart draws attention to these types of moves by identifying trending up moves and correcting up moves, as well as trending down moves and correcting down moves.

In summary, when implementing the intermediate swing chart, the analyst is merely following the two-bar up and down movements of the market (Figure 5.12). The intersection of an established downtrending line with a new uptrending line is an intermediate swing bottom. The intersection of an established uptrending line with a new downtrending line is an intermediate swing top. The combination of intermediate swing tops and bottoms forms the intermediate trend indicator chart. The crossing of an intermediate swing top changes the intermediate trend to up. The penetration of an intermediate trend

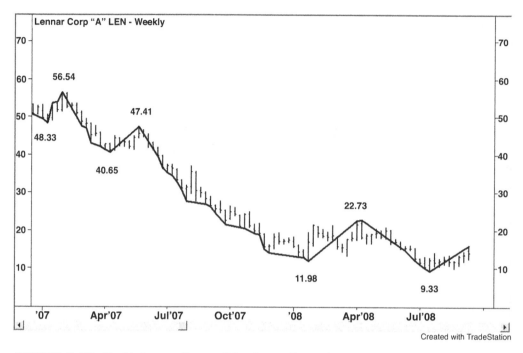

FIGURE 5.12 Weekly Intermediate or 2-Bar Swing Chart. The intermediate trend chart ignores the minor or 1-bar moves and focuses on the 2-bar moves. Copyright © TradeStation.

bottom changes the intermediate trend to down. The market is composed of intermediate uptrends, intermediate downtrends, and intermediate trend corrections.

MAIN TREND INDICATOR

After studying the minor and intermediate swing charts and learning some of their advantages and disadvantages, the analyst may naturally be drawn to the main swing chart. After being made aware of the exigencies relating to trading the minor trend chart and experiencing the relative ease of using the intermediate trend chart, the trader may want to develop an indicator for a longer-term view of the market. While the minor trend indicator is the most active, followed by the intermediate trend indicator, the main trend indicator is the least active. This does not necessarily make it better, however, as the objective of creating these charts is to trade for profits. The minor trend chart has too many sudden changes in trend along with high trading costs, while the main trend chart has low trading costs in terms of commissions, but high costs in terms of missed opportunities. The best way to use this chart is in conjunction with the intermediate trend indicator. For example, in a bull market as determined by the main trend chart (Figure 5.13), it is better to use the intermediate trend indicator for buying opportunities following

FIGURE 5.13 Main or 3-Bar Trend Indicator from High Prices at 21.55, 19.05 and 18.59. The trend line will move down following three consecutive lower-lows.
Copyright © TradeStation.

corrections. Conversely, in a bear market as determined by the main trend indicator, it is better to use the intermediate trend indicator to enter the market following corrections. The construction of the main trend chart should not be treated lightly, as the main trend of every market should be the trader's primary concern.

To be able to analyze a market and trade successfully, the analyst must construct the main trend chart, the intermediate trend chart, and the minor trend chart. The swings of the shorter-term charts make up the swings of the longer-term charts. While each chart has its advantages and disadvantages, combining the charts to generate trades is the best use of these charts. The best way to use these charts is to always trade in the direction of the main trend; use the intermediate trend chart to enter and exit the market in the direction of the main trend; and the more aggressive traders can use the minor trend chart to trigger buys and sells in the direction of the intermediate and main trends. Do not use any one chart as the sole reference for trading. Use a combination of the charts in the direction of the main trend. Following the proper construction of the main trend chart, the trader will have before him a chart that shows each main top and main bottom and the date when each main top and main bottom (Figure 5.14) occurred. In addition, he will be able to determine when main trend changes have taken place and the duration of the main swings in terms of price and time. From this information a simple trading system can be developed.

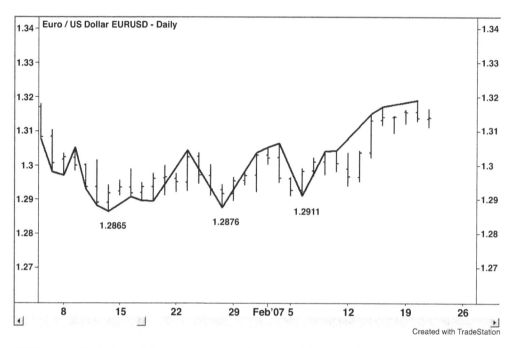

FIGURE 5.14 Main or 3-Bar Swing Bottoms from Low Prices at 1.2865, 1.2876, and 1.2911. A high price becomes a main top when the market posts three consecutive lower-lows. Copyright © TradeStation.

Main Trend Definition

Since the main swing chart can be used to identify the main tops and bottoms for any time period, in order to avoid confusion about whether we are speaking exclusively of the monthly, weekly, daily, or intraday charts, we call each trading time period a bar (Figure 5.15).

The main swing chart follows the three-bar movements of the market from a low price each time the market makes a higher-high than the previous bar for three consecutive time periods, a main trend line moves up from the low three bars back to the new high. This action makes the low price from three bars back a main bottom. From a high price each time the market makes a lower-low than the previous bar for three consecutive time periods, a main trend line moves down from the high three bars back to the new low. This action makes the high price from three bars back a main top. The combination of a main trend line from a main bottom and a main trend line from a main top forms a main swing. This is important information, because when stop placement is discussed, traders will be told to place stops under main swing bottoms, not under lows, and over main swing tops, not over highs. Learn and know the difference between a low and a main swing bottom, and a high and a main swing top.

Once the first main swing is formed, the trader can anticipate a change in the main trend. If the main swing chart begins from the first trading month, week, or day and the

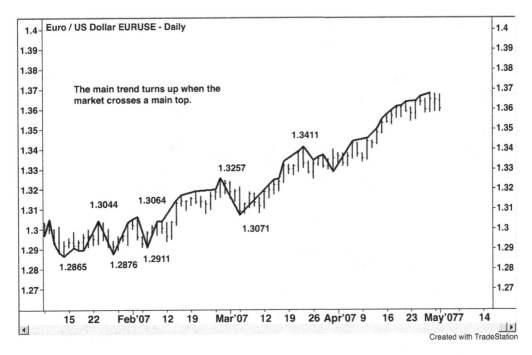

FIGURE 5.15 Main or 3-Bar Trend Indicator
Copyright © TradeStation.

main trend line moves up to a new high, this does not mean that the main trend has turned up. Conversely, if the first move is down, this does not mean the main trend is down. The only way for the main trend to turn up is to cross a main top, and the only way for the intermediate trend to turn down is to cross a main bottom. In addition, if the main trend is up and the market makes a main swing down that does not take out the previous main swing bottom, this is a correction. If the main trend is down and the market makes a main swing up that does not take out the previous main swing top, this is also a correction. A market is composed of two types of up and down moves. The main swing chart draws attention to these types of moves by identifying trending up moves and correcting up moves, as well as trending down moves and correcting down moves.

In summary, when implementing the main swing chart (Figure 5.16), the analyst is merely following the three-bar up and down movements of the market. The intersection of an established downtrending line with a new uptrending line is a main swing bottom. The intersection of an established uptrending line with a new downtrending line is a main swing top. The combination of main swing tops and bottoms forms the main trend indicator chart. The crossing of a main swing top changes the main trend to up. The penetration of a main trend bottom changes the main trend to down. The market is composed of main uptrends, main downtrends, and main trend corrections.

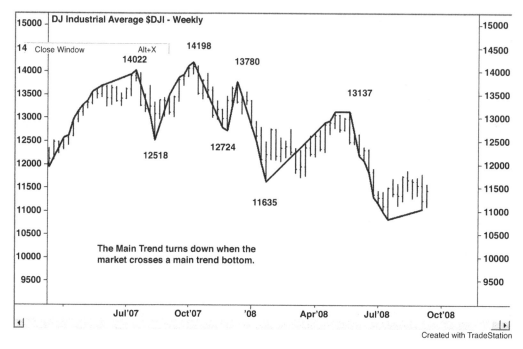

FIGURE 5.16 Main or 3-Bar Trend Indicator
Copyright © TradeStation.

TREND INDICATOR CONSTRUCTION

There are two ways to construct the trend indicator chart. The first way is to create the chart manually. The second is to have a charting program create the chart. It is highly suggested to create the chart manually at first to get a feel for the information the chart is revealing. Only after mastering the creation and interpretation of the trend indicator chart should one computerize this technique. Once computerized, the trader will have the ability to analyze quickly more markets and time periods. This will help the trader learn more about the characteristics of each market especially the size and duration of the swings.

In order to manually construct a trend indicator chart the following must be available: a bar chart, price and time data, a red pen, a green pen, a black pen, and a ruler. The black pen is used to update the chart, the green pen is used to track the upward movement of the trend line, and the red pen is used to track the downward movement of the trend line. Since a poorly drawn line may be misinterpreted, the ruler is used to keep the lines straight. Use the price and time data to ensure the proper marking of highs and lows, as relying on visual estimation invites faulty identification, which can also have an adverse effect on the research.

It is best to start the trend indicator chart from the first trading bar of the contract, because by the time the contract being analyzed becomes the actively traded market, the analyst will have constructed all of the swings of the contract and derived valuable information about price and time from the activity charted. This chart serves as a finger-print of the market, because each individual market has unique patterns contained in the total chart by which it can be identified. This is why precise and accurate data must be maintained at all times.

The Inside Bar

An important fact to note when tracking the swings of the market is the occurrence of the inside move and the outside move. Since this chart pattern holds true for all time periods (monthly, weekly, and daily) and all trend indicators (minor, intermediate, and main), we refer to it as an *inside bar* (Figure 5.17). The inside bar occurs when the high is lower than the previous high and the low is higher than the previous low. When charting the swings of the market, the analyst ignores the inside bar and waits to see the trading range of the next bar. Since the inside bar is ignored, the analyst must always look at the preceding bar to determine if the trend line should be moved up or down. This bar is known as the *last active bar* or *reference bar*. If the trend line was moving up before the

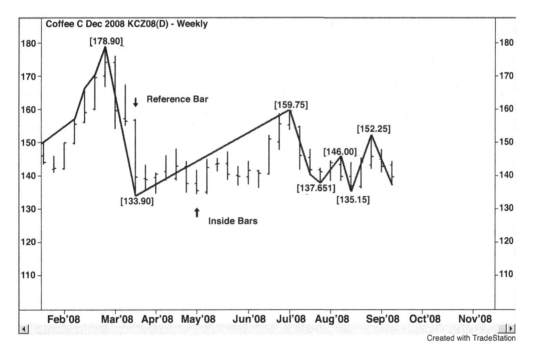

FIGURE 5.17 Inside Moves. Inside moves are ignored during the construction of the trend indicator chart.
Copyright © TradeStation.

inside bar and the current rally takes out the high of the last active bar, then the trend line moves up. If the trend line was moving up before the inside bar and the market moves below the low of the last active bar, then depending on the type of swing chart being used the trend line moves down. If the trend line was moving down before the inside bar and the break takes out the low of the last active bar, then the trend line moves down. If the trendline was moving down before the inside bar and the market moves above the high of the last active bar, then depending on the type of swing chart being used the trend line moves up. In summary, the trader ignores the inside bar and refers to the last active bar to determine the direction of the trend line's movement.

The Outside Bar

The outside time period (Figure 5.18) occurs when the high of the current time period is higher than the previous time period and the low of the current time period is lower than the low of the current time period. Contrary to the inside bar, the order of occurrence of the high and low on an outside move day is critical and should be noted. If the minor trend line is moving up and the first move of the outside move day is to the high, the minor trend line moves up to the high, then down to the low. The intermediate and main trend indicator charts will read this move as 1-bar up. If the minor trend line is moving

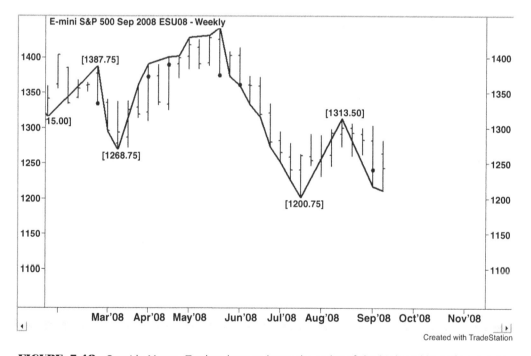

FIGURE 5.18 Outside Moves. Traders have to know the order of the high and low of an outside bar.
Copyright © TradeStation.

up and the first move of the outside move day is to the low then up to the high, the minor trend line moves down to the low then to the high. This action moves the intermediate and main trend indicator line up while the down move is ignored. Furthermore, if the minor trend line is moving down and the first move of the outside move day is to the high, the minor trend line moves to the high, then to the low. The intermediate and main trend indicator charts treat this action as a one-day move up. Finally, if the minor trend line is moving down and the first move of the outside move day is to the low, the minor trend line moves to the low, then to the high. The intermediate and main trend indicator charts follow the first move down to the low.

It is critical that the correct order of the high and low of an outside move day be recorded properly, because the market will either be continuing the trend or the trader will be forced to move the stop to a new level. When back-testing the minor trend indicator on historical data and the order of an outside day cannot be confirmed, it is safe to assume that the price closest to the opening occurred first and the price closest to the close occurred last.

Pay close attention to the intermediate and main trend indicator charts when the market has an outside move because a swing top or swing bottom may be taken out if the outside move is large. This action will change the trend to up or down without having a 2- or 3-bar move.

STOP ORDERS

Although stop orders are discussed later in the book with more specific examples, the general rule to follow is to place them under bottoms and above tops. This is because when the stop is hit, the trend will change. On the other hand, stop loss orders that are placed under lows and above highs are caught more often and simply take the trader out of the market. Another, more basic reason why this type of popular stop should be avoided is that the trader is simply placing the stop within the normal swing of the market. When using the swing chart to enter a market to trade the trend, never consider using a stop set at a specific dollar amount, as it will almost certainly get taken out during the normal course of trading. If using the swing chart to trade a breakout to the upside, then the trader is encouraged to test various stop loss points under the breakout price since he is trading market momentum. If using the swing chart to trade a breakout to the downside, then the trader is encouraged to test various stop loss points over the breakdown price. Since the trader is entering such a move because of downside momentum, any rally that regains the old swing bottom should be stopped out.

The stop points established are set by the market. The construction and study of the swing chart in advance will therefore help a trader determine if the specific market he wants to trade creates price swings he can afford to trade. If the trader cannot afford the stop generated, then he is undercapitalized to trade the specific market and should find another one he can afford to trade in with his limited capital.

The price level the market is trading at often determines the size of the swing and ultimately the size of the stop. For example, markets trading near highs have wider swings than markets trading near low prices. Stops should be placed one, two, or three price units above or below swing tops and bottoms. Which stop placement is indicated depends on the position of the market relative to the price level and the current market volatility. For example, when the market is trading at a historically low level, a stop should be placed closer to the swing top or swing bottom than when a market is trading at a historically high level. Use the long-term charts to determine the position of the market, and place the stop accordingly.

When specific markets are discussed, rules should be created to determine the proper stop placement relative to the swing top or swing bottom and in accordance with the current trading level of the market.

USING THE INFORMATION GENERATED

Keep a record of all swings, as these points can become important support and resistance points during the life of the current market or historical support and resistance points in future years. Besides being important price points, the dates of the swing tops and bottoms can become important timing points during the life of the current market or historical timing points in future years.

Now that the swing tops and bottoms have been identified, record the swings in terms of price and time from top-to-top, top-to-bottom, bottom-to-top, and bottom-to-bottom. This information can be used to determine whether or not a market is expanding or contracting. Swings should also be grouped by price levels and calendar dates. This will give the trader an idea of the behavior of the market at various price levels during particular periods. In addition to cyclical information, this chart contains important seasonal data. Traders should also analyze the strength of up moves from various price levels as well as their corresponding corrections. Conversely, traders should study the strength of down moves from various price levels and their corresponding corrections. A spreadsheet program can be used to organize this information so that the changes in price and time can be easily calculated. It is important to keep a record of these swings because they can become valuable in forecasting future price and time swings.

Depending on the trader's perspective, the minor, intermediate, and main swing charts should be created in order to determine the trend of every time period studied. This means the trader should create a minor, intermediate, and main trend indicator for the intraday charts he uses as well as the longer time periods. The general rule is to gather as much information about the trading characteristics of the market as possible. Further analysis will show that all of these charts are interrelated. Thus, creating all of them will not be wasted effort. By creating these charts the trader is given a top-down perspective: a top or bottom on the monthly chart is the most important, followed by a top or bottom on the weekly chart, then a top and bottom on the daily chart, and finally a top and bottom on the hourly chart.

CHARACTERISTICS OF THE TREND INDICATOR CHART

After creating a trend indicator chart and studying the tops and bottoms, the following should be strongly noted in order to understand the interrelationship of the charts. This concept is addressed again when percentage retracements and Gann angles are discussed.

Interrelationships of Time Periods and Swings
- A swing top on a monthly chart is always a top on the weekly, daily, or hourly charts.
- A swing top on a weekly chart is always a top on the daily and hourly charts, but not always on the monthly chart.
- A swing top on the daily chart is always a top on the hourly chart, but not always on the weekly or monthly charts.
- A swing top on the hourly chart is not always a top on the daily, weekly, or monthly charts.
- A swing bottom on a monthly chart is always a bottom on the weekly, daily, or hourly charts.
- A swing bottom on a weekly chart is always a bottom on the daily and hourly charts, but not always on the monthly chart.
- A swing bottom on the daily chart is always a bottom on the hourly chart, but not always on the weekly or monthly charts.
- A swing bottom on the hourly chart is not always a bottom on the daily, weekly, or monthly charts.
- Uptrends and downtrends on the monthly chart are composed of a series of swings from the weekly, daily, and hourly charts. Study how many weekly, daily, or hourly swings on average it takes to form a monthly uptrend or downtrend.
- Uptrends and downtrends on the weekly chart are composed of a series of swings from the daily and hourly charts. Study how many daily or hourly swings on average it takes to form a weekly uptrend or downtrend.
- Uptrends and downtrends on the daily chart are composed of a series of swings from the hourly chart. Study how many hourly swings on average it takes to form a daily uptrend or downtrend.
- Uptrends and downtrends on the hourly chart are composed of a series of swings from the other intraday time periods, such as the 30-minute, 15-minute, or 5-minute chart. Study how many time period swings on average it takes to form an hourly uptrend or downtrend.

Interrelationships of Types of Swings
- A minor swing uptrend is made up of a series of minor swings.
- A minor swing downtrend is made up of a series of minor swings.
- An intermediate swing uptrend is made up of minor and intermediate swings.
- An intermediate swing downtrend is made up of minor and intermediate swings.
- A main swing uptrend is made up of minor, intermediate, and main swings.

- A main swing downtrend is made up of minor, intermediate, and main swings.
- An intermediate swing top is always a minor top, but a minor top is not always an intermediate top.
- An intermediate swing bottom is always a minor bottom, but a minor bottom is not always an intermediate bottom.
- A main swing top is always a minor top and an intermediate top, but a minor top and an intermediate top are not always a main top.
- A main swing bottom is always a minor bottom and an intermediate bottom, but a minor bottom and an intermediate bottom are not always a main bottom.

SUMMARY

The Trend Indicator or Swing Chart, which can be used for any time period, can be created for the Minor or 1-Bar Swing, the Intermediate or 2-Bar Swing, or the Main or 3-Bar Swing.

The trend indicator chart follows the swings of the market. Traders simply follow the up-and-down movements of the market by raising or lowering the trend line. The crossing of the top and the bottom changes the trend to up or to down, not the movement of the trend line. This action creates uptrends, downtrends, and corrections. Changes in direction turn lows into bottoms and highs into tops. Inside bars should be ignored during the construction of the trend indicator chart. In contrast, outside-bar moves should be watched carefully, as the order of the high or low of the outside bar is critical to the structure of the trend indicator chart. When an outside bar occurs, traders should note which came first, the high or the low.

Avoid placing stops over highs and under lows; instead, place them over tops and under bottoms. The placement of the stop should also be relative to the historical trading position of the market. Studying and analyzing the data created by the swing charts can help the trader determine the duration of the swings in terms of price and time from top-to-top, top-to-bottom, bottom-to-top, and bottom-to-bottom. This information can then be used to judge whether a market is expanding or contracting. In addition, market behavior at various price levels and time periods can help a trader determine the nature of a market. Finally, the trader should have a working knowledge of the interrelationships of the monthly, weekly, daily, and intraday charts and the minor, intermediate, and main trends to gain a better understanding of support and resistance.

CHAPTER 6

Pattern: Swing Chart Trading

A fter building a trend indicator chart and watching how the market performs, the next step is learning how to build a simple trading system. The simplest system to build is one that places the trader in the trade mechanically. Learning the characteristics of a market and each trend indicator is the key to success when using the swing trading method to enter and exit the market. This chapter focuses on the techniques for building trading strategies using the swing charts. Initiating trades from extreme levels, initiating a trade on a reversal stop, and various methods of trading are discussed.

REVIEWING THE TREND INDICATOR CHART RULES

Minor Trend Indicator Charts

The minor or one-day trend indicator chart is easy to construct, as it simply follows the one-day up and down movement of the market (Figure 6.1).

The minor trend line moves up from a low price following a higher-high than the previous bar. When this occurs, a line is drawn from the low one bar back to the high price on the current bar. This action makes the low one bar back a minor bottom. As the market continues to move higher, the trend line moves up to each new high. This process continues until the market posts a price lower than the previous low. When that happens, the minor trend line moves down from the high on the previous bar to the low on the current bar, which makes the last high a minor top. This is the basic formation needed for trading the one-day or minor trend indicator.

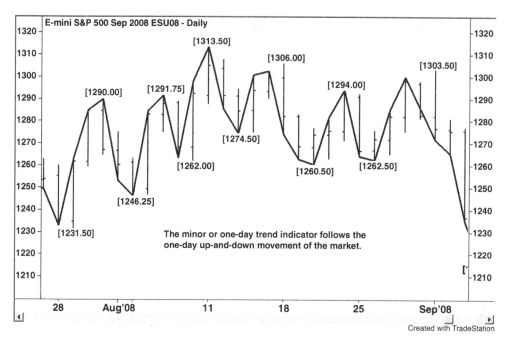

FIGURE 6.1 Minor Trend Indicator Chart
Copyright © TradeStation.

Intermediate Trend Indicator Charts

The intermediate or two-day trend indicator chart is also easy to construct. It is very similar to the minor or one-day trend indicator chart except that it follows the two-day movement of the market (Figure 6.2).

The intermediate trend line moves up from a low price following two consecutive higher-highs than the previous bar. When this occurs a line is drawn from the low two bars back to the high price on the current bar. This action makes the original low two bars back an intermediate bottom. At this point it is no longer necessary to have two consecutive higher-highs to move the trend line up. As the market continues to move higher, the trend line moves up to each new high. This process continues until the market posts two consecutive lower-lows. When that happens, the intermediate trend line moves down to the lower-low on the current bar, which makes the high two bars back an intermediate top. This is the basic formation needed for trading the two-day or intermediate trend indicator.

Main Trend Indicator Charts

The main or three-day trend indicator chart is built in a similar fashion to the one-day and two-day trend indicator charts except that it follows the three-day movement of the market (Figure 6.3).

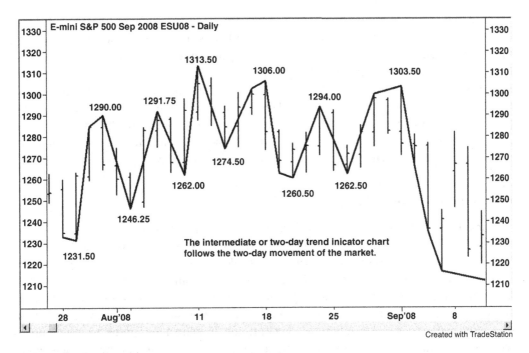

FIGURE 6.2 Intermediate Trend Indicator Chart
Copyright © TradeStation.

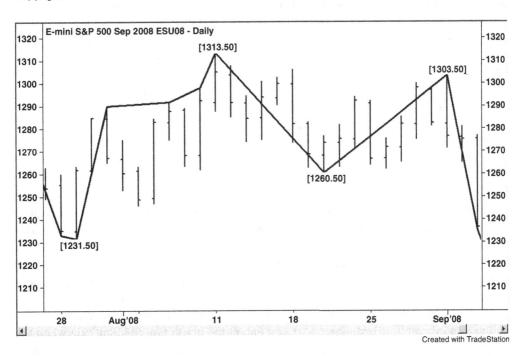

FIGURE 6.3 Main Trend Indicator Chart. The main or 3-day trend indicator chart follows the 3-day movement of the market.
Copyright © TradeStation.

The main trend line moves up from a low price following three consecutive higher-highs than the previous bar. When this occurs, a line is drawn from the low three bars back to the high price on the current bar. This action makes the original low three bars back a main bottom. At this point it is no longer necessary to have three consecutive higher-highs to move the trend line up. As the market continues to move higher, the trend line moves up to each new high. This process continues until the market posts three consecutive lower-lows. When that happens, the intermediate trend line moves down to the lower-low on the current bar, which makes the high three bars back a main top. This is the basic formation needed for trading the three-day or main trend indicator.

Common Characteristics

It is best to start the three trend indicators from the first day the contract comes on the board. This way the trader charts all of the price swings, and the trend will be known before the contract becomes active. During periods of inactivity or light trading, such as during the first few months of trading, the market sometimes only has a closing price. Treat this price as a high or a low, depending on whether it is above or below the last trading day's range. As this chart is being developed, write in the prices and their dates above the swing tops and below the swing bottoms. If using a computer program, make sure the price of the top or bottom as well as the size and duration of the swing is identified on the chart. This information is necessary because it provides the trader with a permanent history of the financial instrument's main tops and bottoms.

Enter the history on a spreadsheet where the distance in terms of price and time can be calculated. It is important to record this information so that the trader can see the changes from top-to-bottom, bottom-to-top, top-to-top, and bottom-to-bottom. This information should be maintained in terms of both price and time so that the trader learns the duration and distance of each swing, which she needs to know for forecasting future market swings. In addition a permanent record of the tops and bottoms can be used for cycles and historical tops and bottoms.

The trader should also be aware of market activity at various price levels. For example, the size and duration of the swings at both low and high levels should be noted. The most likely observation is that trading activity is tight and narrow at lows and wide at high levels. This information helps the trader determine in which section of the move the market is trading. By gathering swing data and studying the size and duration of the swings from top-to-top, the analyst can learn from the characteristics of a market at a top when a rally is coming to an end, which can prevent him from entering a new position at a very high level or at the end of a major swing. Conversely, similar information can be gleaned from studying the size and duration of bottoms-to-bottoms, and can prevent the trader from initializing a position at an extremely low level or at the end of a major down cycle.

In regard to these three trend indicators, the same rules govern when a trader enters and exits a market. For instance, the trader enters the market on the long side when the market crosses the last swing top. She continues to maintain her long position as long as the market continues to make higher tops and higher bottoms, with a protective and reversal stop under the last swing bottom. She does the opposite for a short position, for example, entering the market on the short side when the market crosses the last swing bottom. This type of trading technique is encouraged when the market has reached an extreme level in terms of price and time.

BASIC TRADING INSTRUCTIONS

After constructing the trend indicator charts and studying the swing tops, swing bottoms, and stop placement, it is fairly simple for a trader to initiate trades using this trading tool. Following is a generic explanation of how to use the trend indicator to enter the market.

Using the trend indicator only to enter a market allows the trader to be guided in and out of the market by the changes in the trend. Following the proper construction of the trend indicator charts, determine the current position of the market relative to its historical range or the range of the current active contract, as this trading tool works best when the market is at a historical high or low or following a prolonged move up or down.

The trend indicator can be initiated at any point on the chart, but certain levels have proved to be more successful than others. Starting the trend indicator from an extreme level will probably be more successful than starting the trend indicator in the middle of a major campaign. The following are explanations of trend indicator trades initiated from two major price levels.

Initiating a Trend Indicator Buy Signal from an Extreme Low. From a flat position and following a prolonged move down in terms of price and time and when the market is at an extremely low price level, place a buy stop for one contract or 100 shares over the last swing top, then wait for the market action to reach the stop and fill the order (Figure 6.4). After receiving the fill, place a sell stop order under the last swing bottom. If the market continues to rally, then stay in the position as long as the market continues to make higher-highs and higher-lows, with the sell stop maintained under the last swing bottom. Throughout the life of the rally, the market may develop a series of higher-tops and higher-bottoms. When this happens, continue to follow the market up by moving the sell stop and placing it under each new swing bottom and locking in profits along the way. Once the market forms a swing top and breaks the last swing bottom, the position is stopped out, and the trader is flat.

Initiating a Trend Indicator Sell Signal from an Extreme High. From a flat position and following a prolonged move up in terms of price and time and when the market is at an extremely high price level, place a sell stop for one contract or 100 shares under the last swing bottom, then wait for the market action to reach the stop and fill the order (Figure 6.5). After receiving the fill, place a buy stop order over the last swing top. If the market continues to break, then stay in the position as long as the market continues to make lower-lows and lower-highs with the buy stop maintained

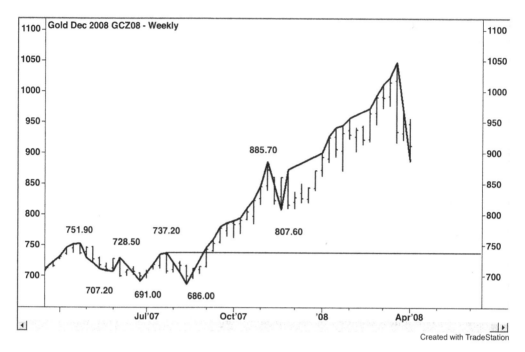

FIGURE 6.4 Initiating a Trend Indicator Buy Signal from an Extreme Low. The intermediate trend turned up on a trade through 737.20.
Copyright © TradeStation.

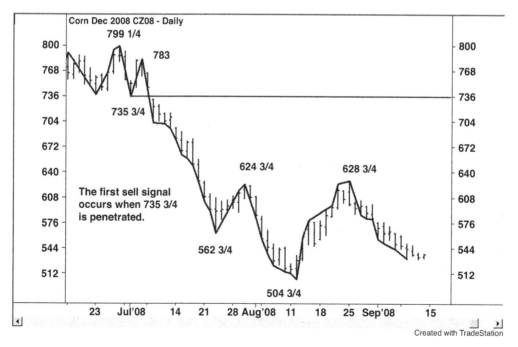

FIGURE 6.5 Initiating a Trend Indicator Short Signal with a Sell Stop
Copyright © TradeStation.

over the last swing top. Throughout the life of the break, the market may develop a series of lower-tops and lower-bottoms. When this happens, continue to follow the market down by moving the buy stop and placing it over each new swing top and locking in profits along the way. Once the market forms a swing bottom and breaks the last main top, the position is stopped out, and the trader is flat.

Reversal Stops

Initiating a Buy Signal with a Reversal Buy Stop As mentioned earlier, the safest time to initiate a buy is following a prolonged move down in terms of price and time or when the market has reached an extremely low price level (Figure 6.6). While this is often the most successful pattern to trade, more active traders may choose to buy following the liquidation of a short position. After a buy stop and reversal is reached, the trader simply follows the upward swings of the market and moves the sell and reversal stops up each time a new swing bottom forms. He maintains the same long position as long as the market continues to make higher tops and higher bottoms. The trade is liquidated, and the position reversed when the last swing bottom is crossed and the sell stop is hit.

A long position triggered by a buy stop and reversal is often more risky than a buy signal generated following a prolonged move down in terms of price and time or from an

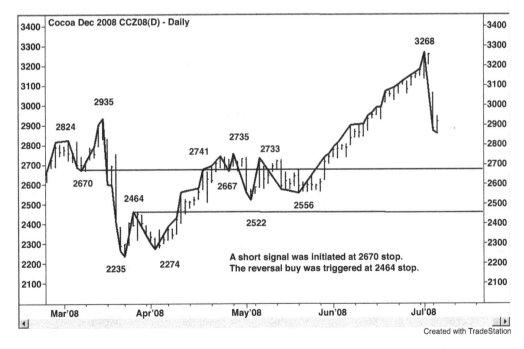

FIGURE 6.6 Initiating a Buy Signal with a Reversal Buy Stop
Copyright © TradeStation.

extremely low level. This is because the buy is often triggered at a poor price level such as the middle of the contract range. Choppy, two-sided trading may occur at this level, and whipsaw-like trading may be common. The frequency of loss therefore increases because of losing trades and high commission costs. It should be noted that the characteristic described is more common with the minor trend indicator than with the intermediate and main trend indicators. Through study and research the trader will determine which trend indicator is best suited for her trading style. This topic was discussed in more detail in Chapter 5.

The best time to enter a long position on a buy reversal signal is following a prolonged move down in terms of price and time that has taken the market to a historically low price level while the trader was in a short position and riding the trend indicator down. In this case, the trader will have excess capital to work with, since the original position was a profitable short position. In other words, the trader is risking the market's money.

Initiating a Short Signal with a Reversal Sell Stop   Just as with the reversal stop buy signal discussed earlier, initiating a short signal with a reversal sell stop is more risky than initiating a short position from an extremely high level (Figure 6.7). This is because the trader has little control over the price level at which the position may be triggered. If the short is triggered at or near a historical support level or major percentage

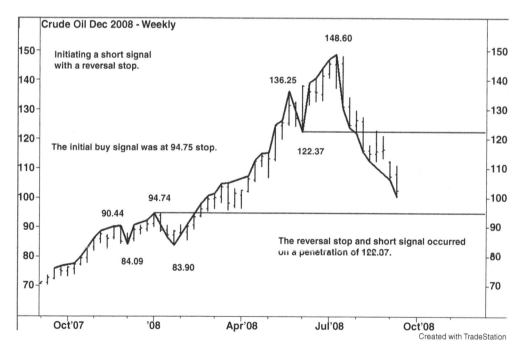

FIGURE 6.7   Initiating a Short Signal with a Reversal Sell Stop
Copyright © TradeStation.

retracement zone, the trader may find himself trading on both sides of the market for several time periods until the market can break away from the support prices. This type of signal is recommended for aggressive traders who wish to trade more actively and can withstand whipsaw trading activity and increased commission costs.

The best time to use a short reversal signal is following a prolonged move up in terms of price and time that has taken the market at or near a historically high price level while the trader was in a long position and riding the main trend indicator up. Traders using both long and short reversal signals must always be aware of the fact that swing trading can be adversely affected by whipsaw markets and that it may take a series of several small losses before the trade develops into a long-term move.

TWO WAYS TO DETERMINE A CHANGE IN TREND

After careful study and analysis I have determined two different ways to set up a change in trend. Although both involve the crossing of a previous swing top or bottom, one indicates a change in trend that is likely to be followed by a retracement while the other indicates a follow-through move following the change in trend.

The basic definition of a change in trend is from a downtrend the market crosses the last swing top and from an uptrend the market crosses the last swing bottom. The basic definition of an uptrend is a series of higher-tops and higher-bottoms and of a downtrend, a series of lower-tops and lower-bottoms. Remember this is not just higher-highs and higher-lows or lower-highs and lower-lows.

A change in trend to down occurs when the market breaks the last trend bottom. This bottom can either occur before the last swing top or after the last swing top. It is very important to note that when a market crosses the last swing bottom before the last swing top, the trend changes to down, but this formation is likely to be followed by a sharp retracement up to set up a secondary lower top (Figure 6.8). This retracement is safe to short with a stop loss above the last swing top. The key to utilizing this formation is to anticipate a retracement before the down move continues.

The second type of change in trend to down occurs when the market breaks the last swing bottom made after the last swing top (Figure 6.9). When this pattern takes place, the last swing bottom is crossed following a retracement of the break from the top. The market not only changes the trend to down, but simultaneously forms a secondary lower top. This pattern often leads to an immediate breakdown in the market.

Think of the reversal of this pattern when the market is forming a bottom. A change in trend to up occurs when the market crosses the last trend top. This top can either occur before the last swing bottom or after the last swing bottom. It cannot be emphasized enough that it is very important to watch how the trend changes to up following a prolonged move down. Note that when a market crosses the last swing top created before the last swing bottom, the trend changes to up, but this formation is likely to be followed by a sharp retracement down to set up a secondary higher bottom (Figure 6.10). This

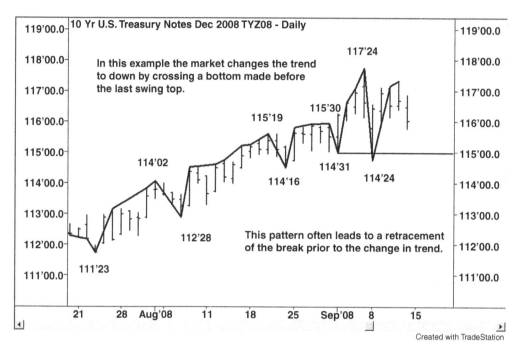

FIGURE 6.8 Two Ways to Determine a Change in Trend
Copyright © TradeStation.

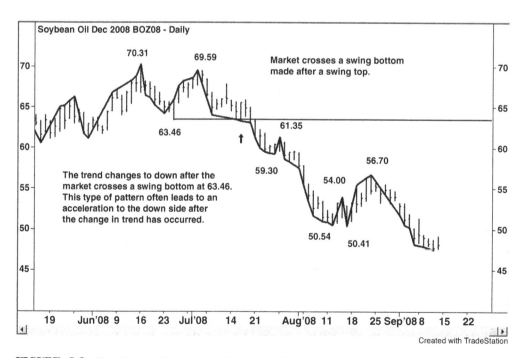

FIGURE 6.9 Two Ways to Determine a Change in Trend
Copyright © TradeStation.

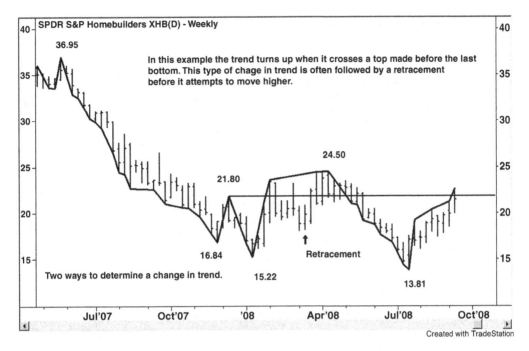

FIGURE 6.10 Two Ways to Determine a Change in Trend. The market crosses a swing top made after a swing bottom.
Copyright © TradeStation.

retracement is safe to buy with a stop loss below the last swing bottom. The key to utilizing this formation is to anticipate a retracement before the up move continues.

The second type of change in trend to up occurs when the market breaks or crosses the last swing top made after the last swing bottom. When this pattern takes place, the last swing top is crossed following a retracement of the rally from the bottom (Figure 6.11). The market not only changes the trend to up, but simultaneously forms a secondary higher bottom. This pattern often leads to a breakout to the upside.

It is very important for the analyst and trader to distinguish between these two types of bottoming or topping action. The logic behind these two patterns is based on how traders look at risk in the market. Most professional traders do not try to pick bottoms in falling markets or tops in runaway markets, but instead allow the market to stop moving in the direction of the prevailing trend before trading in the direction of the change in trend. This is the equivalent of a soccer player stopping the ball before kicking it. If the player tries to kick a moving ball, he usually does not have as much control over its direction. Instead he settles the ball with his foot, then kicks it while he has control.

Before a trader initiates a new position he usually looks for a "lean" or a big order he can lean on in case the position moves against him. I like to say that "a trader finds his out or exit on the trade by looking to the left on the chart." This being said, in the first explanation of a change in trend to up when the last top before the last bottom is

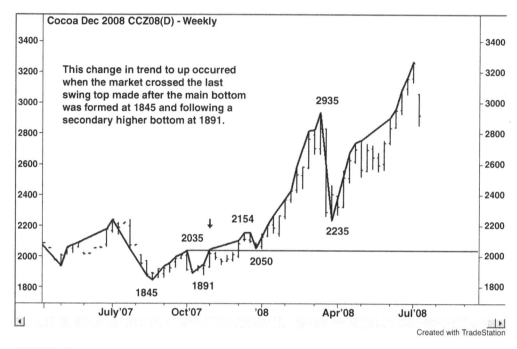

FIGURE 6.11 Two Ways to Determine a Change in Trend. The market crosses a swing top made after a swing bottom.
Copyright © TradeStation.

crossed, that rally is caused by shorts being taken out or buy stops being hit. After these short sellers are taken out of the trade, the market breaks back, and the new buyers step in because they have the last main bottom to lean on.

In the second type of bottoming action, the buyers have already come in on the retracement of the first leg up from the bottom. They used the last main bottom as their lean and are now getting long ahead of the change in trend to up. What is basically happening when tops or bottoms are being formed on a swing chart is that order size has shown up on either the bid or the offer to stop the move causing traders to take action.

OTHER SWING CHART TRADING STRATEGIES

After building a swing chart and watching how the market performs, the trader often begins to think of different ways to trade the swings. This is because the perception of higher volatility and shorter swings in today's markets has put the fear of getting caught with a large position in a whipsaw market into the trader's head. This fear often discourages traders from considering a long-term trend position. Buying strength and selling weakness has also discouraged many traders out of fear of buying the top or selling the bottom. Traders need to study and research the market in order to learn how to apply swing trading strategies, and a properly constructed swing chart along with market timing can help them plan a strong long-term trading campaign.

Swing trading strategies often fail today because the trader does not give the market enough time to develop the long-term trend. This is because many traders only look at the nearby contract to trade and ignore the deferred contracts because they believe that a market with low open interest cannot be traded. Deciding which market to trade depends on individual trading style. Thus, short-term or day traders have to trade in the market that has the most liquidity, while fear of poor fills and slippage keeps many traders out of deferred contracts.

If you want to attempt to trade the longer-term, then you have to look to the deferred contracts, which means you cannot be afraid of trading a futures contract six months to one year in the future. Forex traders should note that long-term swing trading seems suited for this market because of the size and duration of the moves that take place (Figure 6.12). As we have just said, this confidence is gained through study and research of the market. In other words, for a trader to be successful at swing trading he must overlook the possibility of a short-term bad fill and focus on the long-term potential of the market.

The action of the market is relative. Short-term traders rely on fast-moving markets because it is their intention to move in and out quickly, and they need the volatility to accomplish this. A swing trader, on the other hand, accepts the fact that the position may take time to develop and is not worried about day-to-day market activity. Thus, if your intention is to trade the long term, you must buy the data and build the charts to study.

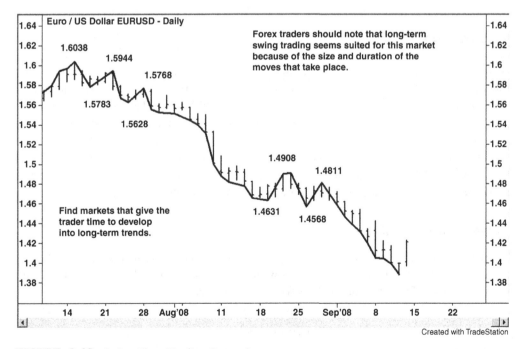

FIGURE 6.12 Swing Chart Trading Strategies
Copyright © TradeStation.

When analyzing futures markets, traders often spend the majority of their time with the most actively traded commodity market. Ideally, however, the trader should be looking at the most actively traded and another chart at least six months out. The longer the time frame, the more likely the trader will find a futures contract to swing-trade. With stocks and Forex markets since there is no expiration, the trader does not have this problem. The monthly and weekly charts usually offer the best indication of which market to swing-trade. These charts offer the trader the ability to see which markets are trading at extreme levels and so are most likely to lead to valid long-term swings.

As mentioned earlier, swing trading today often fails because the trader does not allow enough time for the trend to develop. If you trade the nearby contract, a swing position will often fail because the rollover occurs too soon in the development process. When trading soybeans, for example, a swing that started in October with November soybeans will not have enough time to develop as it will be interrupted by the rollover to January soybeans. If you are going to attempt to swing-trade a position in November soybeans, it makes sense to start trading in at least April or May to give yourself a chance to catch a meaningful continuous move. The process of rolling from one contract to the other often confuses the trader, especially when rolling from old crop contracts to new crop contracts. This constant rollover can force the analyst to concentrate on properly rolling from one contract to the next rather than on the actual trading action.

In summary, if you want to have success in swing trading the long-term trend of a market, you must trade a deferred contract, accept the possibility of a short-term bad fill due to low liquidity, and research and plan the trading strategy.

SWING TRADING RULES

When deciding to trade the long-term swings, look for a market at or near a historically low or high level. Volatility is often low at or near an extremely low level, especially if the market is completing a prolonged move down. With the volatility low and trading ranges tight, stop loss orders can be more easily controlled. Volatility is usually high and ranges wide at or near an extremely high price. This means that stops will be wider so adjustments may have to be made to maintain control of the position in order to control the initial risk. This is one of the characteristics you learn when you study the swing size and duration data you create each time you make a swing chart.

Swing Trading Strategies

There are several different ways to swing-trade with the Trend Indicator Charts. Remember these trading strategies can be used with the Minor, Intermediate, and Main Trend Indicator Chart. They include the following four strategies:

1. Buy/sell when a trend top/bottom is crossed.
2. Buy/sell at fixed price intervals in the direction of the trend.

3. Buy/sell at fixed time intervals in the direction of the trend.

4. Buy/sell a combination of the three trend indicator charts.

Buy/Sell When a Trend Top/Bottom is Crossed The long swing trade begins with a simple crossing of a swing top following a prolonged down move in terms of both price and time (Figure 6.13). The short swing trade starts with the penetration of a swing bottom at or near an extremely high price or after a prolonged rally in terms of price and time.

A successful swing trade does not just happen by accident, but must be planned. After executing the first trade to begin the swing, the trader simply follows the swings of the market by adding to the initial position in the direction of the trend as the market takes out higher tops or lower bottoms in the case of a short swing trade.

A long swing trade means the trader is buying strength. A short swing trade involves selling weakness (Figure 6.14). In each case, the trader must be aware that there will be normal countertrend upswings and countertrend downswings in the market that will not change the trend. This action can turn a profitable position into a breakeven or losing position because of the average price of the total position.

During the normal course of a prolonged trend trade there will be several swings. The trader has the choice to add to his initial position at each subsequent swing point or the trader may choose to maintain only his initial position. In this case, the trader merely follows the swing up or down by trailing a stop below swing bottoms for long positions or above swing tops for short positions.

Swing Trading at Fixed-Price Levels A second way to trade the swing charts is to buy or sell at fixed price levels after the first buy or sell signal has been triggered. The safest way to determine which fixed interval to use is by studying the past history of the stock's swings (Figure 6.15). Remember, in a swing trade from a trend bottom the trader is buying strength, and in a swing trade from a trend top the trader is selling weakness. If the average upswing in a stock is $5.00, then do not start trading the swing after a $5.00 rally. Instead look to buy at a price such as the midpoint of the current upswing from which the market is likely to accelerate to the upside. The idea is to buy with the trend, but at a better price than buying on a breakout over a swing top. This better price can be a predetermined price increment, such as a percentage retracement point, a Gann angle, or a fixed increment. (Retracement points and Gann angles are discussed in more detail in Chapters 8, 9, and 10.) The information learned from building and studying the historical swings of a specific market is necessary for building a successful swing trading strategy. Use the historical data to learn the characteristics of the swings.

When using this strategy in a down trending market, the trader is looking to establish his position by shorting at a better price than selling under the next swing bottom (Figure 6.16). This order entry area may be a percentage retracement level, a Gann angle, or at a fixed increment.

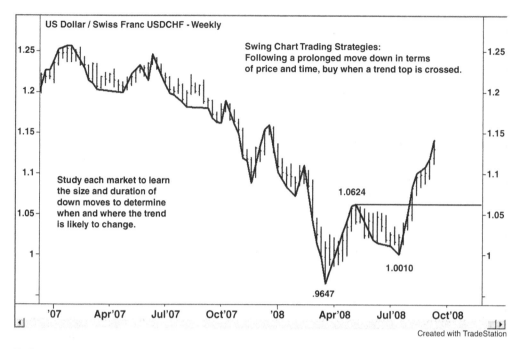

FIGURE 6.13 Swing Chart Trading Strategies. Buy when a trend top is crossed. Copyright © TradeStation.

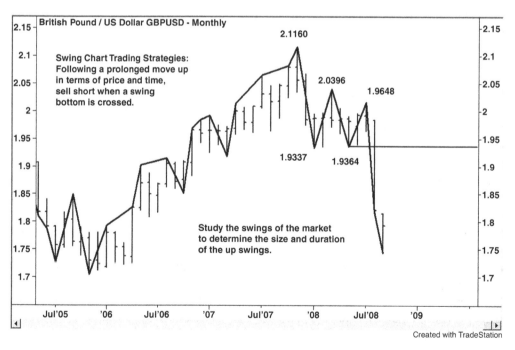

FIGURE 6.14 Swing Chart Trading Strategies. Short when a trend bottom is crossed. Copyright © TradeStation.

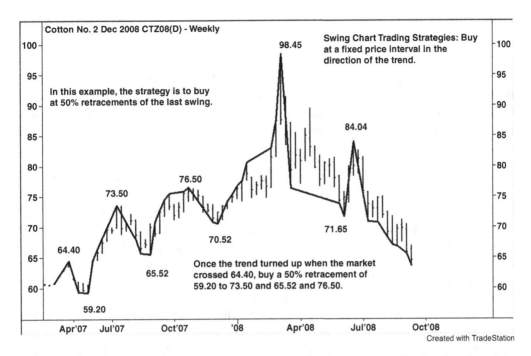

FIGURE 6.15 Swing Chart Trading Strategies. Buy a fixed price interval in the direction of the trend.
Copyright © TradeStation.

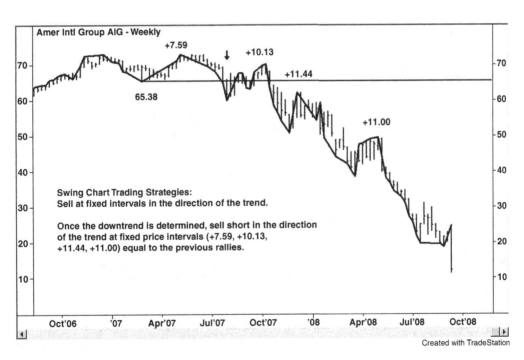

FIGURE 6.16 Swing Chart Trading Strategies. Short a fixed price interval in the direction of the trend.
Copyright © TradeStation.

Using this swing trading method often exposes the trader to normal swings against the trend. This can turn profitable positions into breakeven or losing positions. Before a trade is initiated a trader must assess his stop loss order against his entry. Developing a position-sizing model based on sound money management rules is suggested.

Swing Trading at Fixed Time Intervals   The expression "beating the market" is often used in trading. However, fixed-time interval swing trading actually goes with the rhythm of the market rather than trying to beat it. If, as determined by the information gathered from previous swings, the market has tended to correct a certain number of time periods from a top, then if the trend is up, buy when the market trades lower for an equal amount of time as the previous break (Figure 6.17). For example, if the first swing is 10 days up and 4 days down and the second swing is 15 days up and 4 days down, then look to buy the next 4-day break following a rally.

After the trend has turned down, the trader should look to initiate short positions when the market rallies an amount of time equal to the previous rally (Figure 6.18). For example, if the first swing is 10 days down and 4 days up and the second swing is 10 days down and 4 days up, then look to short the next 4-day rally following a break.

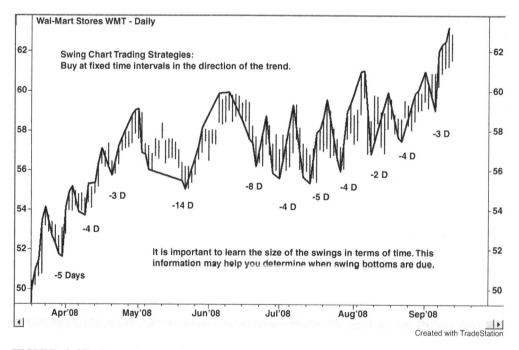

FIGURE 6.17   Swing Chart Trading Strategies
Copyright © TradeStation.

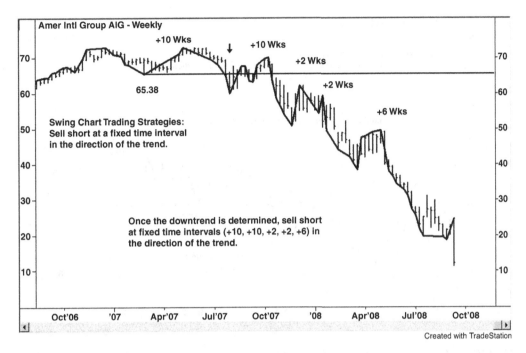

FIGURE 6.18 Swing Chart Trading Strategies
Copyright © TradeStation.

For this swing strategy to work, it is important that the market continue to trade in the same manner as previous swings. If a rally fails, for example, to equal a previous rally in terms of time, or the subsequent break is greater than the previous break, then time is indicating a possible change in trend to down.

If a market fails to break more than or equal to a previous break in terms of time, or the subsequent rally is greater than the previous rally, then time may be indicating a developing change in trend to up.

Keep in mind that you are attempting to trade with the time movement of the market. When time is up or the pattern changes, then consider that the trend has changed.

Buy/Sell a Combination of the Three Trend Indicator Charts

Swing Trading Using a Combination of the Minor Trend Indicator and the Intermediate Trend Indicator Another way to swing-trade the market is to use the minor trend indicator to enter the market in the direction of the intermediate trend (Figure 6.19). All trades triggered by the minor swing chart will be in the direction of the intermediate trend. Protective stops can be placed below the last intermediate trend bottom or below the minor bottom. Stops placed under the intermediate trend bottom are less likely to get caught. Stops placed under minor trend bottoms may get caught under choppy

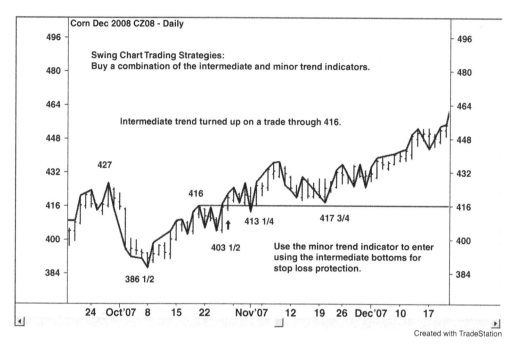

FIGURE 6.19 Swing Chart Trading Strategies
Copyright © TradeStation.

conditions although the intermediate trend remains intact. It becomes a matter of personal preference in deciding under which bottom to trail the stop. The answer relies on the trader's study, experimentation, and back-testing of this strategy.

Initiating a short position is just the opposite of the long position strategy. For a short position, the swing trader waits for the intermediate trend indicator to signal a downtrend and then uses the minor trend indicator to enter a short position (Figure 6.20).

This is an aggressive trading style and should be initiated at extremely low price levels for longs or extremely high price levels for shorts. This type of strategy is often used when the intermediate trend has produced a wide range and the trader wants to use a smaller risk to enter the position.

Swing Trading Using a Combination of the Minor Trend Indicator and the Main Trend Indicator The entry technique for this strategy is the same as the intermediate/minor trend indicator combination (Figure 6.21). In this strategy, the trader waits for the main trend to turn up or down and uses the minor trend indicator to initiate the entries. This strategy is popular because often the main trend swing is very wide and the trader would rather risk taking a few small losses than one big loss if wrong. Often when using this entry strategy the minor trend bottom or top will form in an important retracement area or on a Gann angle. This is just one example of how the swing, retracement, and Gann angle charts get linked together.

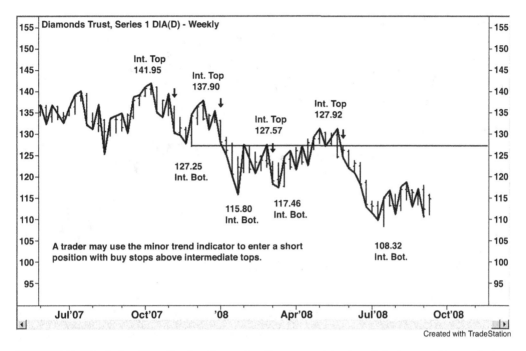

FIGURE 6.20 Swing Chart Trading Strategies. Short a combination of the intermediate and minor trend indicators.
Copyright © TradeStation.

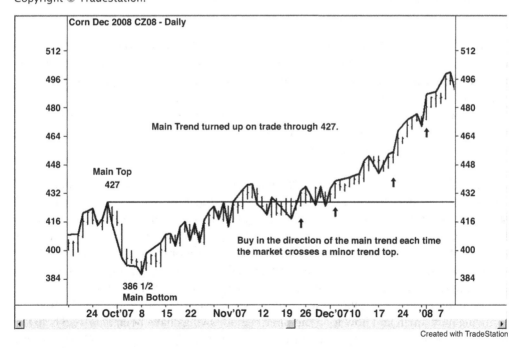

FIGURE 6.21 Swing Chart Trading Strategies. Buy a combination of the main and minor trend indicators.
Copyright © TradeStation.

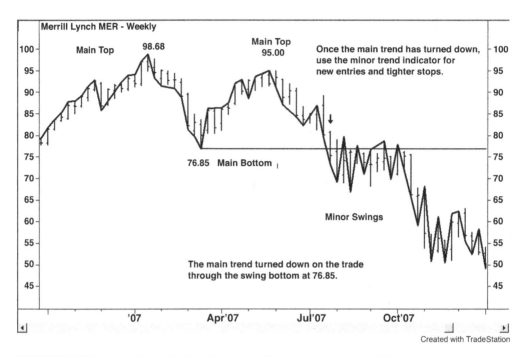

FIGURE 6.22 Swing Chart Trading Strategies. Short a combination of the main and minor trend indicators.
Copyright © TradeStation.

This trading strategy is quite popular when a market is in a prolonged uptrend and downtrend and the stop loss order is too far away for reasonable risk. The trader waits for a minor swing to set up in the direction of the main trend then goes long or short when the minor trend top or bottom is crossed (Figure 6.22). Traders have to remember that although they are trading in the direction of the main trend, this entry is based on the minor trend entry rules, which could mean a series of small losses or choppy trading until the uptrend or downtrend resumes.

Swing Trading Using a Combination of the Intermediate Trend Indicator and the Main Trend Indicator   This swing trading strategy may produce the strongest results because of the strength of the two trend indicators. Using the intermediate trend indicator as the trigger for the trade in the direction of the main trend may produce better results because this type of entry produces fewer false breakouts than the minor trend entry (Figure 6.23).

To make this strategy a success it is suggested that the trader know something about the swing characteristics of the intermediate main trend indicators. Ideally this trade will be initiated at a key support level such as a retracement zone or on a Gann angle. Knowing how much and how long the intermediate swings have been may also help the trader determine the validity of the buy or sell signal (Figure 6.24). Again learning how to combine different charts, retracement zone, Gann angles, and price and time swing information will help improve the success of the trade.

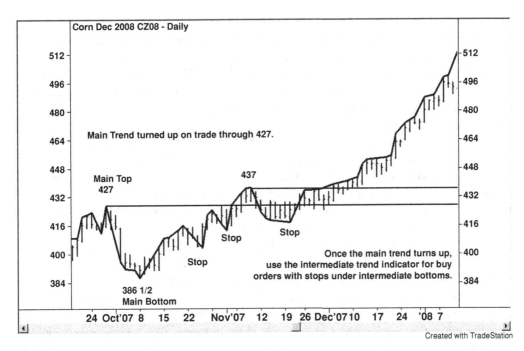

FIGURE 6.23 Swing Chart Trading Strategies. Buy a combination of the main and intermediate trend indicators.
Copyright © TradeStation.

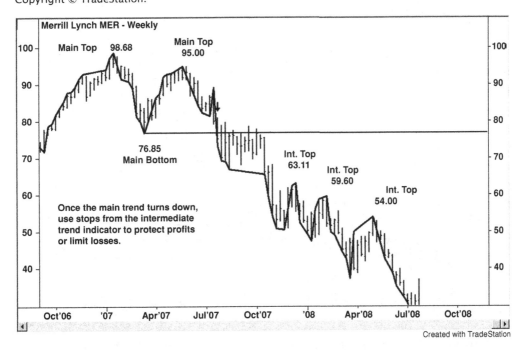

FIGURE 6.24 Swing Chart Trading Strategies. Short a combination of the main and intermediate trend indicator.
Copyright © TradeStation.

Other Trend Combinations   Another way to trade the trend is to use the monthly, weekly, and daily charts as substitutes for the main, intermediate, and minor trend indicators.

In this strategy use the same trend indicator, but vary the time period. For example if the monthly intermediate trend is down, then use the weekly intermediate trend indicator to look for sell signals. In another example, if the weekly main trend indicator is up, then use the daily main trend indicator to search for buy signals. The top-down approach is used to apply this strategy. In other words, the trader starts at the highest time period and then works down to the next time level for the actual trade execution. This can be done for time periods such as monthly down to weekly or daily down to hourly.

On this chart (Figure 6.25) the monthly intermediate trend is up. The trader will use the weekly chart to enter the long side of the market in the direction of the monthly trend. If the trader enters the trade on the monthly swing chart at $407\frac{1}{4}$ the suggested stop is 370. Using this technique the trader has the option to use the weekly chart to try to enter at a better price or use the weekly chart to trail stops tighter. The idea is to trade the weekly chart in the direction of the monthly trend while attempting to improve the entry price or lock in profits by trailing stops more frequently.

The monthly chart of General Motors (GM) turned down when the market crossed 29.10 (Figure 6.26). Once this trend is determined by the higher time period, the trader uses the lower time period chart to enter the short position. The position may be added at the old bottom, a percentage retracement point, or at fixed price and time intervals.

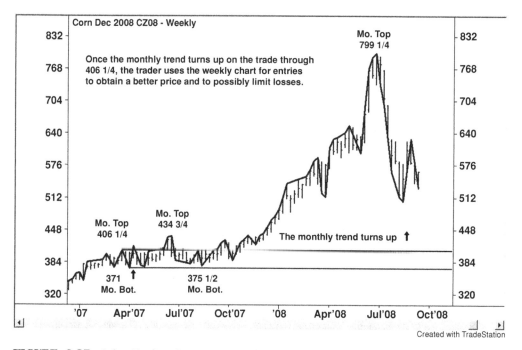

FIGURE 6.25 Other Trading Strategies. Monthly trend up; Buy using the weekly chart. Copyright © TradeStation.

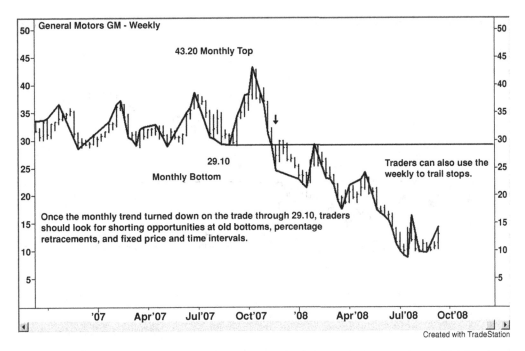

FIGURE 6.26 Other Trading Strategies. Monthly trend down; short using the weekly chart. Copyright © TradeStation.

Alternatively, if the short is executed at 29.10 with a stop loss at 43.20, the trader has the option to trail stops using the faster-moving trend indicator on the weekly chart rather than leave the stop above the slower-moving monthly trend indicator.

In this example, the McDonald's Corp. (MCD) monthly chart (Figure 6.27) has been clearly in an uptrend since the trade through 35.99. Once the trader determines the dominant trend he wants to use, he uses the shorter time period to execute entries. The trader can use the daily chart to wait for buying opportunities on fixed price or time pullbacks as well as new breakouts on the swing chart. This combination may be popular with those who like a lot of activity as the daily chart has a tendency to show numerous swings. Staying focused on only accepting trades in the direction of the monthly trend is the key to using this strategy successfully.

Some markets, like the AT&T (T) chart, have wide ranges on the monthly chart (Figure 6.28). This turns off many traders as the large spread, although correct in determining the change in trend points, is often too wide to accept for risk management purposes. Traders who prefer to use monthly/daily combinations must accept a higher frequency of trades. Focusing on key retracement levels and having the patience to wait for trades to these levels often helps the trader to become more successful. Once again the idea is to determine the main trend and only then trade in the direction of that trend.

The intermediate trend on the 2008 December U.S. Treasury Bond chart (Figure 6.29) turned up on the weekly chart when the market crossed 115'04. The top at 115'04 was a

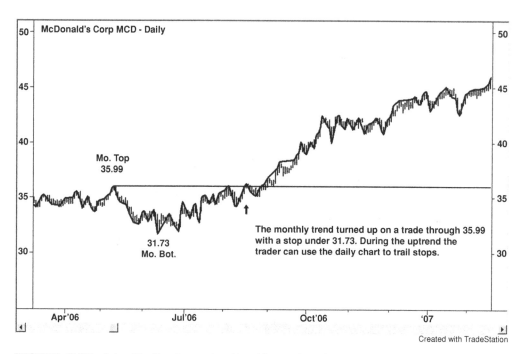

FIGURE 6.27 Other Trading Strategies. Monthly trend up; buy using the daily chart. Copyright © TradeStation.

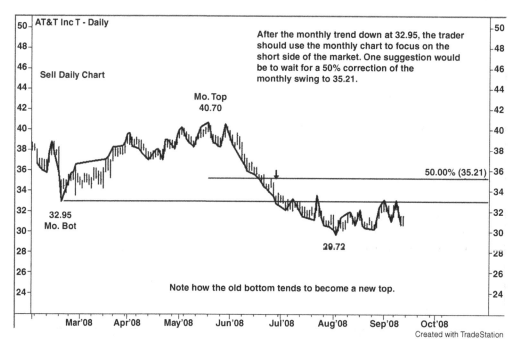

FIGURE 6.28 Other Trading Strategies. Monthly trend down; short using the daily chart. Copyright © TradeStation.

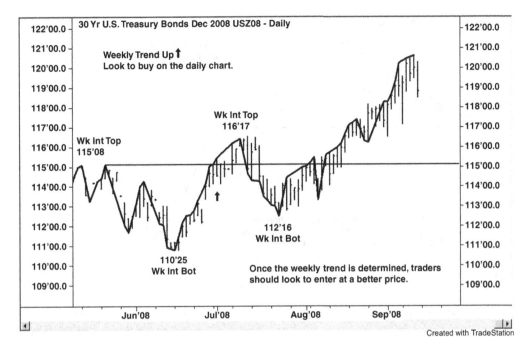

FIGURE 6.29 Other Trading Strategies. Weekly trend up; buy using the daily chart. Copyright © TradeStation.

top made before the last swing bottom at 110'25 so the trader should expect a pull back to set up a secondary higher bottom. Once the intermediate trend turned up the trader should start watching the daily chart to find a better entry than 115'04. The trader can use a fixed price such as a 50 percent retracement of the last intermediate swing, a fixed time interval such as a previous swing, or the crossing of a swing top inside of the last swing. All of these entries are valid as long as the trader can enter at a price better than his original entry on the weekly chart. The trader can also use the daily swing chart breakouts to enter with stops under the daily swing bottoms.

In some cases like the 2008 Daily September Euro contract (Figure 6.30), once the weekly trend turns down, the market accelerates to the downside. Often the trader is unable to trail his initial stop using the larger time frame chart. In this example, the trader would shift down to the daily chart to trail his stops on the initial short position. If the trader were unable to do this in a logical fashion, then he risks giving back a substantial amount of the gains or placing the stop in a poor position, which would cost him further gains.

The next example (Figure 6.31) shows a combination of the daily/hourly 2008 September E-Mini S&P chart. Traders often choose to trade the trend of the larger time frame. This is because trading in the direction of the larger time frame gives the trader the ability to trade with more clarity and conviction. On this chart the daily trend took a long time to turn up. This type of countertrend rally is often followed by a correction

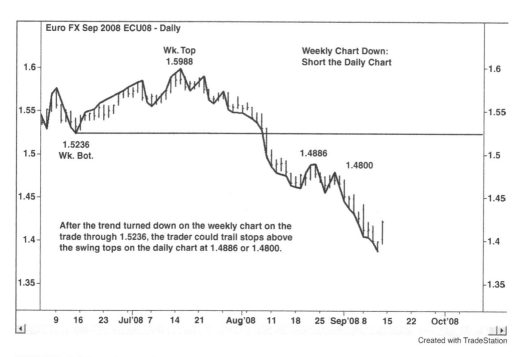

FIGURE 6.30 Other Trading Strategies. Weekly trend down; short using the daily chart. Copyright © TradeStation.

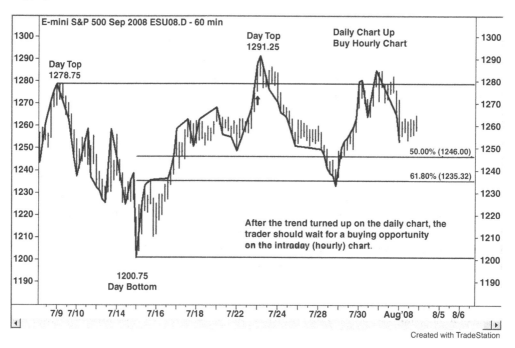

FIGURE 6.31 Other Trading Strategies. Daily trend up; buy using the hourly chart. Copyright © TradeStation.

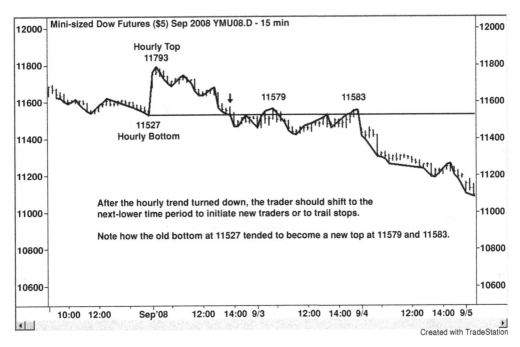

FIGURE 6.32 Other Trading Strategies. Hourly trend down; short using the 15-minute chart. Copyright © TradeStation.

because early longs take profits at the old top. Day traders using this strategy have to be aware of the retracement of the last swing up on the daily chart and use the hourly chart to enter at a favorable price level. In this example the target zone was the 50 percent to 61.8 percent area.

Finally, traders can also use a combination of the Hourly/15-minute chart. This strategy is in keeping with the top-down approach to trading. The higher time period hourly trend (Figure 6.32) turned down on the trade through 11527. Day-traders should be aware of the points where the larger time periods change trend, as these prices often become new support or resistance. Since the old main bottom on the hourly chart was 11527, this price has to be watched on the 15-minute chart for potential resistance and shorting opportunities.

SWING CHART NEGATIVES

The Whipsaw Market

The biggest negative factor affecting the swing chart trader is the whipsaw market. A whipsaw is a series of false changes in trend characterized by rallies and breaks that do not follow through to the upside or downside and change direction after one or two bars following the last change in trend (Figure 6.33).

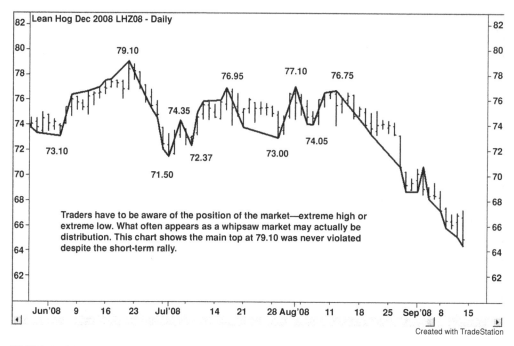

Traders have to be aware of the position of the market—extreme high or extreme low. What often appears as a whipsaw market may actually be distribution. This chart shows the main top at 79.10 was never violated despite the short-term rally.

FIGURE 6.33 Whipsaw Market: Topping Action
Copyright © TradeStation.

In order to prevent this from happening, filters can be built. Such a filter can be as simple as increasing the size of the stop placement above a top or below a bottom. This would require that the market make a minimum price move before you shift the trend line indicator or change the minor trend indicator from one day to two or three days.

Filters have to consider the price level at which the market is currently trading. High price levels, for example, need wider stops above swing tops because of greater volatility and wider ranges. At low price levels, ranges tend to be narrower, and volatility is not as great (Figure 6.34).

Other filters that could be considered would be conventional overbought/oversold indicators such as the Relative Strength Indicator (RSI) or the Slow Stochastic Oscillator. For example, if the main trend was in a prolonged decline and the trader noticed that the RSI was showing an oversold condition, then the trader may begin to watch for a change in trend on the swing chart. Any combination of overbought/oversold indicator and swing chart could prove beneficial as long as the trader does not initiate a position until the trend indicator has officially turned up or down.

Lost Motion

When researching filters to use with swing charts, the trader will encounter a concept Gann referred to as "lost motion." *Lost motion* can best be defined as the amount of

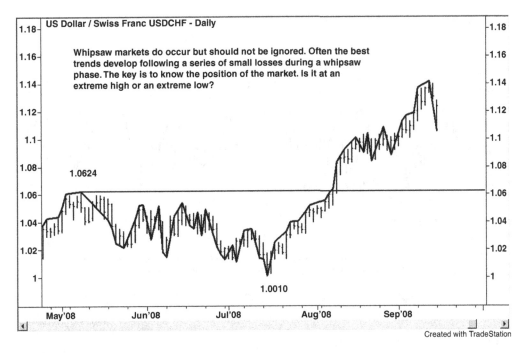

FIGURE 6.34 Whipsaw Market: Bottoming Action
Copyright © TradeStation.

penetration a market allows above a swing top without changing the trend to up or below a swing bottom without changing the trend to down (Figure 6.35).

As we said in the generic examples of how the swing chart operates, you should buy when the market crosses a swing top and sell when the market crosses a swing bottom. The word "crosses," however, was not defined. This is because each market has its own lost-motion figure.

In the soybean market, for example, a swing top is often crossed by between 3 and 5 cents before the market turns down and resumes the downtrend. This means that stops placed 1 to 3 cents over a swing top can get caught without continuing higher.

The same is true for a stop placed under swing bottoms. At times the market will take out a swing bottom by as much as 5 cents before turning around and resuming the main uptrend.

It is important that the trader record the occurrences of lost motion so that she can strategically place stops that when hit will change the trend to up or down. This can be accomplished by keeping accurate charts of this "false breakout." Mark on the chart when failed breakouts occurred. They are most likely to show up near extreme tops and extreme bottoms. The analyst should note that these figures can be kept historically, so that a large database of these phenomena can be developed and kept for reference. From these data, the analyst should be able to determine the maximum, minimum, and average of lost motion for each market.

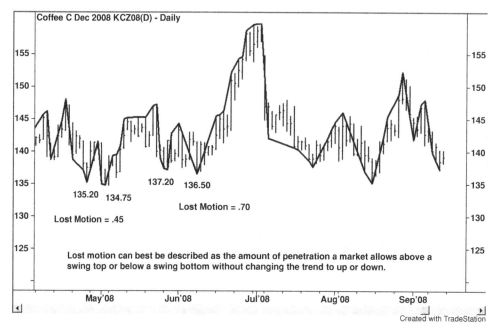

FIGURE 6.35 Lost Motion: Bottoms
Copyright © TradeStation.

In addition to the historical perspective, the chartist should keep a record of the lost motion unique to the current active chart. By charting the swings of a market from the first day of trading, the trader will have an accurate record of its lost motion before it becomes the actively traded contract.

Traders should also note the lost motion of a market at particular price levels. For example, the lost motion of a particular stock may be higher when the equity is trading in the $40.00 to $50.00 range than it is when trading between $20.00 and $30.00. Lost motion seems to be a function of the volatility of the market. Therefore studies of volatility and Average True Range may be helpful in determining the proper stop placement (Figure 6.36).

The concept of lost motion is very important because it also occurs when using percentage retracements and Gann angles to find support and resistance. For instance, a market will often penetrate a 50 percent price or Gann angle, then recover and resume the trend. The lost motion discovered by studying the swing charts can often be used as a starting point when researching this phenomenon on a percentage retracement or Gann angle chart.

SUMMARY

This concludes our discussion of swing charts and how to use them to trade. It is important to know that swing trading can be accomplished with all three trend indicator

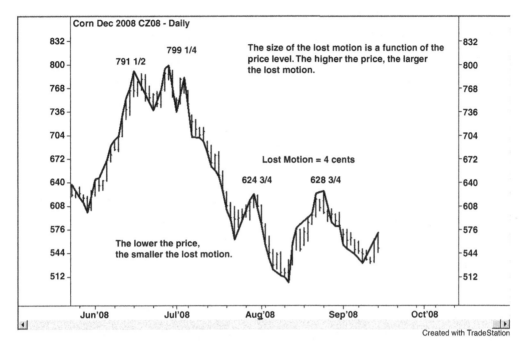

FIGURE 6.36 Lost Motion: Price Levels
Copyright © TradeStation.

charts individually or in combination. To be successful using these trading strategies the trader must know the swing characteristics of each market he trades. This includes size and duration of rallies and breaks and lost motion. Knowledge of lost motion helps the trader avoid whipsaw conditions and aids in the proper placement of stops. All of the suggested swing trading strategies work best at extreme low or extreme high levels. Buying or shorting from these levels allows traders to trade in moves as they develop from the beginning and gives them the opportunity to trade the entire trend. All the suggested trading strategies emphasize trading with the trend by buying strength and selling weakness according to the swings, buying and selling at fixed price intervals, buying and selling at fixed time intervals and buying and selling combinations of the trend indicators.

The swing chart technique is a very important part of Gann analysis, as all of the other charts begin with the construction of the swing chart. In order to draw Gann angles properly, you must have properly identified tops and bottoms. To find percentage retracement levels, you must have identified tops and bottoms. Finally, in order to count time periods for cycles, you must have the proper starting points in the form of swing tops and swing bottoms.

CHAPTER 7

Pattern: Other Chart Formations

In Chapters 5 and 6, covering the construction of the trend indicator charts and using them for trading and stop placement was discussed in a simplified manner. The method explained was mechanical and assumed the trader would follow the swings of the market exclusively. Because conditions change based on market conditions, the trader must be aware of certain situations that give her the option to ignore the trend indicator stops and move the stops prematurely. The following are examples of times when the trend indicator may be overruled. These situations include double bottoms and tops, prolonged moves in price, swing balancing, and signal tops and signal bottoms.

THE DOUBLE BOTTOM

After making a trend indicator chart, the analyst will notice that this swing chart makes some common chart patterns more easily identifiable. One of the easiest patterns to recognize is the double-bottom formation. Buying against a double bottom is often safest, because a stop placed under a double bottom is caught less often. This is especially true if the double bottom was formed at an extremely low level or following a prolonged move down in terms of both price and time. An exact match of the bottoms is not necessary to form a double bottom: for example, the second bottom may be slightly above the first bottom. Studying historical charts on how a double bottom is formed on each trend indicator chart can provide the chartist with the correct amount of tolerable price difference. A double bottom that has the second bottom slightly above the first bottom is known as a *secondary higher bottom,* and it often indicates that higher markets are to follow. This is a very common pattern before the start of a big rally, especially after the first bottom was followed by a large spike to the upside (Figure 7.1).

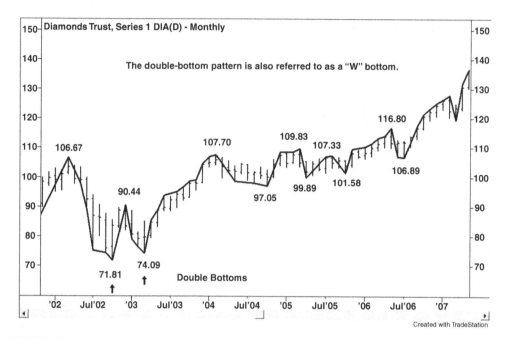

FIGURE 7.1 The Double Bottom. The double-bottom pattern is also referred to as a "W" bottom. Copyright © TradeStation.

The double-bottom pattern is also referred to as a "W" bottom because the combination of a trend indicator bottom, trend indicator top, and trend indicator bottom forms a W. This pattern can trigger two trading opportunities: a countertrend buy following the formation of the second bottom and after a breakout over the last swing top. In each trade, stop loss protection is placed under the last trend indicator bottom.

When deciding to use the double-bottom formation to trigger trading signals, the trader must remember that although this formation can be described the same way for each time indicator from minor to main, the strength of each bottom is different.

Double bottoms on the minor trend indicator chart occur more frequently than on the intermediate and main trend indicator charts. They are also not as strong compared to this formation on the intermediate and main trend indicator charts due to the frequency of the indicator.

Double bottoms on the intermediate trend indicator chart occur less frequently than on the minor trend indicator chart, but more frequently than on the main trend indicator chart. A double bottom on the intermediate chart is stronger than the same formation on the minor trend indicator chart, but weaker than the same formation on the main trend indicator chart.

Double-bottom formations on the main trend indicator chart occur less frequently than on the minor trend indicator chart and the intermediate trend indicator chart, and are stronger than on these other charts.

The strength of the double bottom is once again a function of time. The greater the distance between double bottoms, the more important the formation. This is especially true if the double bottom has started after a prolonged move down in terms of price and time or at a historically low level. A double bottom formed at an extremely high price level often sets up the first selling opportunity when penetrated. Traders should watch for elongated double-bottom formations, and pay particular attention to where they are taking place.

THE DOUBLE TOP

Another formation easily recognizable following a properly constructed trend indicator chart is the double-top formation. Selling against a double top is often safest, because a stop placed over a double top is caught less often. This is especially true if the double top was formed at an extremely high level or following a prolonged move up in terms of both price and time. An exact match of the tops is not necessary to form a double top, for example, the second top may be slightly below the first top. Studying historical charts on how a double top is formed can provide the chartist with the correct amount of tolerable price difference. A double top that has the second top slightly below the first top is known as a *secondary lower top*, and it often indicates that lower markets are to follow. This is a very common pattern before the start of a large break, especially after the first top was followed by a large spike to the downside (Figure 7.2).

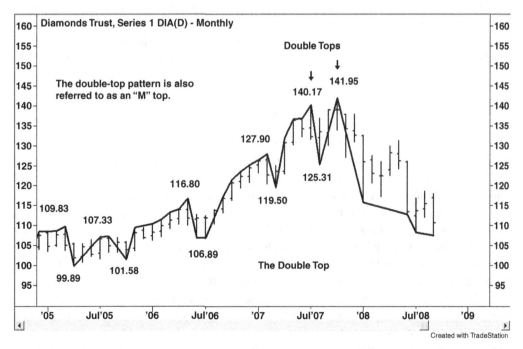

FIGURE 7.2 The Double Top. The double-top pattern is also referred to as an "M" top. Copyright © TradeStation.

The double-top pattern is also referred to as an "M" top because the combination of a trend indicator top, trend indicator bottom, and trend indicator top forms an M. This pattern can trigger two trading opportunities: a countertrend sell following the formation of the second top and after a breakout under the swing bottom. In each trade, stop-loss protection is placed over the last trend indicator top.

When deciding to use the double-top formation to trigger trading signals, the trader must remember that although this formation can be described the same way for each time indicator from minor to main, the strength of each top is different.

Double tops on the minor trend indicator chart occur more frequently than on the intermediate and main trend indicator charts. They are also not as strong compared to this formation on the intermediate and main trend indicator charts due to the frequency of the indicator.

Double tops on the intermediate trend indicator chart occur less frequently than on the minor trend indicator chart, but more frequently than on the main trend indicator chart. A double top on the intermediate chart is stronger than the same formation on the minor trend indicator chart, but weaker than the same formation on the main trend indicator chart.

Double-top formations on the main trend indicator chart occur less frequently than on the minor trend indicator chart and the intermediate trend indicator chart, and are stronger than on these other charts.

The strength of the double top is once again a function of time. The greater the distance between double tops, the more important the formation. This is especially true if the double top has started after a prolonged move up in terms of price and time or at a historically high level. A double top formed at an extremely low price level often sets up the first buying opportunity when penetrated. Traders should watch for elongated double-top formations, and pay particular attention to where they are taking place.

PROLONGED RALLY OR BREAK RULE

Although trading using the trend indicator charts is rule-based and almost completely mechanical, at times existing market conditions overrule these factors. This is especially true when placing trailing stops following a prolonged move up in terms of price and time: for example, seven consecutive bars of trading in the same direction.

Gann suggested that after seven consecutive bars of higher-highs and higher-lows, traders should move the sell stop from below the last trend indicator bottom to below the low of the seventh day up. Conversely, he suggested that following seven consecutive bars of lower-highs and lower-lows, traders should move the buy stop from over the last trend indicator top to above the high of the seventh day down.

The stop selection can vary depending on the personal preferences of the trader. For example, following a seven-day rally the trader may want to enter a stop close only under the close of the seventh day instead of the low. In the case of a seven-day break, the trader may want to enter a stop close only over the close of the seventh day instead of the high.

Each market has specific characteristics. For example, some markets have a tendency to rally only five consecutive days instead of seven before topping, or five consecutive days instead of seven before bottoming. By studying the historical swing charts of a specific market, a trader can determine the optimal stop required. The number of completed swings a market has made may also trigger the early movement of a stop. For example, the swing action of a market may have a tendency to move in groups of three or five. In this case, a trader may elect to move the stop up to under a low instead of a swing bottom following a three or five swing up move or over a high instead of a swing top following a three or five swing down move.

BALANCING SWINGS

There is another exception to the stop placement rule, the balanced swing chart, which involves the calculation of previous swing moves. For example, if the last swing was 19 cents up and 6 cents down, then following the next 19-cent rally, the stop would be moved up from below the last swing bottom to just under a 6-cent correction from the last high price. This type of trailing stop would require the trader to constantly monitor a market making new highs in order to move the stop to the correct place. This stop is designed to get caught after a rally equals or exceeds a previous rally and breaks more than the previous break (Figure 7.3).

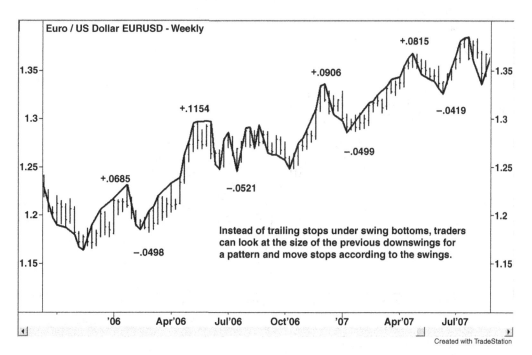

FIGURE 7.3 Balancing Swings
Copyright © TradeStation.

The situation is reversed for buy stops. For example, if the last swing was $10.00 down and $3.00 up, then following the next $10.00 break, the stop would be moved down from above the last swing top to just over a $3.00 correction from the last low price.

Overbalancing Price and Time

From the swing charts, the trader should calculate the size and duration of the swings. In a declining market, by definition the declines tend to grow longer and the rallies shorter in terms of both price and time. As a market nears a bottom, the frequency of the swings begins to increase, as do the duration of the rallies in terms of both price and time. This action should be observed and noted as a clue to when a market will bottom; it should be watched particularly when a market has reached a historically low price level.

Note the formation of the bottoming action in the Weekly U.S. Dollar/Japanese Yen market in Figure 7.4. After two prolonged moves down in terms of price and time of −16.93 and −18.93, this market posted a rally of 9.98. The rally was greater than the previous rally of 7.45. This was the first clue that a good bottom was formed and the market was getting ready to rally. The second sign that this market was ready to move higher was the break of −3.13. This move was less than the previous down move in terms of price and time. Although this market could not maintain the same size of the first rally from the low, the rally remained intact for several weeks as each subsequent rally made

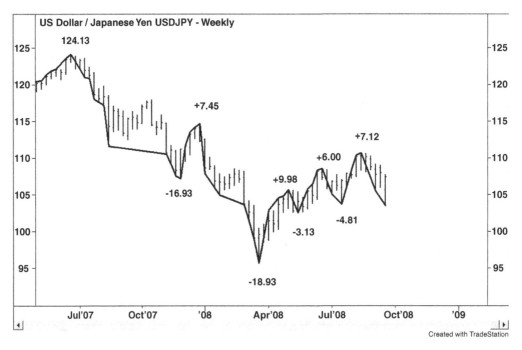

FIGURE 7.4 Overbalancing Swings
Copyright © TradeStation.

a higher swing top and a higher swing bottom while exceeding each break in terms of price and time.

Often the first clue to a bottom is an expanded range day to the upside. This move may occur in one, two, or three days from the bottom. Even before it crosses a swing top, the market shows signs of a bottom. Traders should keep a record of the first swing up from a bottom. This information often repeats from year to year and could be called a characteristic of a particular market, each market having its own. Records should be kept of these characteristics, as they are often a clue to the size and duration of an impending rally. This type of move often occurs seasonally or cyclically. This is why historical dates of bottoms must be kept. The longer the first rally from a bottom in terms of price and time, the stronger the impending rally. Confidence can be gained by knowing that the size of the rally from a bottom often determines the strength of the next rally. This is important for trading against the trend, when buying the next break in anticipation of a double bottom.

Overbalancing means that the current rally has exceeded the previous rally in terms of price and time. An overbalance of time is the most important indication of a change in trend. Although the price movement of a market from a bottom is a good indicator of a near-term change in trend, the longer the market spends above the last swing bottom in terms of time, the greater the probability of a change in trend in the near term. This is known as building a support base of time instead of using price alone to build it.

A quick rally that overbalances or crosses a swing top fails more often if a solid time base has not been formed. Sometimes this is called a *quiet market*. Traders are often quoted as saying, "Never short a quiet market." When setting up the bottom for the next rally, it is better for the market to build a support base over several time periods with small ranges rather than with one large move over a short period of time.

Although it was noted earlier that inside bars should be ignored when building a swing chart, it does not mean that they have no importance. Disregarding the inside bar is only valid during the construction phase of the swing chart, as valuable information can be obtained from a series of inside days.

The same is true for a top. Following a strong, long-lasting uptrend in terms of both price and time, a market often has a day when the first break from the high exceeds the previous break from a high in terms of both price and time. If the first break from a top is an expanded range day, or if the last day of a two- or three-day break from an extreme high is an expanded range day, then watch for a series of inside days to overbalance time in order to set up the impending break that is likely to lead to a change in trend. Remember that despite a sharp break from a top that exceeds a previous break in terms of price, the market needs to overbalance time in order to trigger an acceleration to the downside, which can change the trend.

This agrees with what was said about support-base building. Inside days usually follow an expanded range day. An expanded range day from an extreme bottom is often indicative of a major bottoming formation. This may not be enough, however, to attract new buying that can change the trend to up and cause an acceleration to the upside. This is because the market needs to overbalance time. The series of inside days that usually follow an expanded range day from an extreme bottom help accomplish this formation. It is important that the trader watch for a series of inside days near a bottom for a sign that the main trend is getting ready to turn higher and that the market is getting ready to accelerate to the upside.

Outside moves can be used to indicate impending trend changes. An outside move tends to temporarily stop a rally or break, thus allowing time or price to catch up with the current trading situation. Often a series of inside moves occurs within the framework of the outside range. This formation should be watched carefully for indications of base building, which could lead to the start of a rally, or top building, which could trigger a decline. Crossing the high end of the outside move day can lead to the start of an uptrend, while crossing the low of the outside move day can lead to the start of a downtrend. Once again, the position of the market in terms of price and time often determines the strength of the breakout move.

In summary, the height of the market is often determined by the length of the base, and vice versa for tops. Following a prolonged move down in terms of price and time, especially following an expanded range down, watch for a series of inside moves to signal bottoming action. Conversely, following a prolonged move up in terms of price and time, watch for a series of inside moves to signal topping action. The same is true of a series of inside moves following an outside move.

It should be noted here that buying and selling based on breakouts over these types of tops or bottoms do not change the trend to up or down, but are actually exceptions to the strict trend indictor rules. Buying or selling breakouts in the direction of the trend most often leads to a successful trade; however, totally ignoring the formation is not recommended. To make it successful, this formation needs to be studied and practiced.

Forecasting Price Moves

Learning how to read the swings of a market can also be an important forecasting tool. Forecasts started from major tops and bottoms can use previous swing price data to determine with reasonable accuracy where a market could go and when. This technique also helps the trader identify whether a market is behind and has to catch up with the trading pattern, or if it is behind and has to make an adjustment to once again balance the formation.

For example, if the last rally was 40 points in 5 days, then from a bottom, the trader can anticipate a 40-point move in 5 days. If the market moves 60 points in 2 days, then the trader can anticipate a 20-point correction over the next 3 days, before the trend resumes. In addition, if a market rallies only 30 points in 4 days, then the trader can anticipate a 10-point rally the last day of the swing so the market can balance. It takes time to make this type of analysis, because the trader has to know the swing characteristics of the market being traded, and these can only be discerned from records of the swings.

Once a trader becomes proficient with this form of analysis, he should be able to forecast expanded range days or inside days. In other words, he should be able to forecast when a market is likely to move and when it is likely to sit in a range. This can be

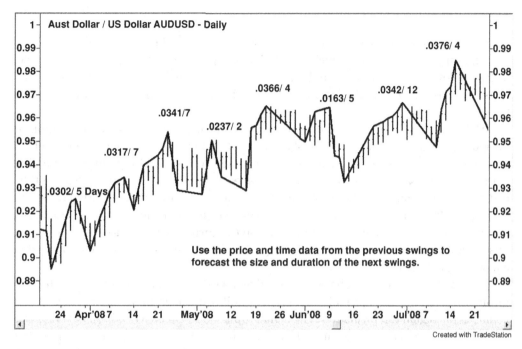

FIGURE 7.5 Forecasting Price Moves
Copyright © TradeStation.

accomplished either by trading on active days or by sitting in a range before the market takes off.

In Figure 7.5 one can see the importance of keeping records of previous up and down swings as they often forecast the next up or down move. The idea behind knowing the size and duration of the swings is to give the trader clues as to what to expect from each rally or break. A trader who maintains good records of the swings can often anticipate the start of a top or a bottom before the market actually turns. In the Australian Dollar/ U.S. Dollar chart in this example one can see the consistency of the .03+ rally in 5 to 7 days. If the trader is trading the uptrend and wants to attempt to capture large portions of the swing instead of trading under each swing bottom, he must know the size and duration of the previous swings. This methodology works well with longer-term charts because of the infrequency of the minor swings. The longer-term chart allows the trader to focus his attention on the larger moves.

SIGNAL TOPS AND SIGNAL BOTTOMS

The two most important exceptions to the trend indicator rules are the signal top and the signal bottom. I have studied this formation extensively and have concluded that this is a universal pattern. In other words, it does not matter which market is traded: at some point they all post either a signal top or signal bottom at major tops or major bottoms.

The Signal Top

A signal top can be defined as follows: following a prolonged move up in terms of both price and time, a market has a higher-high than the previous time period, a lower-close, a close below the time period's midpoint, and a close below the opening. If this occurs, consider it as a sign that the market has topped and that the trend is getting ready to turn down.

The signal top is one of the most powerful indicators of a major top formation. It most often occurs at or near historical tops and often becomes the contract high, which is why it is important to chart, observe, and note the historical tops of a commodity market. As was said earlier, this is accomplished using the yearly, quarterly, monthly, and weekly continuation charts of the same contract month. These charts come into play most often when a market has had a strong vertical rally and is trading at an area that has not yet been identified as resistance on the current active chart. In other words, this type of top most often occurs following a breakout over an old contract high and at a new contract high.

This signal alone may not be enough to trigger a sell, because often there is no follow-through break, and the uptrend resumes. The follow-through break is necessary, as it confirms the signal top formation. The signal top is often called a *closing price reversal top* or a *key reversal top*, but these terms are not as specific as signal top, as neither mentions the close below the day's midpoint, the close below the opening, or the follow-through break, nor the prolonged move up in price and time.

To understand its importance, we need to break the signal top down into its components.

A prolonged move in price is an important part of determining the significance of a signal top. This type of signal must occur following a strong rally in terms of price. As stated earlier, a record should be kept of the size of past rallies in terms of price, because a market often repeats them. Study the past to see if the current rally equals or exceeds a previous rally at the time of the signal top day. Knowing these historical swings in advance can help the trader anticipate the signal top day. In addition to studying the size of the price swings, a trader should know if the market is approaching a historically high price level.

A prolonged move in terms of time is also an important indication of an impending signal top day. As stated earlier, time is most important in determining a change in trend or a top, so knowing the past history of a market's rallies in terms of time can provide important information as to when or if a valid signal top is or will be taking place. Historical swing chart data such as the duration of bottoms to tops and tops to tops can provide this information. If a market is approaching a swing level in terms of time, which has stopped a rally before, then anticipate a signal top.

A higher-high and a lower-close occur quite often even in the midst of a strong rally. Without a prolonged move in price or time and a follow-through break, this pattern may trigger a false topping signal. Research will show that when this pattern fails it is because the market has failed to achieve at least one of the following: a balancing of a price swing, a balancing of a time swing, or a follow-through to the downside the next time period.

Although a reversal down can occur following a prolonged move up in terms of price and time, a higher-high and a lower-close, and a follow-through the next time period, there can be different degrees of strength to this signal. For example, the market may have all of the preceding factors, and a close below the day's midpoint, but not be below the opening price. While the best signal top is called a *triple-signal top*, a higher-high and lower-close, with only a close below the midpoint or only below the opening price, are called a *double-signal top*.

Tops with this type of formation should be studied to determine the strength of the signal in predicting major top formations. The same is true for the signal top days that close lower and below the opening price, but not below the day's midpoint.

The following is a list of the various strengths of signal tops, from strongest to weakest, and assuming a prolonged rally in terms of price and time:

1. A higher-high and a lower-close, a close below the opening, and a close below the day's midpoint.

2. A higher-high and a lower-close, and a close below the day's midpoint.

3. A higher-high and a lower-close, and a close below the opening.

4. A higher-high and a lower-close.

The main thing to watch for is a higher-high and a lower-close following a prolonged move up in terms of price and time and a follow-through break. The degree of strength of the top should be determined by whether or not the close is below the midpoint and/or below the opening. Once again, records of how a major top was formed should be kept. These tops should be referred to frequently to determine the strength and reliability of the expected break.

Remember also that while there is an important signal as to the top of the market, it does not automatically change the trend to down, but only temporarily freezes the market and puts it in a position to break to the downside. This break is not a change in trend, although it can lead to one. Records should be maintained to determine how much penetration of the low at the time of the signal top is needed to confirm a valid signal top. This amount varies by market and must be known to avoid false sell signals.

When using the trend indicators to enter and exit positions, traders should move the stops up from under swing bottoms to just below the low of the signal top bar to lock in any profit and to get taken out when the market confirms the signal top with a follow-through break.

Variations in the signal top formation can provide different results. For example, a close below the period's midpoint is suggested, but further filtering of the strength of this signal can be determined if the market closed in the lower 25 percent or 10 percent of the day's range. To make this signal more useful in forecasting major tops, the signal should be observed and tested using a program such as TradeStation.

Time indicators can also be strengthened. Besides looking at the duration of the rally in terms of price, a trader may want to compare signal tops that occur at cyclical or seasonal times. Price analysis may also be filtered by observing and testing signal tops that occur at historical price levels, major percentage retracement points, and major Gann-angle formations.

Although a signal top does not actually change the trend to down mechanically, countertrend traders who are comfortable with their market research on this signal can enter into a countertrend short-term position by selling weakness upon confirmation of the signal top. This often carries a large dollar risk because it is against the trend and because a stop loss has to be placed above the signal top.

An additional countertrend selling strategy is to sell a 50 percent retracement of the first leg down from the signal top. This move may take two or more days to develop, but is one of the most common trading patterns. This strategy can be altered to include 33 percent or 67 percent retracements. Combined with former main tops, balance points, or Gann angles, retracement sells can produce major entry or exit points that can turn a market or change the trend from up to down.

Figure 7.6 is a good example of the signal top. Following a prolonged move up in terms of price and time, the 2008 December Corn reached a record high and posted a signal top. By identifying the signal top, the long trader is able to exit his trade by moving his stop to under the low of the signal top day instead of waiting for the

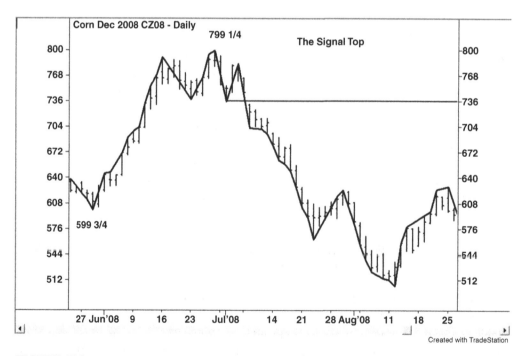

FIGURE 7.6 The Signal Top
Copyright © TradeStation.

swing bottom to be violated. This allows the trader to capture more of the swing and eliminates some of the giveback that is associated with trailing stops according to the swing chart.

The Signal Bottom

A signal bottom can be defined as follows: following a prolonged move down in terms of both price and time, a market has a lower-low than the previous time period, a higher-close, a close above the time period's midpoint, and a close above the opening. If this occurs, consider this a sign that the market has bottomed and that the trend is getting ready to turn up.

The signal bottom is one of the most powerful indicators of a major bottom formation. It most often occurs at or near historical bottoms and often becomes the contract low, which is why it is important to chart, observe, and note the historical bottoms of a commodity market. As was said earlier, this is accomplished using the yearly, quarterly, monthly, and weekly continuation charts of the same contract month. These charts come into play most often when a market has had a strong vertical break and is trading at an area that has not yet been identified as support on the current active chart. In other words, this type of bottom most often occurs following a breakout under an old contract low and at a new contract low.

This signal alone may not be enough to trigger a buy, because often there is no follow-through rally and the downtrend resumes. The follow-through rally is necessary, as it confirms the signal bottom formation. The signal bottom is often called a *closing price reversal bottom* or a *key reversal bottom*, but these terms are not as specific as signal bottom, as neither mentions the close above the day's midpoint, the close above the opening, or the follow-through rally, nor the prolonged move down in price and time.

To understand its importance, we need to break the signal bottom down into its components.

A prolonged move in price is an important part of determining the significance of a signal bottom. This type of signal must occur following a strong break in terms of price. As stated earlier, a record should be kept of the size of past breaks in terms of price, because a market often repeats them. Study the past to see if the current break equals or exceeds a previous break at the time of the signal bottom day. Knowing these historical swings in advance can help the trader anticipate the signal bottom day. In addition to studying the size of the price swings, a trader should know if the market is approaching a historically low price level.

A prolonged move in terms of time is also an important indication of an impending signal bottom day. As stated earlier, time is most important in determining a change in trend or a bottom, so knowing the past history of a market's breaks in terms of time can provide important information as to when or if a valid signal bottom is or will be taking place. Historical swing chart data such as the duration of bottoms to tops and bottoms to bottoms can provide this information. If a market is approaching a swing level in terms of time, which has stopped a rally before, then anticipate a signal bottom.

A higher-high and a higher-close occur quite often even in the midst of a strong break. Without a prolonged move in price or time and a follow-through rally, this pattern may trigger a false bottoming signal. Research will show that when this pattern fails it is because the market has failed to achieve at least one of the following: a balancing of a price swing, a balancing of a time swing, a follow through to the upside the next time period.

Although a reversal up can occur following a prolonged move down in terms of price and time, a lower-low and a higher-close, and a follow-through the next time period, there can be different degrees of strength to this signal. For example, the market may have all of the preceding factors, and a close above the current range's midpoint, but not be above the opening price. While the best signal bottom is called a *triple-signal bottom,* a lower-low and higher-close, with only a close above the midpoint or only above the opening price, are called a *double-bottom top.*

Bottoms with this type of formation should be studied to determine the strength of the signal in predicting major bottom formations. The same is true for the signal bottom days that close higher and above the opening price, but not above the current range's midpoint.

The following is a list of the various strengths of signal bottoms from strongest to weakest, and assuming a prolonged break in terms of price and time:

1. A lower-low and a higher-close, a close above the opening, and a close above the day's midpoint.
2. A lower-low and a higher-close, and a close above the day's midpoint.
3. A lower-low and a higher-close, and a close above the opening.
4. A lower-low and a higher-close.

The main thing to watch for is a lower-low and a higher-close following a prolonged move down in terms of price and time and a follow-through rally. The degree of strength of the bottom should be determined by whether or not the close is above the midpoint and/or above the opening. Once again, records of how a major bottom was formed should be kept. These bottoms should be referred to frequently to determine the strength and reliability of the expected rally.

Remember also that while there is an important signal as to the bottom of the market, it does not automatically change the trend to up, but only temporarily freezes the market and puts it in a position to break to the downside. This break is not a change in trend, although it can lead to one. Records should be maintained to determine how much penetration of the high at the time of the signal bottom is needed to confirm a valid signal bottom. This amount varies by market and must be known to avoid false buy signals.

When using the trend indicators to enter and exit positions, traders should move the stops down from above swing tops to just above the high of the signal bottom bar to lock in any profit and to get taken out when the market confirms the signal bottom with a follow-through rally.

Variations in the signal bottom formation can provide different results. For example, a close above the signal bottom range's midpoint is suggested, but further filtering of the strength of this signal can be determined if the market closed in the upper 25 percent or 10 percent range of the signal bottom time period. To make this signal more useful in forecasting major bottoms, the signal should be observed and tested using a program such as TradeStation.

Time indicators can also be strengthened. Besides looking at the duration of a break in terms of price, a trader may want to compare signal bottoms that occur at cyclical or seasonal times. Price analysis may also be filtered by observing and testing signal bottoms that occur at historical price levels, major percentage retracement points, and major Gann-angle formations.

Although a signal bottom does not actually change the trend to up mechanically, countertrend traders who are comfortable with their market research on this signal can enter into a countertrend short-term position by buying strength upon confirmation of the signal bottom. This often carries a large dollar risk because it is against the trend and because a stop loss has to be placed below the signal bottom.

Figure 7.7 is an example of a signal bottom in the 2008 December 30-Year Treasury Bond market. Note how the market went through a prolonged move down in terms of price and time and traded near an extreme low, in this case the contract low. After the signal bottom was formed the market had the all-important follow-through rally. This

FIGURE 7.7 The Signal Bottom
Copyright © TradeStation.

rally triggered short-covering all the way through the previous swing top and changed the trend to up. After the trend was changed to up, the market retraced about 50 percent of the first leg up from the reversal bottom. This is a very common pattern as the first leg up is short-covering and the new buyers come in after the break.

An additional countertrend buying strategy is to buy a 50 percent retracement of the first leg up from the signal bottom. This move may take two or more days to develop, but is one of the most common trading patterns. This strategy can be altered to include 33 percent or 67 percent retracements. Combined with former main bottoms, balance points, or Gann angles, retracement sells can produce major entry or exit points that can turn a market or change the trend from down to up.

These two exceptions, signal tops and signal bottoms, to the standard stop rule are designed for aggressive traders who want to lock in profits before the market retraces all the way up over a swing top or through a swing bottom. It should be noted that these stops when executed do not represent a change in trend, but are often important indicators of changes in trend that are going to take place in the very near future. These stops are also very effective in active, fast-moving markets when the market makes several large swings over a short period of time.

OTHER IMPORTANT FORMATIONS

In addition to the signal top and signal bottom formations, the market often indicates an impending change in trend by closing on or near a low or high.

Closing Near a Low

Following a prolonged move down in terms of price and time, or when the market is trading near a historically low level, the market will often have an expanded range bar down and settle on the low or within one or two price units of the low. The next period the market opens higher and never trades under the close of the low day.

This action does not change the trend, but is a strong sign that the market is getting ready to change trend or build a support zone.

Closing Near a High

Following a prolonged move up in terms of price and time, or when the market is trading near a historically high level, the market will often have an expanded range bar up and settle on the high or within one or two price units of the high. The next period the market opens lower and never trades over the close of the high day.

This action does not change the trend, but is a strong sign that the market is getting ready to change trend or build a resistance zone. These top formations should be researched and studied for the accuracy of their forecasting ability.

OTHER POPULAR PATTERNS

One key to successfully trading the markets is to study and experiment with different trend indicators and patterns. Gann often mentioned in his books and courses the importance of study and experimentation. He was constantly looking for new ways to analyze and trade the markets. The theme that developed over time, however, was the importance of the trend indicator. Because of computers today, the trader is offered the opportunity to study and experiment with many different trend indicators and pattern recognition programs. If a trader settles on the Gann Swing Indicator, as his main trend indicator then he may want to experiment with other technical tools to confirm the trend or to exit the trend.

Confirmation of the trend may come in the form of a moving average crossover used in conjunction with the Gann Swing Indicator for example. Other chart patterns may be used to identify exits to established swings. In this chapter, the use of exceptions to the trend indicator rules was mentioned. These included signal top and signal bottom formations. In addition to these patterns, Candlestick trading patterns can be used to provide valid confirmations or exit strategies. Once again it is highly suggested that the trader study and experiment how Candlestick patterns can be used to improve the success of the Gann Trend Indicator. A Doji pattern, for example, may be used in conjunction with the Trend Indicator chart. Although this pattern is not necessarily a change in trend indicator, it may help the trend trader exit a position well before the trend indicator signals an exit. Other Candlestick patterns that may prove to be beneficial to the Trend Indicator trader are the Hanging Man, Hammer, Shooting Star, and Inverted Hammer. The key is to study and experiment how Candlestick patterns can be used to improve the success of the trend indicator chart.

SUMMARY

Although many traders would like to create purely mechanical trading systems to trade the trend, sometimes conditions exist that may help the trader maximize trading profits and minimize risk. In my opinion, this is exactly what the exceptions to the trend indicator rules accomplish. While a trader often gets caught up in the art of trading using the trend indicator only, he or she must realize that trading successfully involves making strategic adjustments. The ability to identify certain signals such as double bottoms and tops, prolonged moves in price, swing balancing, and signal tops and bottoms will help the trader to determine impending changes in trend before the trend indicator is activated.

This concludes the chapter on chart patterns that are the exceptions to the swing chart rules. In learning about both the chart and the exceptions, pay particular attention to the signal tops and signal bottoms, as the majority of major tops and bottoms formed will occur in this fashion.

CHAPTER 8

Price: Horizontal Support and Resistance

G ann used a number of methods to determine support and resistance. Using his methodology, he determined that support and resistance exist horizontally and diagonally. The horizontal support consists of swing tops, swing bottoms, and percentage retracement points. They are known as *horizontal* support and resistance points because when drawn on a chart, they extend far to the right. The swing chart support and resistance move on into infinity while the percentage levels remain intact as long as the market remains inside of the range that created them. Diagonal support and resistance, on the other hand, are created by Gann angles. The intersection of the two methods becomes a strong support or resistance level.

THE SWING CHARTS

In the chapters on the trend indicators, we learned how to build swing charts using the minor trend, the intermediate trend, and the main trend. On each of these charts, we identified tops and bottoms. As we move toward more advanced price and time studies, we will learn that these prices are not only important in the short term, but also extend out into infinity.

Swing Tops

After a market has posted a top, this top should be extended to the right on the chart. This is done by drawing a red line from the top out to the right. This line represents the top extended over time. As the market continues to trade, it may trade up to or over this line several times. The first time the market reaches this top, selling pressure should be expected. Watch for topping action in the form of a double-top formation or a signal top.

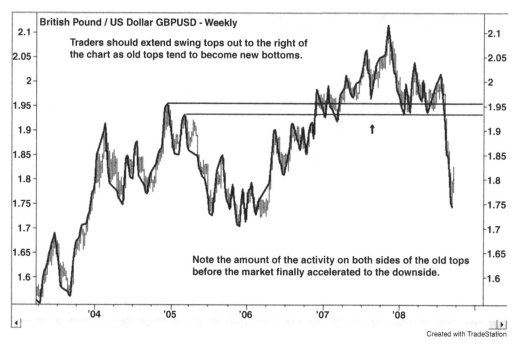

FIGURE 8.1 Swing Tops as New Bottoms
Copyright © TradeStation.

When the market crosses the top, the trend changes to up or continues the current trend. The top that is crossed now becomes a level to watch for bottoms. One of Gann's favorite rules was "old tops become new bottoms." This action is important to watch because often a market will cross a top, take out the stops, then return to the top. If it is a valid top formation, this old top should hold as a new bottom (Figure 8.1).

Each top is important to track because each is related to future tops. This is why tops should be extended into infinity (that is, the future). Although it may be difficult to keep track of the minor tops, the intermediate and especially the main tops should be extended.

Swing Bottoms

After a market has posted a bottom, this bottom should be extended to the right on the chart. This is done by drawing a red line from the bottom out to the right. This line represents the bottom extended over time. As the market continues to trade, it may trade down to or under this line several times. The first time the market reaches this bottom, buying pressure should be expected. Watch for bottoming action in the form of a double-bottom formation or a signal bottom.

When the market crosses the bottom, the trend changes to down or continues the current trend. The bottom that is crossed now becomes a level to watch for tops. Another of Gann's favorite rules was "old bottoms become new tops." This action is important to

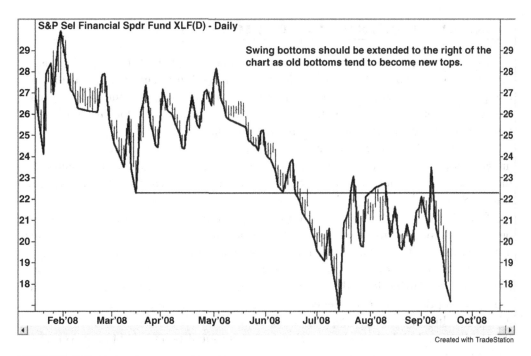

FIGURE 8.2　Swing Bottoms as New Tops
Copyright © TradeStation.

watch because often a market will cross a bottom, take out the stops, then return to the bottom. If it is a valid bottom formation, this old bottom should hold as a new top (Figure 8.2).

Each bottom is important to track because each is related to future bottoms. This is why bottoms should be extended into infinity. Although it may be difficult to keep track of the minor bottoms, the intermediate and especially the main bottoms should be extended into the future.

Besides determining future tops and bottoms, the swing charts are used to forecast future price action by following the swings of the market. In order to determine possible future price direction, keep a record of the size of the rallies. It is important to study the past upswings so that future upswings can be forecast. Conversely, keep a record of the previous downswings to forecast future downswings.

Constructing the swing chart is the first step to price and time analysis, because it sets in motion all of the other technical analysis tools. Together a swing bottom and a swing top form a trading range. This range contains key support and resistance points that must be determined for successful trading. In Chapter 9, we look at those important support and resistance points. The first section describes how to calculate and interpret the percentage retracement levels while the second section deals with other horizontal price levels such as price multiples, pivot price calculations and moving averages.

PERCENTAGE RETRACEMENT PRICE LEVELS

The most important percentage retracement point is 50 percent of the range. This is the price most often traded while a market is inside a range. When a market is in an uptrend, this price is support when the market is trading over this price. If the market breaks under this level, it indicates weakness and a further decline, but does not change the trend to down such as when it crosses a swing bottom.

When a market is in a downtrend, the 50 percent price is resistance when trading under this price. If the market breaks over this level, it indicates strength and a further rally, but does not change the trend to up such as when it crosses a swing top (Figure 8.3).

In addition, a market can trade both sides of a 50 percent price for several time periods while trading inside the range. This particular action should be closely watched, as these swings often demonstrate the lost motion or momentum of a market.

Lost motion was defined earlier in relation to swing-chart trading and stop placement. Here we define it as the average penetration of a price through a percentage retracement price that the market can tolerate prior to regaining the percentage retracement price. In other words, it represents the average amount measured in price in which the market can break through a percentage retracement point prior to recovering the percentage retracement point.

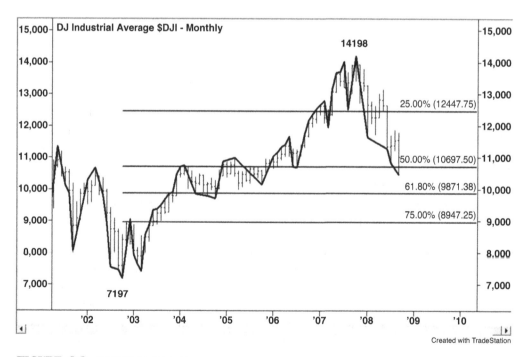

FIGURE 8.3 Retracement Levels
Copyright © TradeStation.

For example, assume the market is in an uptrend and the swing chart creates a main range with a 50 percent point at $10.00. During the first day of the week the market breaks to a low price of $9.90. The second day of the week the market rallies back to post a high of $10.12 and a low of $10.01. This action creates a minor bottom at $9.90. The lost motion of this range is the difference between the percentage retracement point and the low price prior to the formation of the minor bottom and the regaining of the percentage price:

$$\$10.00 - \$9.90 = 10 \text{ cents}$$

This lost motion number is important to know because it aids in stop placement when buying against the 50 percent price during an uptrending market. A stop placed under the price determined by the lost motion is least likely to get hit, and if it does, the market is most likely to continue lower.

The preceding is a simplified example of how to determine the lost motion figure in a market. More sophisticated methods can be developed by taking the average of a series of lost motion points linked with the same 50 percent price or all 50 percent prices in general. It should be noted that the lost motion figure changes according to the price level of a market. For example, at low prices, volatility tends to be low, so the lost motion figure may be relatively lower than the lost motion figure at a high price level, where volatility tends to be high.

It is very important to maintain accurate records of the lost motion amount for each commodity traded at various price levels. Over time the analyst should be able to develop a solid understanding of how a market behaves when trading through a 50 percent price. This research can prove to be invaluable when developing a trading system and when placing stops to cut losses.

At this point it is important to note what actually causes lost motion. Once a range is made and the 50 percent price calculated, it can be assumed that every trader has identified the same price. The common mistake that most traders make is to place an order at that price assuming they are going to catch the low of the break. In reality it is not the price that stops the market, but the size of the order at the bid that turns the market. The market normally trades toward size; therefore, if the large bidder is not at the exact 50 percent price, the market will trade through it. Most individual traders do not place orders large enough to stop a market that is breaking. In other words, passively bidding at a 50 percent retracement price without knowing the downside momentum or the size of the orders at this price will often lead to the trader absorbing a paper loss as the market trades through his price or worse yet getting stopped out. It is not that important to buy at the exact 50 percent price as it is to catch the rally from this price. This is why professional traders find more success in letting the market test the 50 percent price or go through it to see if size will show up to stop the break. Once size shows up on the bid and the market stops going down, a trader often finds more success in buying the 50 percent price on the way back up. I am sure you've seen this action take place quite a few times at 50 percent prices. The key is not to assume that the 50 percent price is going to stop a break, but to be ready when the momentum shifts after this price is tested. For day-traders it is important to watch the electronic tape to determine if buyers are present and offers are being taken out.

As we said at the beginning of the section, the most important percentage retracement point is 50 percent of a major range. This major range can be the all-time range or the next two or three all-time ranges. In addition, the 50 percent price of a contract range along with 50 percent prices of a main range on the monthly chart, the weekly chart, or the daily chart can provide invaluable support or resistance. Like other price and time concepts discussed in this book, combinations or clusters of 50 percent prices can provide direction as well as solid support and resistance.

The bigger the range the better the 50 percent price, as the market is expected to remain inside the larger ranges for a lengthy period of time. The longer the market spends inside a range, the more the trader can learn about the 50 percent price. This is especially beneficial when building a database of lost motion. Price clusters created by "ranges within ranges" are very important, as the 50 percent points of each range are often very close in price and form very solid support or resistance points from which to buy or sell.

While the 50 percent retracement point is the most important support level inside a range, other important percentage retracement levels include the 25 percent or $^1/_4$ retracement level and the 75 percent or $^3/_4$ retracement level. If these points do not provide enough information to properly determine support or resistance, the $^1/_3$ and $^2/_3$ retracement levels may suit the trader's needs.

The key to working with percentage retracements is to work with the major ranges down to the minor ranges. Use historical major ranges first to determine the historically significant major percentage retracement points. This helps to determine the market's major position relative to time. A market trading under the all-time 50 percent level may be bottoming, while a market trading over the all-time 50 percent level may be topping. When looking to forecast the start of major moves, use the all-time ranges. When looking to enter the market for a trade, concentrate your effort on the current major ranges as determined by the monthly, weekly, and daily charts. It is very important to look for clusters of support and resistance, as these points will be most significant when you want to enter into a long or short position.

When trading using the 50 percent price, always trade in the direction of the main trend. If the main trend is up, then look to buy breaks into the 50 percent price. If the main trend is down, then look to sell rallies into the 50 percent price. Finally, it is most important to determine the minimum level of lost motion for each market traded at various price levels. This is the most important analysis tool available for placing protective stops.

The percentage retracement levels are horizontal support and resistance price levels. This is because once identified, these prices remain fixed as long as the market remains inside the range that created it. This is why it is important to work with all-time price ranges and the top-down approach on the current charts. These prices, once formed, are unlikely to get broken; therefore, the percentage retracement levels are likely to last longer. The longer they last, the more valuable information about lost motion and stop placement is learned. This information can help in building a successful trading system.

In addition to the percentage retracement price levels, the swing tops and swing bottoms are important support and resistance points that can be extended into the future on the charts. Once a market passes a top or a bottom, it still remains important. This is because there is a strong tendency for old tops to become new bottoms during uptrends and old bottoms to become new tops during downtrends. It is for this reason that old tops and bottoms should be extended out into the future.

The lost motion rule can also be applied to the old support/new resistance and old resistance/new support trading scenario. Research and analyze how far a market is allowed to penetrate an old top to the downside before regaining it and reestablishing support. In addition, study and record how far a market is allowed to penetrate an old bottom to the upside before regaining it and reestablishing resistance. Accurate determination of lost motion is the key to determining a safe stop.

The strongest horizontal support and resistance points occur when the old top or the old bottom is also a percentage retracement price. This combination makes for solid support or resistance. The simplest rule to follow during an uptrend is to buy a break back to a combination of an old top and a 50 percent price. Conversely, the simplest rule to follow on a break is to sell a rally back to a combination of an old bottom and a 50 percent price. Compare and combine, when possible, the stop selection chosen when trading this combination, and be sure to allow the market plenty of room to work, without exposing yourself to unnecessary risk.

OTHER RETRACEMENT LEVELS

Although the 50 percent retracement is most important it is also important to divide the range into other retracement prices. Some traders prefer to divide the market into 8ths and 10ths. Others prefer to use the 38.2 percent and 61.8 percent Fibonacci retracement levels as key prices. All are perfectly acceptable as the point of using retracement levels is to create horizontal price levels that when combined with diagonal angles create price clusters of support and resistance.

The key retracement areas divided into 8ths include:
12.50, 25.00%, 37.50%, 50.00%, 62.50%, 75.00%, 87.50%
The key retracement areas divided into 10ths include:
10%, 20%, 30%, 40%, 50%, 60%, 70%, 80%, 90%
These percentage levels work best in large ranges. The most important range to use with these percentage levels is the all-time range. Simply be aware of where all these retracement areas are at all times. This may help explain why a market is finding support or resistance at a certain price when it is not apparent on the currently active chart.

MULTIPLES OF BOTTOMS AND DIVISIONS OF TOPS

Horizontal support and resistance can also form at multiples of bottoms and divisions of tops. At a minimum when an analyst calculates a multiple of a bottom, he doubles

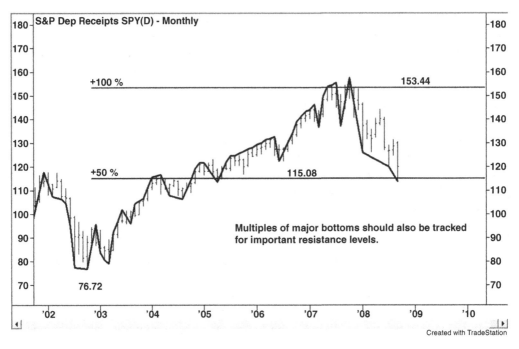

FIGURE 8.4 Multiples of Bottoms
Copyright © TradeStation.

the price. This is a multiple of 100 percent. For example, if a major bottom was formed at $75.00 then a multiple of 100 percent would equal $150.00. This form of analysis was important in determining resistance in the crude oil market during 2008. Other multiples include 200 percent, 300 percent, 400 percent, and so on. In order to determine these multiple price levels it is important to know the all-time low of a market, as multiples of these prices come up most often. As with the other horizontal support and resistance levels, once these numbers are calculated it is important to place them on a chart and see how a market reacts to the price levels (Figure 8.4).

Just as multiples of major historical bottoms can develop into major support or resistance areas, it is important to calculate percentage divisions of major historical tops. At a minimum, traders should at least know 50 percent of the all-time high of a market. This price can become significant support or a downside target following a large break. The same divisions that were used for the range should be used to calculate the divisions of the all-time high. Take this price and calculate price zones in 8ths and 10ths (Figure 8.5).

PIVOT PRICE CALCULATIONS

Another reason for identifying horizontal support and resistance is to create possible areas of interest. An area of interest is a zone where strong trading activity is likely to

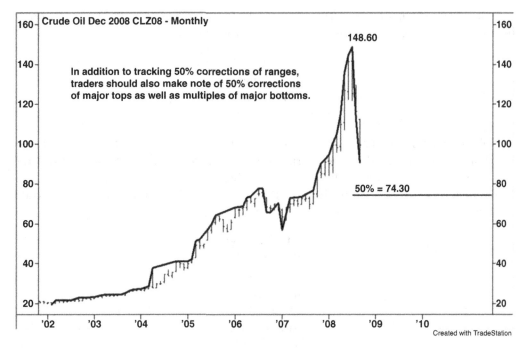

FIGURE 8.5 Retracements of Major Tops
Copyright © TradeStation.

take place, for example, the zone created by 50 percent and 61.8 percent prices is likely to create activity or interest. Other areas of interest can be created by using the Classic Pivot and retracement prices.

One of the more popular ways to determine support, resistance, and price targets today is the calculation of the Classic Pivot. This method has also been called the Floor Trader Pivot because of its popularity in the trading pits of Chicago. The Classic Pivot is usually used with daily data but can be used with any time period that has an Open, High, Low, and Close and creates additional horizontal support and resistance levels. While these numbers may provide support and resistance when used alone, they can become more powerful when combined with major retracement prices.

To calculate the Daily Classic Pivot Price, the trader needs the previous day's Open, High (H), Low (L), and Close (C). The first price that needs to be calculated is the Pivot Price (PP). The formula is $PP = (H + L + C)/3$.

Resistance is calculated first. There are usually four levels of resistance. These are abbreviated as R1, R2, R3, and R4. The formulas are as follows:

$$R1 = (2 * PP) - L$$
$$R2 = (PP + Range)$$
$$R3 = (PP + (Range * 2))$$
$$R4 = (PP + (Range * 3))$$

Support is calculated next. There are usually four levels of support. These are abbreviated as S1, S2, S3, and S4. The formulas are as follows:

$$S1 = (2 * PP) - H$$
$$S2 = PP - Range$$
$$S3 = (PP - (Range * 2))$$
$$S4 = (PP - (Range * 3))$$

These figures are usually listed in a highest to lowest form in a table, but become more useful when placed on the chart. For example, to calculate the Classic Pivot for the 2008 September E-Mini S&P 500 for September 8, 2008, use the following data from September 7: Open = 1236.50, High = 1245.25, Low = 1216.50 and Close = 1241.00 (Figure 8.6).

$$R4 = 1320.50$$
$$R3 = 1291.75$$
$$R2 = 1263.00$$
$$R1 = 1252.00$$
$$PP = 1234.25$$
$$S1 = 1223.25$$
$$S2 = 1205.50$$
$$S3 = 1176.75$$
$$S4 = 1148.00$$

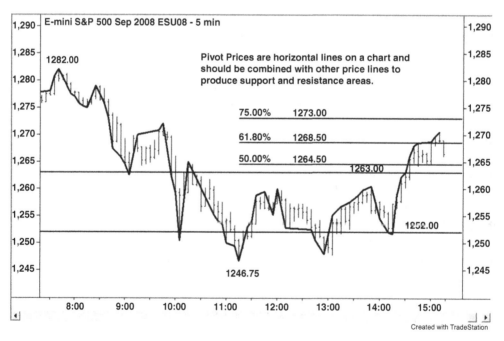

FIGURE 8.6 Pivot Prices
Copyright © TradeStation.

Once these prices are calculated it is suggested that traders draw these prices on their intraday charts as horizontal lines. These lines along with additional horizontal lines such as main tops, main bottoms, and percentage retracement points can create price clusters. These price clusters can become powerful support and resistance levels throughout the day.

MOVING AVERAGES

Moving averages are popular trading tools because of their ease of calculation. To the analyst they just represent another form of price. Often traders who prefer to use moving averages as support and resistance look for two or more moving averages near each other to create important support or resistance zones. These moving averages become more important when they trade at or near other independently determined horizontal support or resistance. Once again the trader is looking for price clusters that may attract order size. Once these areas are highlighted, the trader can determine the strength of each price cluster. One example may be the 200-Day Moving Average trading inside of a 50 percent and 61.8 percent retracement zone. This combination creates an area of interest that may attract a large buyer. The key to using this technique is to be patient and wait for size to show up at the price cluster. Although it is tempting to just place an order at these clusters, the importance of the price cluster is ultimately decided by the size of the buyers in these zones (Figure 8.7).

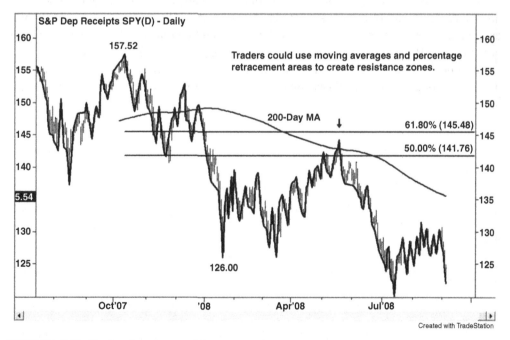

FIGURE 8.7 Moving Averages and Percentage Retracements
Copyright © TradeStation.

SUMMARY

Gann used a number of methods to determine support and resistance levels in his effort to find balance points in the market. One of his most popular methods is the horizontal support and resistance level. Horizontal support and resistance are the straight lines you can draw across a chart from tops, bottoms, and percentage retracement zones. As long as the market continues to trade inside major ranges, these horizontal prices will provide support and resistance into the future.

The most popular retracement price area is 50 percent of a range. Analysts and traders usually divide a range into 8ths and 10ths to find various support and resistance levels. Some traders prefer to use the Fibonacci retracement prices of 38.2 percent and 61.80 percent.

Besides using percentage retracements of ranges, traders should also use multiples of the all-time low or other major lows to set up future support and resistance prices. These multiples are 100 percent, 200 percent, 300 percent, and so on. Traders are also encouraged to use 8ths and 10ths to divide the all-time high or major highs into significant price targets.

The purpose of noting these horizontal points on the chart is to create a frame of the market. All of the trading activity takes place inside of this frame. While some traders prefer to trade only using 50 percent and 61.8 percent retracement levels, it is still important to note all of the others especially when they refer to the all-time low and all-time high.

Another reason for identifying horizontal support and resistance is to create possible areas of interest. An area of interest is a zone where strong trading activity is likely to take place, for example, the zone created by 50 percent and 61.8 percent prices is likely to create activity or interest. Other areas of interest can be created by using combinations of the Classic Pivot and retracement prices or moving averages and retracement prices.

The best way to trade using horizontal prices is to look for price clusters. The best price clusters are created by two or more numbers that have been determined using independent methods.

CHAPTER 9

Price: Gann Angles

T his section of Gann theory is probably the most popular, as many traders use Gann angles in their personal trading and forecasting. These angles are often compared to trend lines, when in fact they are not. A Gann angle is a diagonal line that moves at a uniform rate of speed. A trend line is created by connecting bottoms to bottoms in the case of an uptrend and tops to tops in the case of a downtrend (Figure 9.1).

When creating Gann angle charts, the swing charts once again become significant, as the swing top is the origin of the downtrending angles, and the swing bottom is the origin of the uptrending angles. All three trend indicator charts can be used to determine the placement of the angles, but as in swing-chart trading, too many angles can confuse the trader. Because of this, Gann angles originating from minor tops and minor bottoms are discouraged, as the frequency of the angles creates an almost spiderweb-like appearance. This can lead to a condition called *analysis paralysis*, wherein the analyst is literally kept from making a move in the market because the enormous number of angles masks the support and resistance prices.

The best charts from which to place Gann angles are the intermediate trend chart and the main trend chart, the optimal one being the intermediate chart, as it provides just the right number of angles from which to determine and forecast support and resistance. Angles drawn from the main trend indicator chart are also important, but occur less often. They are strong because they are an extension of the strong bottoms and tops, but their infrequency on this chart often forces the trader to take unnecessary risks.

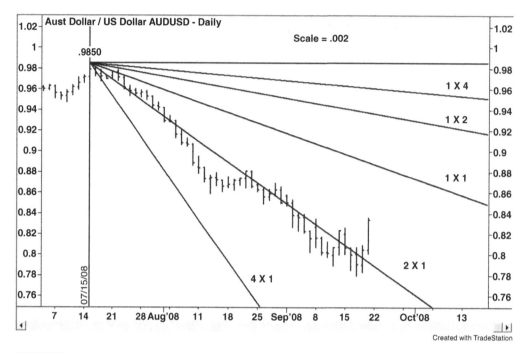

FIGURE 9.1 Downtrending Gann Angle Chart of Daily Australian Dollar/U.S. Dollar
Copyright © TradeStation.

IMPORTANCE OF GANN ANGLES

There are 19 basic geometric forms to explain the angle theory (see Figures 9.2 through 9.20). These forms tend to repeat more often than others, and are considered important because they have withstood the test of time.

1. Square of the range from a low price
2. Square of the range from a high price
3. Strong-position bull market above a 1 × 1 angle
4. Weak-position bull market below a 1 × 1 angle
5. Strong-position bear market below a 1 × 1 angle
6. Weak-position bear market above a 1 × 1 angle
7. Swing chart and angles from a top
8. Swing chart and angles from a bottom
9. Angle at old top, new support
10. Angle at old bottom, new resistance
11. Angles from double tops

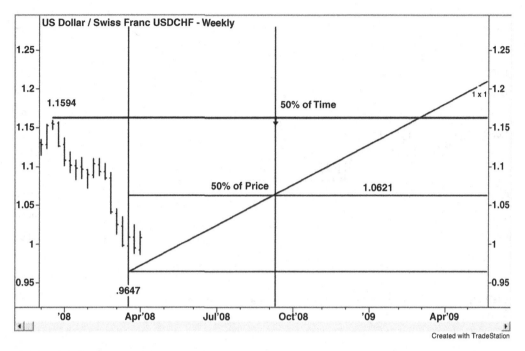

FIGURE 9.2 Square of the Range from a Low Price. The intersection of the Gann angle and 50% of price forms a major support zone.
Copyright © TradeStation.

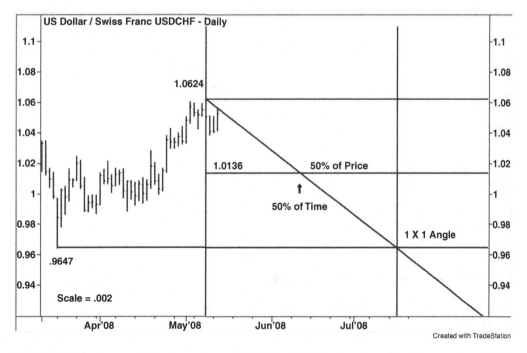

FIGURE 9.3 Square of the Range from a High Price. The intersection of the Gann angle and 50% of price forms a major resistance zone.
Copyright © TradeStation.

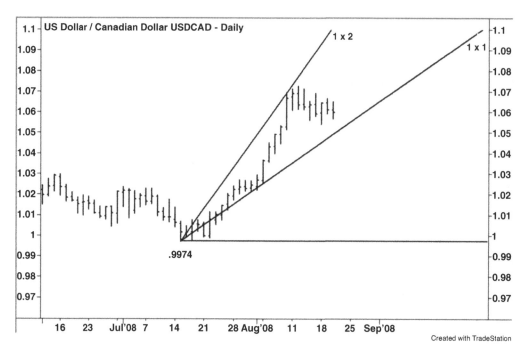

FIGURE 9.4 Strong-Position Bull Market Above a 1 × 1 Angle
Copyright © TradeStation.

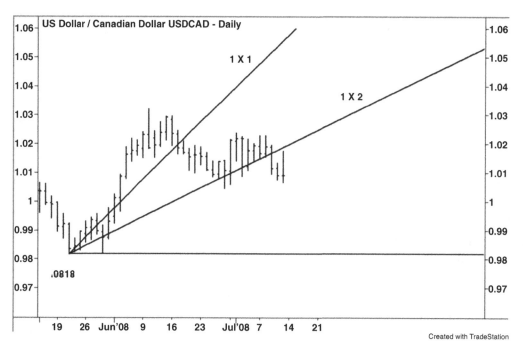

FIGURE 9.5 Weak-Position Bull Market Below a 1 × 1 Angle
Copyright © TradeStation.

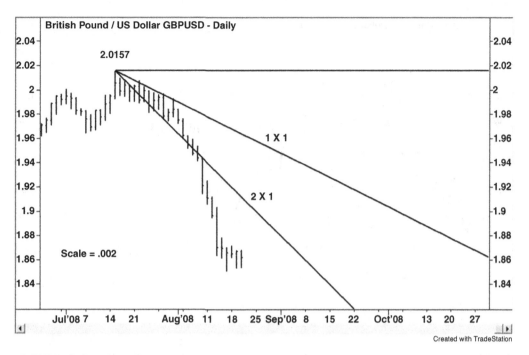

FIGURE 9.6 Strong-Position Bear Market Below a 1 × 1 Angle
Copyright © TradeStation.

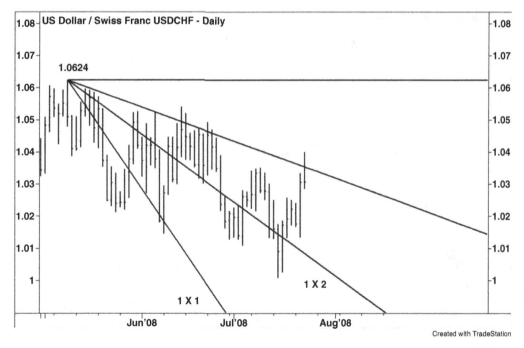

FIGURE 9.7 Weak-Position Bear Market Above a 1 × 1 Angle
Copyright © TradeStation.

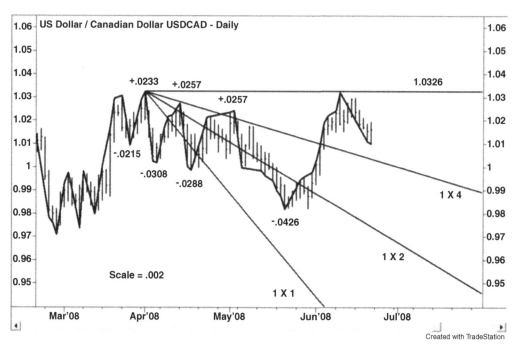

FIGURE 9.8 Swing Chart and Angles from a Top. Use swing charts and angles to forecast price action. Note that here a combination of the swing-chart target and the Gann angle forms support. Copyright © TradeStation.

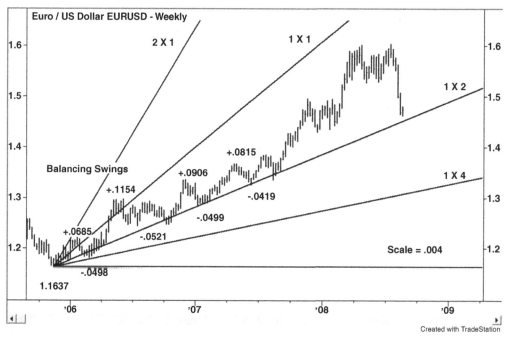

FIGURE 9.9 Swing Chart and Angles from a Bottom. Look for a swing-chart target to balance on a Gann angle. Note here the combination of the swing-chart target and Gann angle. Copyright © TradeStation.

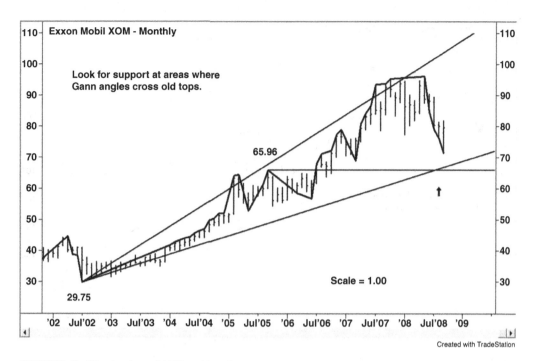

FIGURE 9.10 Angle at Old Top, New Support
Copyright © TradeStation.

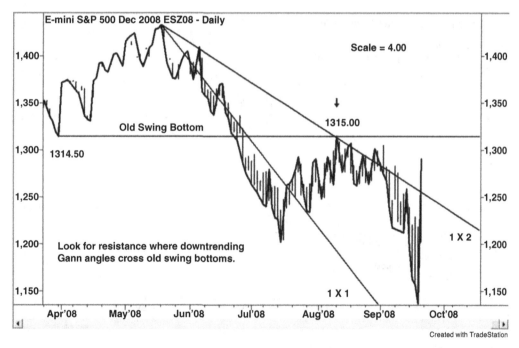

FIGURE 9.11 Angle at Old Bottom, New Resistance
Copyright © TradeStation.

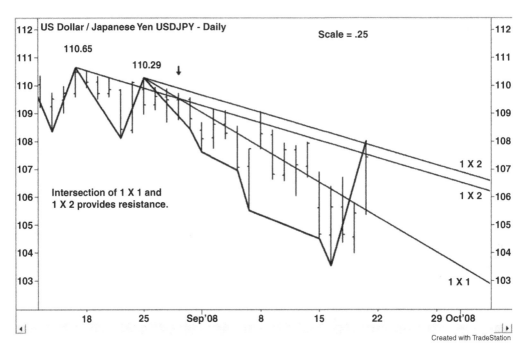

FIGURE 9.12 Angles from Double Tops
Copyright © TradeStation.

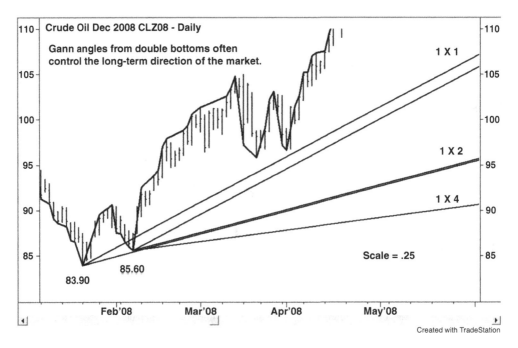

FIGURE 9.13 Angles from Double Bottoms
Copyright © TradeStation.

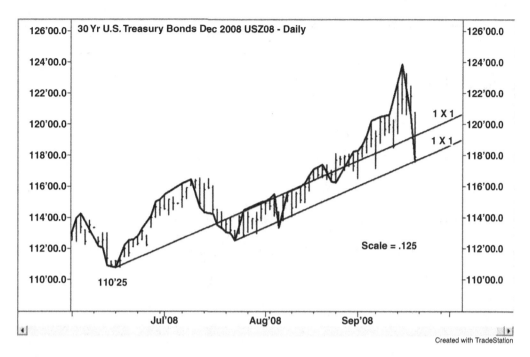

FIGURE 9.14 Uptrending Channel from a Double Bottom. Double bottoms form uptrending channels that guide the markets higher.
Copyright © TradeStation.

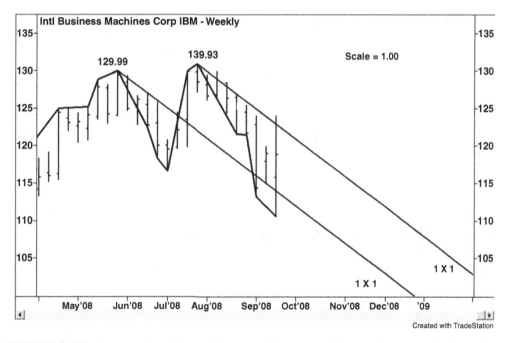

FIGURE 9.15 Downtrending Channel from a Double Top. Double tops form downtrending channels that guide the market lower.
Copyright © TradeStation.

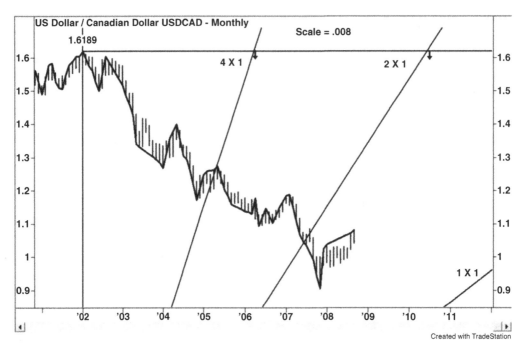

FIGURE 9.16 Zero Angle from a High Price. The high price squares time when the angle from zero reaches the high price.
Copyright © TradeStation.

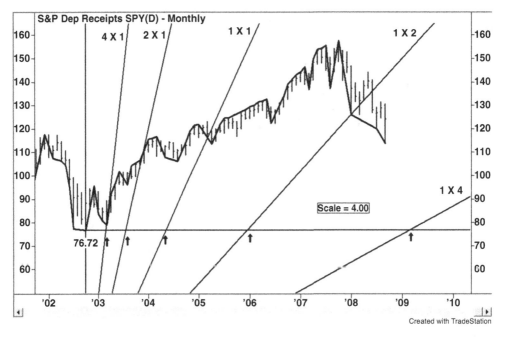

FIGURE 9.17 Zero Angle from a Low Price. The low price squares time when the angle from zero reaches the low price.
Copyright © TradeStation.

164

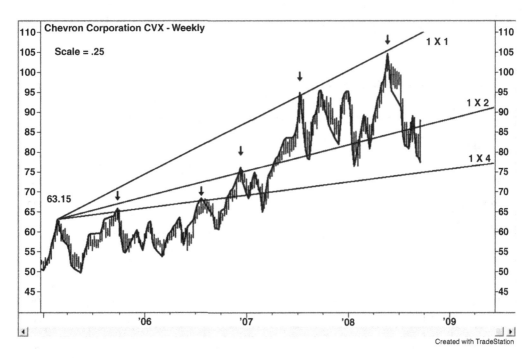

FIGURE 9.18 Angle from a Top Forecasts a Future Top. A 1 × 1 angle drawn up from a top can forecast a future top.
Copyright © TradeStation.

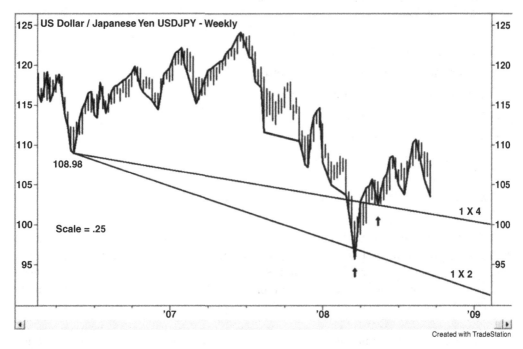

FIGURE 9.19 Angle from a Bottom Forecasts a Future Bottom. A 1 × 1 angle drawn down from a bottom can forecast a future bottom.
Copyright © TradeStation.

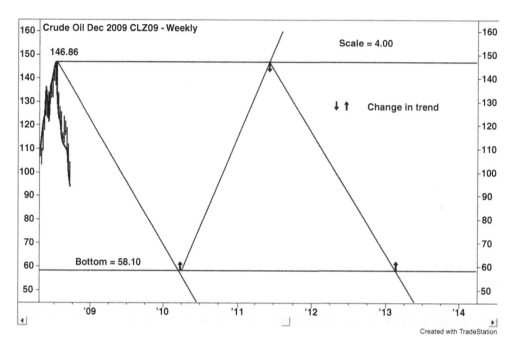

FIGURE 9.20 Angles Repeat as Long as the Market Remains Inside the Range
Copyright © TradeStation.

12. Angles from double bottoms

13. Uptrending channel from a double bottom

14. Downtrending channel from a double top

15. Zero angle from a high price

16. Zero angle from a low price

17. Angle from a top forecasts a future top

18. Angle from a bottom forecasts a future bottom

19. Angles repeat as long as the market remains inside the range

The basic premise behind Gann angles is as follows: if you know the angles that are likely to forecast tops and bottoms many weeks and months ahead of the actual event, you will then be able to trade more successfully. This is because the geometric angles accurately forecast tops and bottoms. The important items to remember before you try this method are as follows:

• Each stock and commodity is unique. You will be required to study and practice using the angles for each market where you are going to trade in order to determine its characteristics. Learn to select the scale that is applicable to each commodity. Arbitrarily selecting any scale will throw the whole chart off.

- The markets are geometric in their design and function. Every point on the chart is geometrically aligned to some other point on the chart. Therefore, the market will obey geometric laws measured by geometric angles.
- Weekly charts are by far the most useful for forecasting, then monthly charts, while the daily charts are best for volatile, active markets.

HOW TO CONSTRUCT GANN ANGLE CHARTS

As mentioned earlier, in order to build a Gann angle chart, the trader must have already built a trend indicator chart. In this section, we will primarily use the intermediate trend indicator chart. This is because the best Gann angle charts are built when following the two-period swings in the market.

Scale

Gann angles move at uniform rates of speed, which makes Gann angle charts sensitive to price scale. A properly constructed chart must be made with the proper scale in order to have any value. As we said earlier, each market has its own unique price scale, and the markets are geometric in design and function. Thus, they will follow geometric laws when charted.

A study of the charts and manuscripts of W. D. Gann shows that he chose a price scale that agreed with a geometric design or formula. When the markets were trading at lower levels, a smaller unit of price was used. When trading at higher levels, a larger unit of price was used.

One rule to remember is to choose a price scale that follows a geometric progression and is in direct relation to the level of the price. If this is practiced, geometric angles will measure price and time in an accurate manner. Price units for daily, weekly, or monthly charts that follow a geometric design can be one of the following:

.01–.02–.04
.02–.04–.08
.04–.08–.16
.002–.004–.008
0.10–0.20–0.40
0.20–0.40–0.80
0.125–0.25–0.50
0.25–0.50–1
2/32–4/32–8/32

It must be remembered that Gann used eight-squares-to-the-inch paper with each fourth line accented as his only charting medium from 1904 until his death in 1955. He chose this chart paper because of its geometric design.

Other papers based on 5 and 10 lines are not acceptable. The Ganntrader 2 software program is also programmed around this specific geometric law.

Gann angles are a function of price and time, which is why the price scale is so important. Since the angles move at a uniform rate of speed, they have predictive value. This is another reason why the proper scale has to be used—if the scale is off, then the prediction will be off.

Table 9.1 lists the price scales that are the best for each futures market. These price scales should be used when building Gann-style charts. They have been tested and have

TABLE 9.1 Optimum Price Scales

Market	Day	Week	Month
Australian dollar/USD	.002 pips	.004 pips	.008 pips
British pound/USD	.002 pips	.004 pips	.008 pips
Cocoa	8 points	16 points	32 points
Coffee	50 points	100 points	200 points
Copper	.25 points	.50 points	1.00 points
Corn	1 cent	2 cents	4 cents
Cotton	25 points	50 points	100 points
Crude oil	.25 points	.50 points	1.00 points
E-Mini Dow Jones	10 points	20 points	40 points
E-Mini Nasdaq	8.00 points	16.00 points	32.00 points
E-Mini S&P 500	4.00 points	8.00 points	16.00 points
Equities	.25 points	.50 points	1.00 points
ETF	.25 points	.50 points	1.00 points
Euro/USD	.002 pips	.004 pips	.008 pips
Eurodollars	2 points	4 points	8 points
Gold	1 dollar	2 dollars	4 dollars
Heating oil	.25 points	.50 points	1.00 points
Live cattle	10 points	20 points	40 points
Live hogs	10 points	20 points	40 points
New Zealand dollar/USD	.002 pips	.004 pips	.008 pips
Oats	1 cent	2 cents	4 cents
Orange juice	50 points	100 points	200 points
Platinum	1 dollar	2 dollars	4 dollars
Silver	1 cent	2 cents	4 cents
Soy meal	50 points	100 points	200 points
Soybean oil	10 points	20 points	40 points
Soybeans	2 cents	4 cents	8 cents
Sugar	4 points	8 points	16 points
Treasury bonds	0.125	0.25	0.50
Unleaded gas	.25 points	.50 points	1.00 points
USD/Canadian dollar	.002 pips	.004 pips	.008 pips
USD/Japanese yen	.25 pips	.50 pips	1.00 pips
USD/Swiss franc	.002 pips	.004 pips	.008 pips
Wheat	1 cent	2 cents	4 cents

yielded accurate results. Study and practice with these scales to see if they suit your trading style. If you want to develop your own scales, then study the two following subsections.

How to Determine the Scale for Markets Not Listed   The easiest way to determine the scale of a market is by taking the difference between top-to-top and bottom-to-bottom and dividing it by the time it took the market to move from top-to-top and bottom-to-bottom. This equation yields the speed of the uptrend and downtrend lines. For example, if the difference between top-to-top and bottom-to-bottom is 50 points and the time is 27 days, then the speed of the trend line connecting these two points is 1.85. The average speed of the trend line can be determined by making this calculation several times. After determining the average speed of the trend line, round it to the next whole number. In this example, if the average uptrend line moves 1.95 per day, then assume the Gann scale is 2. This approach should only be used for markets not on the scale list in Table 9.1.

Equation to Determine the Proper Scale of a Market   The distance between two main bottoms divided by the time between the main bottoms equals the speed or scale of the angle. This same formula can be applied to the distance between two main tops. Once a series of scales has been determined, the trader can determine the average scale and round off to the nearest whole number.

$$\text{Uptrending Scale} = \frac{\text{Main Bottom 2} - \text{Main Bottom 1}}{\text{Difference in Time Between Bottoms}}$$

$$\text{Downtrending Scale} = \frac{\text{Main Top 1} - \text{Main Top 2}}{\text{Difference in Time Between Tops}}$$

Example 1: 2008 Daily May Soybeans   Main bottom November 3, 2006, at 7.02. Main bottom August 16, 2007, at 8.37. The difference in time is 39 weeks.

$$\frac{8.37 - 7.02}{39 \text{ Weeks}} = \frac{1.35}{39 \text{ Weeks}} = 3.46 \text{ cents/week}$$

This is close to the suggested daily scale of 4 cents per week.

Example 2: Daily British Pound/U.S. Dollar   Main top March 14, 2008, at 2.0398. Main top March 27, 2008, at 2.0193. The difference in time is 9 market days.

$$\frac{2.0398 - 2.0193}{9 \text{ Days}} = \frac{.0205 \text{ pips}}{9 \text{ Days}} = .0023 \text{ pips/day}$$

This is close to the suggested daily scale of .002 pips per day (Figure 9.21).

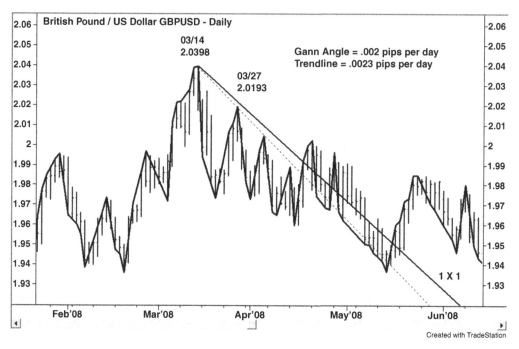

FIGURE 9.21 Daily British Pound/U.S. Dollar Chart
Copyright © TradeStation.

If the bottom-to-bottom and top-to-top data suggested in the chapters on the trend indicator have been maintained, then sufficient information is available to research and analyze the scale of a market properly.

To experiment with the scale, it is necessary to be willing to build a number of charts. The easiest way to determine the proper scale of a market is to use mathematics.

Calculating the Gann Angles

Gann angles are very easy to construct. Since they are a function of price and time, all that is needed to draw them properly are a properly constructed chart, a green pen, a red pen, a calculator, and a ruler.

A properly constructed chart is one that was charted to scale by market day only. Holidays and weekends cannot be included on this chart because there is no price activity during these periods. Each grid has a point value, so using blank grids will throw off the angle, that is, an angle may be higher or lower than expected.

The basic equation for calculating Gann angles is

$$\text{Price} \times \text{Time}$$

Knowing basic algebra helps us calculate either price or time when given two variables. If we know the correct scale and are given a base price and a future price, we can predict when the market will most likely trade this price. If we know the scale to use and are given a base price and a future date, we can predict where the angle will be during that given time period.

Calculating Uptrending Angles

Gann Angles from an Intermediate Bottom Strong Market on the Bull Side of the 1 × 1 Angle

First Important Angle: 1 × 1 The first and most important angle to draw is the 1 × 1 angle, which consists of one unit of price for one unit of time.

Step 1: On a properly constructed chart use your red pen to draw a line from the main bottom across to the right. This line can be extended to the end of the chart. Count and number the bars from the main bottom to the end of the chart. It is easiest to count by 4.

Step 2: From the intermediate bottom, prepare to draw the 1 × 1 angle.

The basic formula is scale multiplied by time plus the main bottom.

Example: 2008 Weekly August Gold market. Scale is 8.00 dollars per week. Intermediate bottom is .679.30 the week ending August 17, 2007.

From the 679.30 intermediate bottom the week ending August 17, 2007, draw a line with the red pen to the right. Extend the line until the contract expiration.

Count the number of weeks from the week ending August 17, 2007, to the week ending August 29, 2008. Identify every fourth or eighth day on the chart (Figure 9.22).

Since the contract expires the week ending August 29, 2008, the distance in time from the bottom on June 14, 2007, is 54 weeks.

Since the scale is 8.00 dollars per week, 54 weeks times 8.00 dollars per week equals 432.00 dollars.

Add this figure to the intermediate bottom. In this case, 679.30 plus 432.00 dollars places the 1 × 1 Gann angle at 1111.30. Take the green pen and draw a 1 × 1 angle from the bottom at 679.30 to 1111.30.

Each day this angle is at an exact point on the chart. For example, the week ending March 14, 2008 is 30 weeks from the intermediate bottom at 679.30. The 1 × 1 angle from the 679.30 bottom the week ending March 14, 2008 is at 919.30 (Figure 9.23).

Alternative Method of Calculating the 1 × 1 Angle or Determining Price If the intermediate bottom and scale are known, it is possible to estimate the date on which the market is likely to trade a specific price. Using the 2008 August Gold market, we know the intermediate bottom is at 679.30. The question is, "Based on the current scale and using the 1 × 1 angle, when is the market most likely to trade 960.30?" (Figure 9.24).

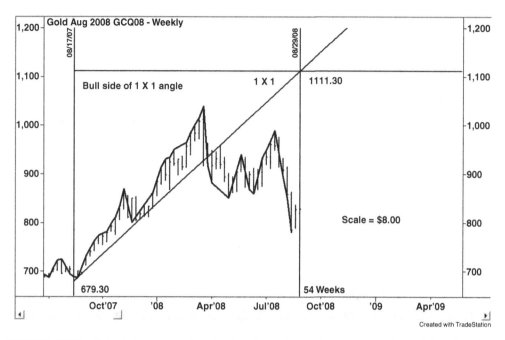

FIGURE 9.22 Calculating Uptrending Angles: Preparing to Draw the 1 × 1 Angle by Identifying Every Fourth or Eighth Day on the Chart
Copyright © TradeStation.

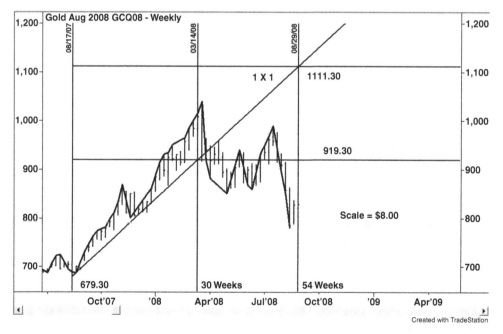

FIGURE 9.23 Calculating Uptrending Angles: Marking the 1 × 1 Angle for a Specific Date
Copyright © TradeStation.

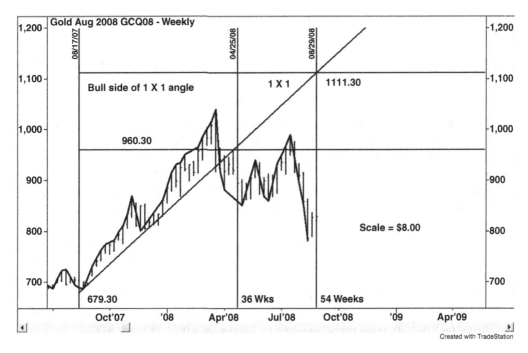

FIGURE 9.24 Alternative Method of Calculating the 1 × 1 Angle
Copyright © TradeStation.

The question is easy to answer. Simply subtract the intermediate bottom from the target price and divide by the scale. This will give you the market day on which the 1 × 1 angle will cross this price. Look for the market day on the chart and find the date associated with it. This does not mean the market will be trading at this price on this date. It just means that if the market follows the 1 × 1 angle, then at a minimum it will be at that price.

Solution

$$960.30 - 679.30 = 281.00$$
$$281.00 \div 8.00 \text{ dollars} = 35.13$$

The answer, 36 weeks, is associated with the week ending April 25, 2008.

Gann Angles from an Intermediate Bottom Strong Market on the Bull Side of the 1 × 1 Angle

Second Important Angle: 2 × 1 The second angle to draw is the 2 × 1 angle, which consists of two units of price for one unit of time.

Step 1: Having placed the 1 × 1 angle on the chart, add the 2 × 1 angle to the chart.
Step 2: From the intermediate bottom, prepare to draw the 2 × 1 angle.

The basic formula is scale multiplied by time plus the intermediate bottom.

Example: 2008 Weekly May Corn market. Scale is .02 per week. Intermediate bottom is $2.93^{1}/_{2}$ the week ending September 15, 2006.

From the $2.93^{1}/_{2}$ intermediate bottom the week ending September 15, 2006, count the number of weeks. Identify every fourth or eighth day on the chart (Figure 9.25).

In this example, the 12th week has been chosen as a reference point.

Since the scale is .02 per week, 12 weeks times .02 per week equals .24. (Up to this point, this is the same calculation as for the 1×1 angle.) Multiply .24 by 2 because you are looking for an angle moving twice as fast as the 1×1. This yields a figure of .48.

Add this figure to the intermediate bottom. In this case, $2.93^{1}/_{2}$ plus .48 places the 2×1 Gann angle at $3.41^{1}/_{2}$. Take the red pen and draw a 2×1 angle from the bottom at $2.93^{1}/_{2}$ to $3.41^{1}/_{2}$.

Each week this angle is at an exact point on the chart. For example, the week ending March 30, 2007, is 28 weeks from the intermediate bottom at $2.93^{1}/_{2}$. The 2×1 angle from the $2.93^{1}/_{2}$ bottom on September 14, 2006 is at $4.05^{1}/_{2}$ (Figure 9.26).

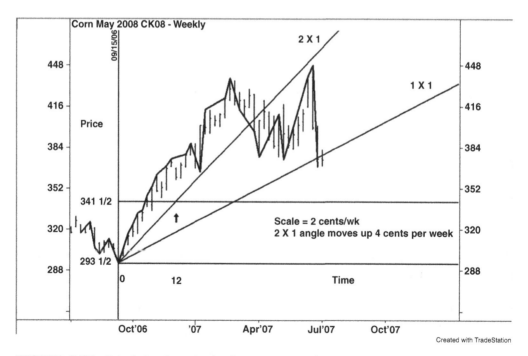

FIGURE 9.25 Calculating Gann Angles from an Intermediate Bottom: 2×1
Copyright © TradeStation.

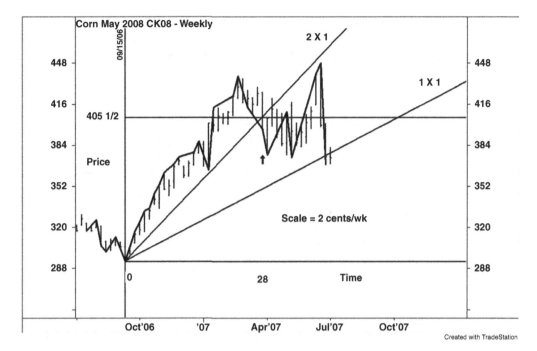

FIGURE 9.26 Calculating Gann Angles from an Intermediate Bottom: Marking the 2 × 1 Angle for a Specific Date
Copyright © TradeStation.

Alternative Method of Calculating the 2 × 1 Angle or Determining Price If the intermediate bottom and scale are known, it is possible to estimate the date on which the market is likely to trade a specific price. Using the 2008 May Corn market, we know the intermediate bottom is at $2.93\frac{1}{2}$. The question is, "Based on the current scale and using the 2 × 1 angle, when is the market most likely to trade $3.61\frac{1}{2}$?"

The question is easy to answer. Simply subtract the intermediate bottom from the target price and divide by the scale. Take this figure and divide by 2 to get the 2 × 1 angle. This will give you the week on which the 2 × 1 angle will cross this price. Look for the week on the chart and find the date associated with it (Figure 9.27). This does not mean the market will be trading at this price on this date. It just means that if the market follows the 2 × 1 angle, then at a minimum it will be at that price.

Solution

$$3.61\frac{1}{2} - 2.93\frac{1}{2} = .68$$
$$.68 \div .02 = 34$$
$$34 \div 2 = 17$$

The answer, 17 weeks, is associated with the week ending January 12, 2007.

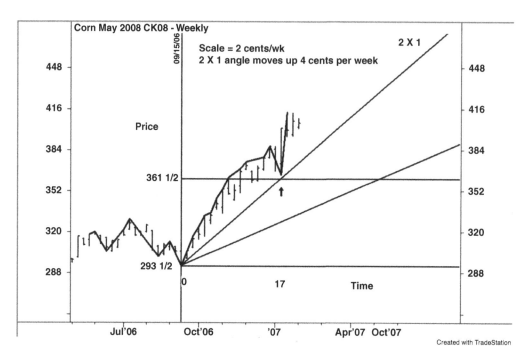

FIGURE 9.27 Alternative Method of Calculating the 2 × 1 Angle
Copyright © TradeStation.

Gann Angles from an Intermediate Bottom Strong Market on the Weak Side of the 1 × 1 Angle

Third Important Angle: 1 × 2   The third angle to draw is the 1 × 2 angle, which consists of one unit of price for two units of time.

Step 1: Having placed the 1 × 1 angle on the chart, add the 1 × 2 angle to the chart.
Step 2: From the intermediate bottom, prepare to draw the 1 × 2 angle.

The basic formula is scale multiplied by time plus the intermediate bottom.

Example: 2008 Daily May Corn market. Scale is .02 per week. Main bottom is $2.93\frac{1}{2}$ the week ending September 15, 2006.

From the $2.93\frac{1}{2}$ intermediate bottom the week ending September 15, 2006, count the number of weeks. Identify every fourth or eighth day on the chart (Figure 9.28).
Since the contract expires the week ending May 16, 2008, the distance in time from the bottom to the week ending May 16, 2008, is 87 weeks.

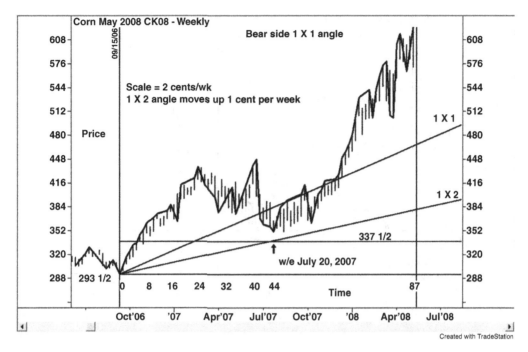

FIGURE 9.28 Calculating Gann Angles from an Intermediate Bottom: 1 × 2
Copyright © TradeStation.

Since the scale is .02 per week, 87 weeks times .02 per week equals 1.74. (Up to this point,
this is the same calculation as for the 1 × 1 angle.) Divide 1.74 by 2 because you are
looking for an angle moving half as fast as the 1 × 1. This yields a figure of .87.

Add this figure to the intermediate bottom. In this case, $2.93\frac{1}{2}$ plus .87 points places the
1 × 2 Gann angle at $3.80\frac{1}{2}$. Take the red pen and draw a 1 × 2 angle from the bottom
at $2.93\frac{1}{2}$ to $3.80\frac{1}{2}$.

Each day this angle is at an exact point on the chart. For example, the week ending July
20, 2007 is 44 weeks from the intermediate bottom at $2.93\frac{1}{2}$. The 1 × 2 angle from
the $2.93\frac{1}{2}$ bottom the week ending September 15, 2006, is at $3.37\frac{1}{2}$.

Alternative Method of Calculating the 1 × 2 Angle or Determining Price   If the intermediate bottom and scale are known, it is possible to estimate the date on which the
market is likely to trade a specific price. Using the 2008 May Corn market, we know the
intermediate bottom is at $2.93\frac{1}{2}$. The question is, "Based on the current scale and using
the 1 × 2 angle, when is the market most likely to trade $3.50\frac{1}{2}$?" (Figure 9.29).

The question is easy to answer. Simply subtract the intermediate bottom from the
target price, and divide by the scale. Take this figure and multiply by 2 to get the 1 × 2
angle. This will give you the week on which the 1 × 2 angle will cross this price. Look
for the week on the chart and find the date associated with it. This does not mean the

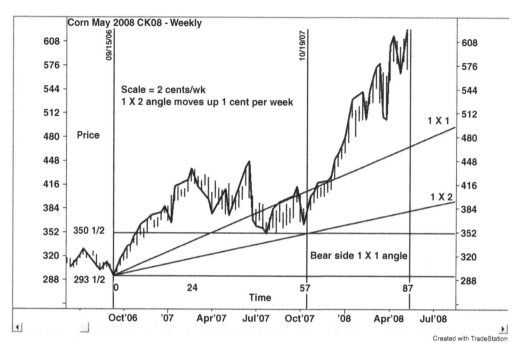

FIGURE 9.29 Alternative Method of Calculating the 1 × 2 Angle
Copyright © TradeStation.

market will be trading at this price on this date. It just means that if the market follows the 1 × 2 angle, then at a minimum it will be at that price.

Solution

$$3.50\,{}^{1}\!/_{2} - 2.93\,{}^{1}\!/_{2} = .57$$
$$.57 \div .02 = 28.5.$$
$$28.5 \times 2 = 57$$

The answer, 57 weeks, is associated with the week ending October 19, 2007.

Calculating Downtrending Angles

Gann Angles Form an Intermediate Top Weak Market on the Bear Side of the 1 × 1 Angle

First Important Angle: 1 × 1 The first and most important angle to draw is the 1 × 1 angle, which consists of one unit of price for one unit of time.

Step 1: On a properly constructed chart use your red pen to draw a line from the intermediate top across to the right. This line can be extended to the end of the chart.

Count and number the bars from the intermediate bottom to the end of the chart. It is easiest to count by four.

Step 2: From the intermediate top, prepare to draw the 1 × 1 angle.

The basic formula is the intermediate top minus the time multiplied by the scale.

Example: Daily New Zealand Dollar/U.S Dollar. Scale is .002 point per day. Intermediate top is .7761 on July 15, 2008.

From the .7761 intermediate top on July 15, 2008, draw a line with the red pen to the right. Extend the line until, for example, October 15, 2008.

Count the number of market days from July 15, 2008. Identify every fourth or eighth day on the chart.

The distance in time from the top on July 15, 2008, until October 15, 2008, is 66 market days (Figure 9.30).

Since the scale is .002 pips per market day, 66 market days times .002 pips per market day equals .1320 pips.

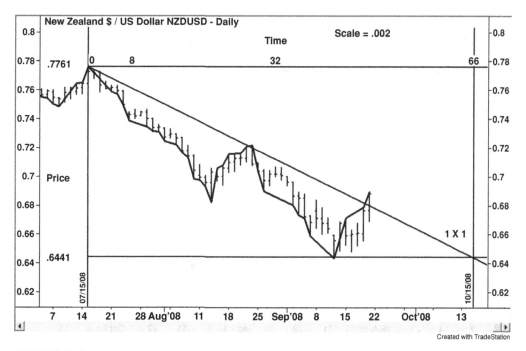

FIGURE 9.30 Calculating Downtrending Angles: Preparing to Draw the 1 × 1 Angle by Identifying Every Fourth or Eighth Day on the Chart
Copyright © TradeStation.

Subtract this figure from the main top. In this case, .7761 minus .1320 pips places the
1 × 1 Gann angle at .6441. Take the green pen and draw a 1 × 1 angle from the top
down to .6441.

Each day this angle is at an exact point on the chart. For example, August 21, 2008, is 27
market days from the intermediate top at .7761. The 1 × 1 angle from the .7761 top
on August 21, 2008 is at .7221 (Figure 9.31).

Alternative Method of Calculating the 1 × 1 Angle or Determining Price   If the intermediate top and scale are known, it is possible to estimate the date on which the market is
likely to trade a specific price. Using the Daily New Zealand Dollar/U.S. Dollar, we know
the intermediate top is at .7761. The question is, "Based on the current scale and using
the 1 × 1 angle, when is the market most likely to trade .6781?" (Figure 9.32).

The question is easy to answer. Simply subtract the target price from the intermediate top, and divide by the scale. This will give you the market day on which the 1 × 1
angle will cross this price. Look for the market day on the chart, and find the date associated with it. This does not mean the market will be trading at this price on this date.
It just means that if the market follows the 1 × 1 angle, then at a minimum it will be at
that price.

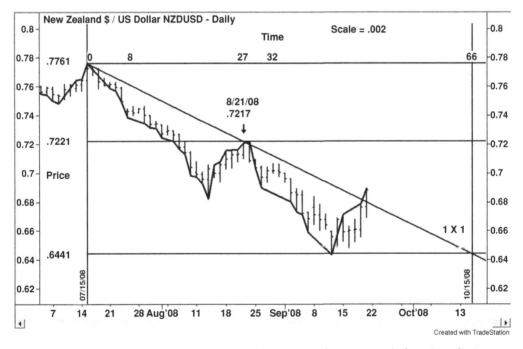

FIGURE 9.31 Calculating Downtrending Angles: Marking the 1 × 1 Angle for a Specific Date
Copyright © TradeStation.

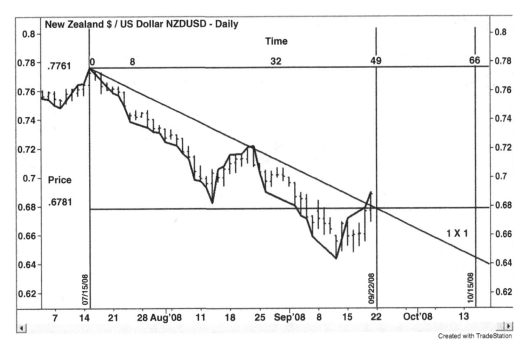

FIGURE 9.32 Alternative Method of Calculating the 1 × 1 Angle
Copyright © TradeStation.

Solution

$$.7761 - .6781 = .0980$$
$$.0980 \div .002 \text{ pips} = 49$$

The answer, 49 market days, is associated with September 22, 2008.

Gann Angles from an Intermediate Top Weak Market on the Bear Side of the 1 × 1 Angle

Second Important Angle: 2 × 1 The second angle to draw is the 2 × 1 angle, which consists of two units of price for one unit of time.

Step 1: Having placed the 1 × 1 angle on the chart, add the 2 × 1 angle to the chart.
Step 2: From the intermediate top, prepare to draw the 2 × 1 angle.

The basic formula is the main top minus scale multiplied by time.

Example: Daily Australian Dollar/U.S. Dollar. Scale is .002 pips per day. Intermediate top is .9850 on July 15, 2008.

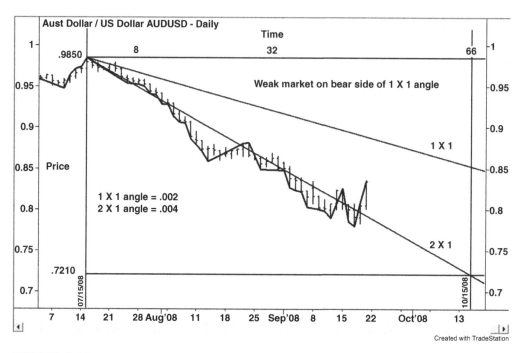

FIGURE 9.33 Calculating Gann Angles from an Intermediate Top: 2 × 1
Copyright © TradeStation.

From the .9850 intermediate top on July 15, 2008, count the number of market days from
    July 15, 2008. Identify every fourth or eighth day on the chart.
The distance in time from the top on July 15, 2008, to October 15, 2008, is 66 market days
    (Figure 9.33).
Since the scale is .002 pips per market day, 66 market days times .002 pips per market
    day equals .1320 pips. (Up to this point, this is the same calculation as for the 1 × 1
    angle.) Multiply .1320 by 2 because you are looking for an angle moving twice as fast
    as the 1 × 1. This yields a figure of .2640 pips.
Subtract this figure from the intermediate top. In this case, .9850 minus .2640 pips places
    the 2 × 1 Gann angle at .7210. Take the red pen and draw a 2 × 1 angle from the top
    at .9850 to .7210.
Each day this angle is at an exact point on the chart. For example, August 7, 2008, is 17
    market days from the intermediate top at .9850. The 2 × 1 angle from the .9850 top
    on July 15, 2008 is at .9170.

Alternative Method of Calculating the 2 × 1 Angle or Determining Price   If the intermediate top and scale are known, it is possible to estimate the date on which the market
is likely to trade a specific price. Using the Australian Dollar market, we know the intermediate top is at .9850. The question is, "Based on the current scale and using the 2 × 1
angle, when is the market most likely to trade .8850?" (Figure 9.34).

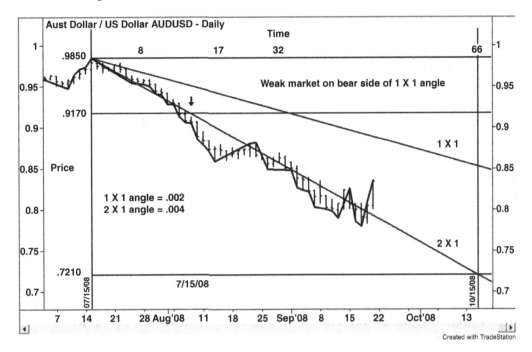

FIGURE 9.34 Calculating a Gann Angle from an Intermediate Top: 2 × 1 for a Specific Date
Copyright © TradeStation.

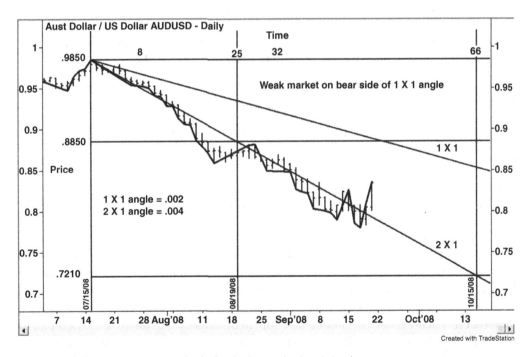

FIGURE 9.35 Alternative Method of Calculating the 2 × 1 Angle
Copyright © TradeStation.

The question is easy to answer. Simply subtract the target price from the intermediate top, and divide by the scale. Take this figure, and divide by 2 to get the 2 × 1 angle. This will give you the market day on which the 2 × 1 angle will cross this price. Look for the market day on the chart, and find the date associated with it. This does not mean the market will be trading at this price on this date. It just means that if the market follows the 2 × 1 angle, then at a minimum it will be at that price.

Solution

$$.9850 - .8850 = .1000$$
$$.1000 \div .002 \text{ pips} = 50$$
$$50 \div 2 = 25$$

The answer, 25 market days, is associated with August 19, 2008 (Figure 9.35).

Gann Angles from an Intermediate Top Weak Market on the Bear Side of the 1 × 1 Angle

Third Important Angle: 1 × 2   The third angle to draw is the 1 × 2 angle, which consists of one unit of price for two units of time.

Step 1: Having placed the 1 × 1 angle on the chart, add the 1 × 2 angle on the chart.
Step 2: From the intermediate top, prepare to draw the 1 × 2 angle.

The basic formula is the intermediate top minus the scale multiplied by time.

Example: Weekly New Zealand Dollar/U.S. Dollar market. Scale is .004 pips per week. Intermediate top is .8215 the week ending February 29, 2008.

From the .8215 intermediate top the week ending February 29, 2008, count the number of weeks from February 29, 2008. Identify every fourth or eighth day on the chart.
The distance in time from the top the week ending February 29, 2008, for example, until December 31, 2008 is 44 weeks (Figure 9.36).
Since the scale is .004 pips per week, 44 weeks times .004 pips per week equals .1760 pips. (Up to this point, this is the same calculation as for the 1 × 1 angle.) Divide .1760 by 2 because you are looking for an angle moving half as fast as the 1 × 1. This yields a figure of .0880 pips.
Subtract this figure from the intermediate top. In this case, .8215 minus .0880 pips places the 1 × 2 Gann angle at .7335. Take the red pen, and draw a 1 × 2 angle from the top at .8215 to .7335.
Each day this angle is at an exact point on the chart. For example, the week ending May 30, 2008, is 13 weeks from the intermediate top at .8215. The 1 × 2 angle from the .8215 the week ending May 30, 2008, is at .7955 (Figure 9.37).

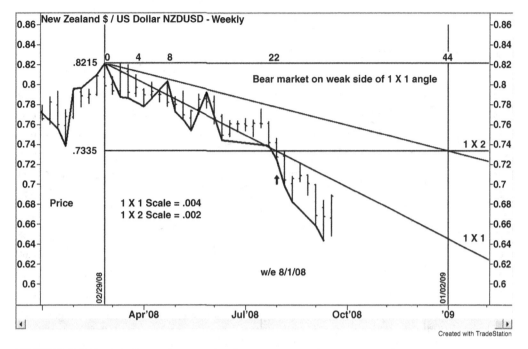

FIGURE 9.36 Calculating Gann Angles from an Intermediate Top: 1 × 2
Copyright © TradeStation.

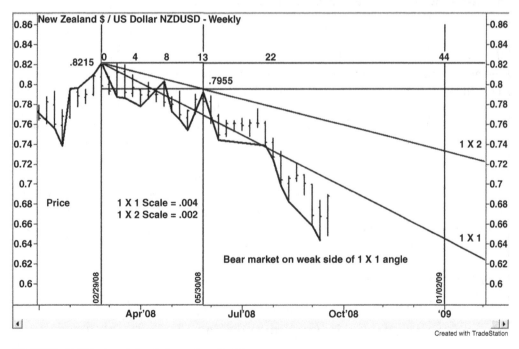

FIGURE 9.37 1 × 2 Angle for a Specific Time
Copyright © TradeStation.

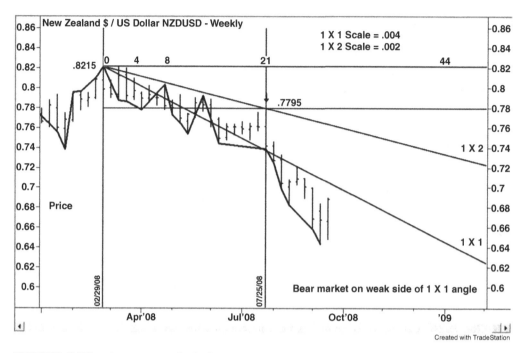

FIGURE 9.38 Alternative Method of Calculating the 1 × 2 Angle
Copyright © TradeStation.

Alternative Method of Calculating the 1 × 2 Angle or Determining Price   If the intermediate top and scale are known, it is possible to estimate the date on which the market is likely to trade a specific price. Using the Weekly New Zealand Dollar market, we
know the intermediate top is at .8215 the week ending February 29, 2008. The question
is, "Based on the current scale and using the 1 × 2 angle, when is the market most likely
to trade .7795?" (Figure 9.38).

The question is easy to answer. Simply subtract the target price from the intermediate top, and divide by the scale. Take this figure, and multiply by 2 to get the 1 × 2 angle.
This will give you the week on which the 1 × 2 angle will cross this price. Look for the
week on the chart, and find the date associated with it. This does not mean the market
will be trading at this price on this date. It just means that if the market follows the 1 × 2
angle, then at a minimum it will be at that price.

Solution

$$.8215 - .7795 = .0420$$
$$.0420 \div .004 \text{ pips} = 10.5$$
$$10.5 \times 2 = 21$$

The answer, 21 weeks, is associated with the week ending July 25, 2008.

Using the same equations, you should also calculate the 8 × 1, 4 × 1, 1 × 4, and 1 × 8 angles if necessary.

Zero Angles

Angles coming up from price 0 are very important and can be easily utilized on the chart you are keeping. This works better with monthly and weekly charts than with daily charts because the time periods are longer. Unless you are working with a daily chart with two or three years worth of data, the 0 angle may never have enough time to become effective.

Example: If you have an important low at 100 and want to bring all of your important angles up from 0 at the time the 100 was made, simply count over to the right 100 squares of time from the actual 100 bottom, and start a 1 × 1 angle upward from 0. You can also count 50 squares for your 2 × 1 angle and 200 for your 1 × 2 angle. Of course, this is if your scale is on the basis of one point. If the scale is something else, you must count accordingly.

The main purpose of this type of charting is to see where price and time equal or square out. This is known as *squaring a low*, and is covered in more detail in Chapter 11.

Example: If you have an important high at 500 and want to bring all of your important angles up from 0 at the time the 500 was made, and your scale was 5, simply count over to the right 100 squares of time from the actual 500 top, and start a 1 × 1 angle upward from 0. You can also count 50 squares for your 2 × 1 angle and 200 for your 1 × 2 angle.

The main purpose of this type of charting is to discover where price and time equal or square out. This is known as *squaring a high* and is covered in more detail in Chapter 11.

How to Use Gann Angles

Putting Gann Angles into Your Trading System   When analysts are speaking Gann, you may hear them say things like, "Stay long until the 1 × 1 angle is broken" or "If it doesn't hold at 50 percent, watch for a change in trend."

At first you may have trouble interpreting such phrases. For example, What do traders mean by "breaking the 1 × 1" and "doesn't hold"? Or, since so much of Gann involves moving from one angle to the next, how far through an angle must the market travel for it to be a significant break?

Identifying a change in trend using geometric angles is a difficult task. Gann never intended his geometric angle rules to stay fixed, since he considered research, testing, and applying them to the markets to be the key to understanding angles. His books and courses are intended as guidelines; he encouraged experimentation.

Constructing geometric angles is easy; interpreting them is a little harder but not impossible. This section should answer any questions about angles and how to construct a trading system.

Developing any trading system is a three-step process:

1. Decide the type of system: trend-following or support-resistance.

   Most trend-following systems are designed to catch larger moves. The biggest fear traders have when using them is that they'll miss the big one. Gann's combination trend-following and support-resistance system suggests that it is virtually never too late to enter the market after a definite signal—even if you miss the bottom or top, the geometric angle will guide you into position.

   The geometric angles also provide valid support and resistance points continually as the market moves up or down away from that bottom or top.

   This is because the geometric angles drawn from a bottom or top are actually an extension of the bottom or top and move at a uniform rate of speed. This touches on the core concept of Gann's theory: Tops and bottoms can forecast future tops and bottoms.

2. Establish entry rules.

   Developing your entry mechanism centers on one of the Gann rules discussed most often: buying or selling when the market touches on an angle.

   The most important angle is the 1×1. Gann said this angle determines the strength and direction of the market, and that you could trade off this angle alone, buying every time price rested on the 45-degree line.

   A contract is always strong when it holds above the 1×1 angle from a bottom, and weak when it is just below the 1×1 line from a top.

   When the market is weak, the best selling opportunity comes when it rallies up to, but not over, the 1×1 line coming down from a two-day top; the best buy exists when the market rests on the 1×1 from a bottom. This can occur a number of times during a prolonged move.

   Remember, angles merely serve as extensions of bottoms or tops. Each time you buy a market resting on the angle, you are, in effect, buying the bottom from which the angles are drawn. As we said earlier, even if you miss the top or the bottom, it is virtually never too late to get in.

   The more important the bottom, the more important the angle drawn from it. It is best to buy at angles from intermediate and main bottoms rather than from one-day bottoms, because the stronger bottom means stronger future angles.

   The Rule of All Angles. Another important guideline is what Gann called the Rule of All Angles: When a market breaks an angle, it will move toward the next angle. This is because, as time passes, an angle's importance weakens and the market eventually breaks through. Therefore a market breaking the 2×1 angle will begin to move toward the 1×1 angle, just as a market breaking the 1×1 angle will eventually reach the 1×2 angle. Conversely, in an up move, an angle

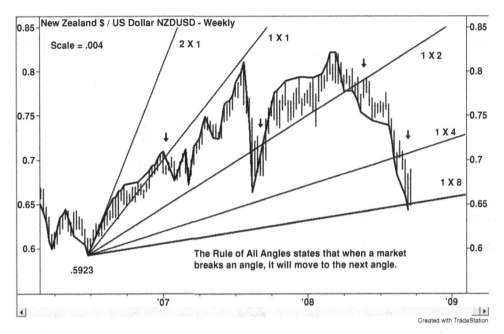

FIGURE 9.39 NZD/U.S. Dollar: The Rule of All Angles
Copyright © TradeStation.

that holds the 1 × 2 angle is likely to rally to the 1 × 1, just as overtaking the 1 × 1 is likely to lead to a rally to the 2 × 1.

As the market forms the bottom, always remember that when the market is above the 1 × 1 angle line, price is ahead of time; when the market is below the 1 × 1, time is ahead of price; and when the market rests on the 1 × 1, time and price are balanced (Figure 9.39).

On a daily chart, when price crosses the 1 × 1 from a bottom, it may not be strong enough to overcome time. This usually causes the market to rest on the 1 × 1 or break under it, only to find support at the 1 × 2. When the time is right and the cycle has run out, the market will usually establish itself on either the 1 × 2, 1 × 1, or 2 × 1 angle. Ideally, the market will follow the 1 × 1.

Early in a bull market you often see prices edge up slowly with small reactions. As well as time working against the market, angles down from one-period and two-period tops offer resistance.

If you trace imaginary lines from these tops, you will notice that they often hold back prices that are creeping up from intermediate and main bottoms. The strongest moves occur when the market crosses angles from both an intermediate top and an intermediate bottom—it takes more strength to break a trend line based on two periods rather than on one period.

When working the geometric angles, it is no surprise to see that the higher the market moves, the wider apart the angles (Figure 9.40). But this also means the

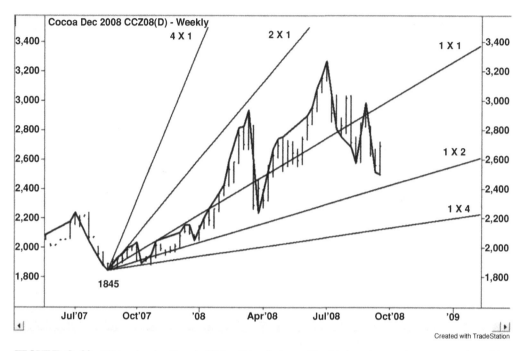

FIGURE 9.40 Wider Angles Equals Wider Price Swings. The higher the market moves, the wider apart the angles. The angles are tight near a bottom.
Copyright © TradeStation.

higher the market travels, the farther it is from its base and, therefore, more vulnerable to correction.

When you combine this with the Rule of All Angles, it is little wonder that the market sells off so sharply after breaking a 2 × 1 angle, only to rally quickly when it reaches the 1 × 1 angle. The converse is true for rallies.

3. Determine placement of stops.

You want to be stopped out only when the trend changes. The key is knowing the extent to which an angle must be penetrated to effect a trend change. Gann provided several ways to determine this.

The rule determining a change in trend from a top involves waiting for a decline exceeding the previous reaction. The rule for a trend change from a bottom involves waiting for a rise that exceeds the greatest rise of a previous rally. When price penetrates an angle by an amount that exceeds a previous penetration, it shows a probable change in trend (Figure 9.41).

This tells you where to place the stop loss order. By studying past movement, you can determine what the "average" move through an angle should be. This is known as *lost motion*, which is discussed in the following section. It was also discussed in Chapter 6. The concept of lost motion is exactly the same when applied to angles.

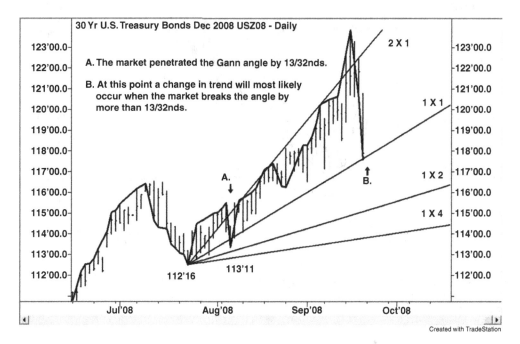

FIGURE 9.41 Rule for Determining a Change in Trend Using Gann Angles
Copyright © TradeStation.

Lost Motion

When applied to angles, lost motion occurs when a price penetrates an important support or resistance angle before it regains the angle and resumes the trend. Throughout the course of an uptrend, the market will follow an uptrending angle moving at a uniform rate of speed. At times the market will break to the downside through an angle, only to recover it within one or two days. The idea is to record the amount the market penetrates the angle before recovering it. This helps determine where to place stop loss orders when buying off of an uptrending angle. The analysis can be done in two parts: the historical tendencies of the lost motion through a specific angle, and the immediate tendencies of the lost motion through a specific angle on the current active start (Figure 9.42).

Determining the historical tendencies of the lost motion through a specific angle requires that a database of these penetrations be maintained. This database is used by the trader to find an average of the minimum penetration, after which he places a stop at this amount plus or minus at least one price unit under the angle. In the case of an uptrending market, the stop is placed at the lost motion figure minus one unit of price under the uptrending angle, while for downtrending markets, the stop is placed at the lost motion figure plus one unit of price over the downtrending angle (Figure 9.43).

Example: Uptrending market with Gann angle at $8.00. Average historical lost motion is 5 cents. Place the stop at least 6 cents under the uptrending angle (Figure 9.44).

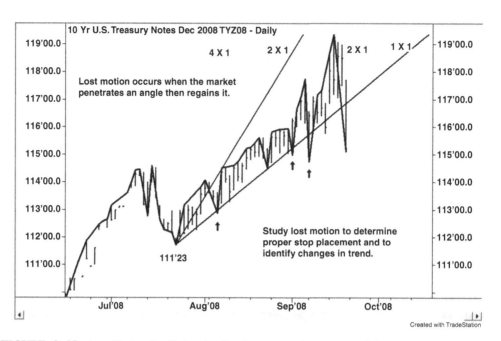

FIGURE 9.42 Lost Motion Applied to Angles. Determine the amount of the lost motion, and then use it to help determine stop placement.
Copyright © TradeStation.

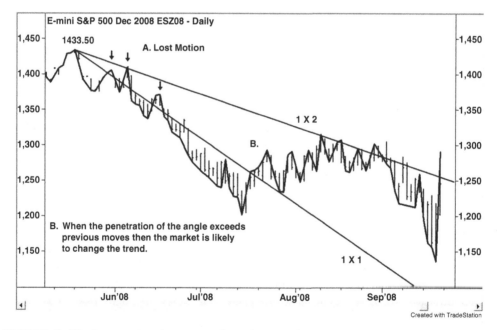

FIGURE 9.43 Determining the Historical Tendencies of Lost Motion through a Specific Angle. Sometimes the market will break an angle, then regain it and rally. Breaking the angle and regaining it establishes the lost motion. Lost motion helps the trader establish a stop loss position.
Copyright © TradeStation.

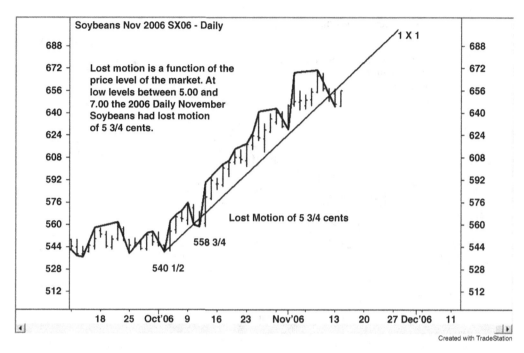

FIGURE 9.44 Lost Motion and a 1 × 2 Angle
Copyright © TradeStation.

Lost motion applied to a current market is slightly different. Because Gann Theory is an adaptive theory, the stops often have to be adjusted to the current market conditions. In other words, dollar stops are not used, but stops related to main bottoms, main tops, percentage retracement points, and Gann angles are placed. When placing a stop using a Gann angle relating to current market conditions, the trader must record the previous penetrations of the angle from which she is attempting to buy or sell. Once this figure is known, she places a stop at this figure plus or minus at least one unit of price. For example, in an uptrending market, if the previous penetration of the angle is 5 cents, then the stop is placed at least 6 cents under the downtrending angle. In a downtrending market, if the previous penetration is 20 tics, then the stop is placed at least 21 tics over the downtrending angle.

Example: Uptrending market with Gann angle at $6.80. Previous penetration was 5 cents. Place the stop at least 6 cents under the uptrending angle.

Example: Downtrending market with Gann angle at 800.25. Previous penetration was 100 points. Place the stop at least 105 points over the downtrending angle.

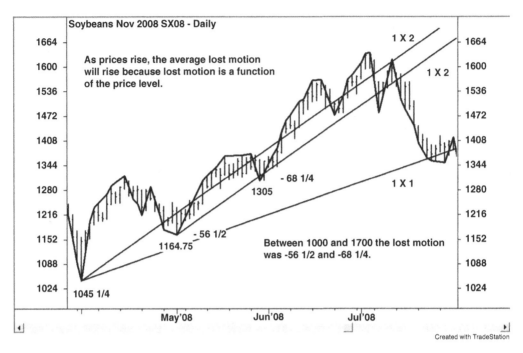

FIGURE 9.45 Lost Motion Is a Function of the Price Level of the Market
Copyright © TradeStation.

The basic idea behind lost motion and Gann angles is to stay with the angle until the market breaks the historical pattern or the immediate pattern. When the angle is penetrated by an amount greater than a previous penetration, the stop loss order protects the trader from a greater loss. Remember that according to the Rule of All Angles once an angle is penetrated, it is likely to continue to the next angle.

Lost motion will vary according to the angle it is applied to and according to the position of the market (Figure 9.45). For example, lost motion will be different for 4×1, 2×1, 1×1, 1×2, and 1×4 angles. In addition, it will vary according to the price level of the market. At low prices, the lost motion will be tighter than at high prices.

After studying lost motion as it is applied to main tops, main bottoms, percentage retracements, and angles, the analyst will most likely come to the conclusion that the average lost motion is the same. This is important to know because it indicates that the combinations of these different price levels with properly placed stops according to the lost motion will yield more successful trading results.

Finally, recall that of the reactions under Gann angles that are not changes in trend, most fall under the Gann label of lost motion. Lost motion describes slight breaks through an angle caused by market momentum. In Gann's day, the average lost motion for grains, for example, was $1^3/_4$ cents. This is why he suggested a 3-cent stop loss order so many times in his books and courses. Traders should study and research the lost motion of each market they choose to trade according to the price level the market is trading. Traders should choose the lost motion increment that seems to mistakenly trigger stops least often.

Through study and practice, you can determine lost motion. They are found in penetrations of tops, bottoms, 50 percent retracement areas, and geometric angles. Any system, including geometric angles, must have rules governing lost motion to place stops accordingly.

This concludes the section on Gann angles. You should now have the basic knowledge necessary to properly calculate the major Gann angles needed to analyze and trade a market. While Gann angles are an important part of determining the strength of the trend, and support and resistance prices, and can be used alone to build trading strategies, they work best when combined with swing tops and bottoms and percentage retracement levels. In the next chapter, the important percentage levels will be discussed, and you will learn how to draw and calculate accurate retracement levels.

SUMMARY

Gann used a number of methods to determine support and resistance levels. The essence of Gann analysis is that important price levels are determined by diagonal and horizontal support and resistance levels. The diagonal price levels are determined by the Gann angles. The horizontal price levels are determined by the swing tops and bottoms and by the percentage retracement points. While each method can yield strong support and resistance points, the combination of the various methods yields the best results. It should also be noted that calculating Gann angles requires precision. Therefore, proper scaling is important in the construction of this type of chart. Finally, an understanding of the concept of lost motion as it applies to Gann angles and percentage retracement points is equally important in developing a trading system.

This chapter emphasized the importance of Gann angles to a trading strategy. The next chapter analyzes pattern and price and their applications.

CHAPTER 10

Combining Pattern and Price

While each of these price indicators can be used by itself, they are best when used in combination with another. Some examples of combinations becoming support are:

- An uptrending Gann angle and a percentage retracement price. This is an especially strong support level when it is the 50 percent price and the uptrending 1×1 angle (Figure 10.1).
- An uptrending Gann angle and an old top. This is especially strong support when it is the uptrending 1×1 angle (Figure 10.2).
- An uptrending Gann angle and an old bottom (Figure 10.3).
- A percentage retracement price and an old top (Figure 10.4).

Some examples of combinations becoming resistance are:

- A downtrending Gann angle and a percentage retracement price. This is an especially strong resistance level when it is the 50 percent price and the downtrending 1×1 angle (Figure 10.5).
- A downtrending Gann angle and an old bottom. This is especially strong resistance when it is the downtrending 1×1 angle (Figure 10.6).
- A downtrending Gann angle and an old top (Figure 10.7).
- A percentage retracement price and an old bottom (Figure 10.8).

The best support is the combination of three price indicators. This formation consists of the uptrending 1×1 angle intersecting the 50 percent retracement price and the swing-chart target. This is strong support because three independent analysis techniques are identifying the same price level.

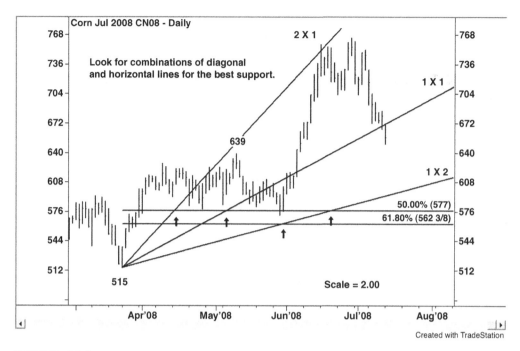

FIGURE 10.1 Diagonal and Horizontal Support: An Uptrending Gann Angle and Percentage Retracement Combination
Copyright © TradeStation.

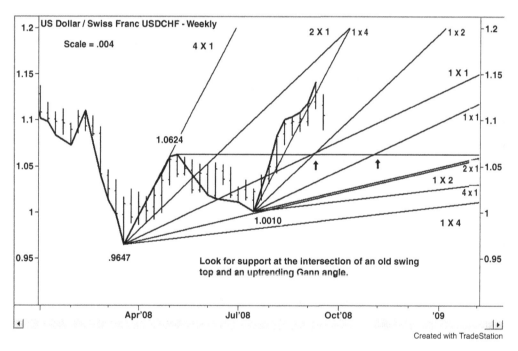

FIGURE 10.2 Diagonal and Horizontal Support: An Uptrending Gann Angle and an Old Swing Top Combination
Copyright © TradeStation.

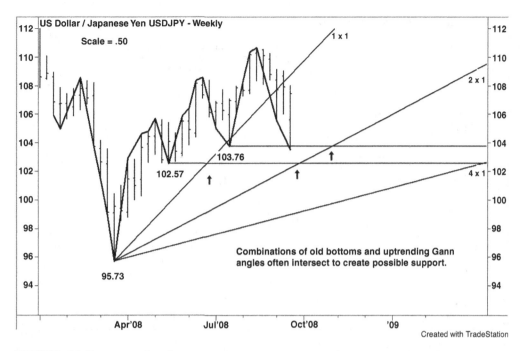

FIGURE 10.3 Diagonal and Horizontal Support: An Uptrending Gann Angle and an Old Swing Bottom Combination
Copyright © TradeStation.

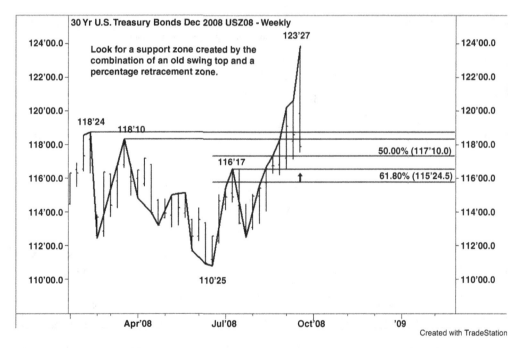

FIGURE 10.4 Horizontal Support: A Percentage Retracement and an Old Swing Top Combination
Copyright © TradeStation.

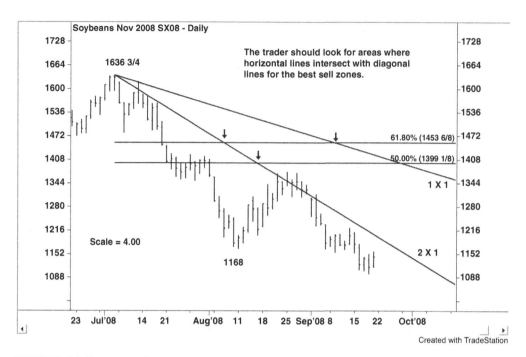

FIGURE 10.5 Diagonal and Horizontal Resistance: A Downtrending Gann Angle and Percentage Retracement Combination
Copyright © TradeStation.

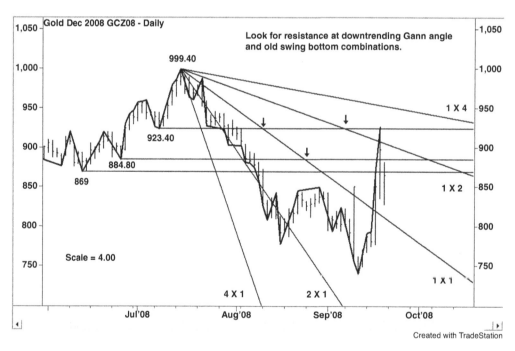

FIGURE 10.6 Diagonal and Horizontal Resistance: A Downtrending Gann Angle and an Old Swing Bottom Combination
Copyright © TradeStation.

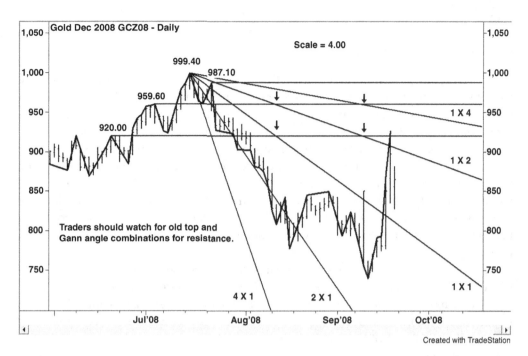

FIGURE 10.7 Diagonal and Horizontal Resistance: A Downtrending Gann Angle and an Old Swing Top Combination
Copyright © TradeStation.

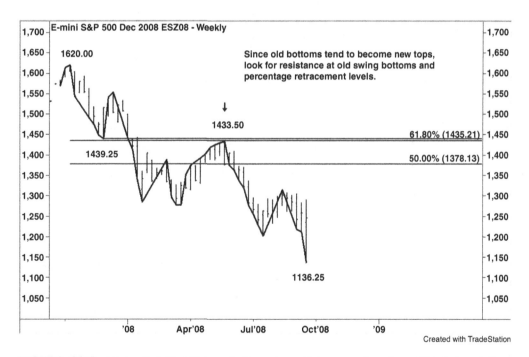

FIGURE 10.8 Horizontal Resistance: A Percentage Retracement and an Old Swing Bottom Combination
Copyright © TradeStation.

It is therefore very important to learn to work with combinations of price indicators, so that you will then have more control over the placement of the stop loss orders. If you trade using the Gann angles and place your stop accordingly, there will be a time when your stop loss may have to be placed at a level equal to the 50 percent price. This may cause your stop to get hit at the same time when support is being reached. Also your stop may have to be placed on a Gann angle if you are buying at a 50 percent price level. Finally, your swing chart may be signaling a corrective break right to the spot where you have placed your stop for a percentage retracement buy or a Gann angle buy. By combining two or sometimes three price indicators, you can place a more powerful stop that is less likely to be reached, but when reached is more likely to indicate a change in trend.

The same formation is true for sell signals. Instead of taking the sell signal individually, trade the combinations in order to place the stops at more strategic levels.

Following the calculation of valid support and resistance levels, you must determine if time is going to be an important factor. The subject of time is covered in the following chapter. Various forms of time analysis are also explained, along with how to apply it to a trading strategy.

CHAPTER 11

Time

G ann considered time the most important factor in determining changes in trend. He measured time in various ways, including natural cycles, anniversary dates, seasonally, swing cycles, and square dates. In this chapter we discuss various ways that time can be used to determine tops, bottoms, and changes. We begin with the most difficult method (natural cycles) and end with the most popular method (the squaring of time). Natural cycles is considered the most difficult concept because it involves the complex topic of financial astrology, which requires hours of outside research before it can be successfully applied. Squaring time is considered the most popular because it involves using charts to forecast tops, bottoms, and changes in trend. Many of the techniques learned in Chapter 9 are applied here. Consequently, research acquired from studying the price activity on a chart will be reinforced using this timing technique. Timing analysis involving seasonal charts and swing charts is also discussed. These concepts also utilize information obtained from charts created using techniques in Chapter 5.

NATURAL CYCLES

A natural cycle is a time period that can be measured and forecast by natural law and cannot be altered by humans.

Celestial Phenomena

The Planets The phenomena or the patterns created by the planets are very important, because they move and create patterns such as conjunctions, squares, trines, and oppositions. For example, two or more planets at the same degree are at a conjunction, two or more planets 90 degrees apart are square, two or more planets 120 degrees apart are trine, and two or more planets 180 degrees apart are at an opposition. These patterns have been classified by financial astrologers as bullish or bearish. The bullish phenomena are conjunctions and trines, while the bearish phenomena are squares and oppositions. Gann and other financial astrologers would search the ephemeris (a table of the planets' movements) to find major planetary patterns to predict tops, bottoms, and market direction. Since the future positions of the planets can be predicted using an ephemeris, it was possible for Gann to construct market forecasts years into the future using planetary rulerships as his guide.

Generally speaking, the business planets are Jupiter and Saturn. Jupiter is considered a bullish planet and Saturn a bearish one. Jupiter is usually considered expansive, hence an expanding market is considered a bull market, while Saturn is considered restrictive and is, therefore, associated with a bear market. Uranus and Mars are associated with volatility and erratic trading. Study and research of these planets and their relationships to market direction is necessary before applying them to trading (Figure 11.1).

Planetary Rulerships   Knowing planetary rulerships is another key to developing a forecast, because the financial astrologer has to associate various markets with the planet or planets that are said to control a specific market's direction. Books are available

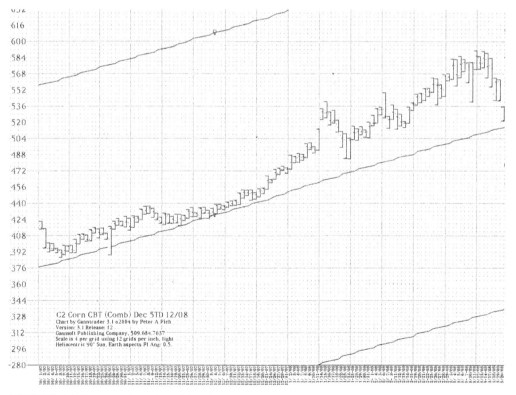

FIGURE 11.1 Natural Cycles of the Planets and the 2008 Daily December Corn Market

that identify these relationships, but these books should only be used as guidelines. Although these accepted relationships are a good starting point, study and practice is required to prove the connections and the relationships before a valid forecasting or trading tool can be constructed. Nonetheless, knowing the planetary rulerships plays an important part in constructing a forecast.

Besides using the movement of the larger planets to predict the major moves in the market, Gann also used minor cycles such as the phases of the moon for the 7-day cycle and movement of the sun for the 30-day cycle. The major moves were primarily predicted by the cycles of the major planets and the phenomena of the major planets. For example, the two-year cycle may have been associated with the orbit of Mars, which takes two years to circle the sun, or the 84-year cycle of Uranus, which takes 84 years to orbit the sun. Finally, Gann also used the cycles of the planetary phenomena to forecast future movement. For instance, the conjunction of Jupiter and Saturn is most often associated with a 20-year cycle.

The 30-Day or Sun Cycle   The sun cycle is a natural cycle because it cannot be changed by man. The actual sun cycle is approximately 365 days, which is very close to a circle or 360 degrees. A complete yearly cycle is measured as 360 degrees or 365 days. In other words, one degree is basically the equivalent of one day. This is the basis for Gann's explanation of cycles.

In addition to the complete sun cycle of 365 days, divisions of the yearly cycle are also important. These divisions include $1/4, 1/3, 1/2, 2/3$, and $3/4$ of the year and are important points for tops, bottoms, or changes in trend. Translated into degrees, they represent 90 degrees, 120 degrees, 180 degrees, 240 degrees, and 270 degrees. Converted into days, they equal 90 days, 120 days, 180 days, 240 days, and 270 days.

Some examples of natural cycles include the Spring Equinox (March 21), Summer Solstice (June 21), Autumnal Equinox (September 21), and Winter Solstice (December 21). These "seasonal dates" are measured by the movement of the sun cycle and are approximately 90 calendar days apart. Although these dates are "quarterly," the man-made quarterly is measured by March 31, June 30, September 30, and December 31, which are not natural quarters or natural dates. These time periods represent the strongest points from a top or bottom from which the next forecasted top or bottom is to occur.

In keeping with the natural cycle of the sun, Gann also assigned importance to the 30-day cycle (Figures 11.2 and 11.3). This is the equivalent of the natural cycle of the sun moving through each sign of the zodiac.

The Seven-Day or Moon Cycle   Another natural cycle Gann recommended to follow is the moon cycle. The moon cycle is a 28-day cycle from new moon to new moon. Key 7-day minor cycles inside of this 28-day main cycle are the different phases of the moon. For example, the 14-day cycle is the new moon to full moon cycle or full moon to new moon cycle.

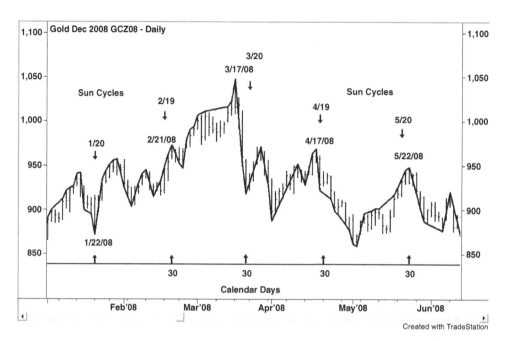

FIGURE 11.2 A 30-Day Cycle. Count 30 days from major tops and bottoms. (The sun cycle is a natural 30-day cycle.)
Copyright © TradeStation.

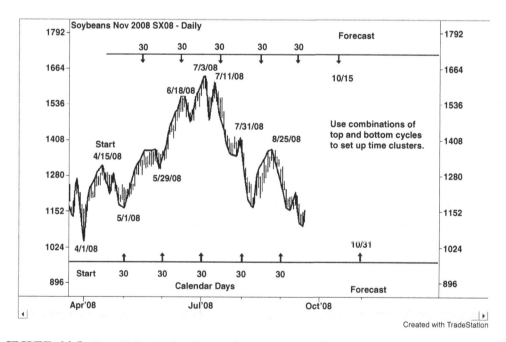

FIGURE 11.3 Two 30-Day Cycles. Two cycles set up a zone for the next likely 30-day bottom.
Copyright © TradeStation.

Financial Astrology   The study of these cycles falls under the heading of financial astrology, which is beyond the scope of this book. Further research and study is needed to understand how to use and apply this method to forecasting tops, bottoms, and changes in trend. It is also very important to know that Gann wrote in a hidden, veiled language at times. This means that those with a thorough understanding of astrology may be able to find the hidden references to astrological cycles throughout original Gann texts and course books.

Gann's Approach

Gann extensively researched the cycles of planets and phenomena. He looked for correlations between the up and down cycles of the market and the up and down movements of the planets. His conclusion after many years of study was that the latitude and longitude of the planets create forces that cause price changes, and that their squares and trines raise and lower prices.

It should be noted at this time that Gann was an active trader as well as a researcher. Therefore, although he had access to and created long-term market forecasts, he updated or adjusted these forecasts according to the short-term movement of the market. This was noted in his forecasts when he told subscribers to adjust tops and bottoms on his original forecasts when market action dictated such a change. For instance, assume he predicted a January 8 top and a February 10 bottom. If January 8 turned out to be a bottom, then he told traders to look for a top on February 10 instead of a bottom. This tells me that the date of the forecast was more important than the predicted top or bottom. It should be stressed that although he was allegedly very accurate in his forecasts, being able to trade the market correctly was much more important than predicting the direction.

How to Apply Natural Cycles to the Market

First of all, the individual who wants to use natural cycles (Figure 11.4) must be familiar with an ephemeris. The law of motion of the planets can be used to forecast the movement and therefore the positions of the planets well into the future. An ephemeris also identifies various phenomena such as planetary conjunctions, squares, trines, and oppositions. Movement of the planets from zodiac house to zodiac house along with phases of the moon are also identified. Finally, the exact latitude and longitude of the planets are pinpointed (Figure 11.5).

Gann used this information to forecast tops and bottoms as well as the strength of bull and bear markets. Using the ephemeris as his guide, he would predict the strength and direction of the market years in advance.

Gann spent many years studying financial astrology based on the books he had in his library and others, a list of which has been published since his death. Many of these books are available today in reprint. In addition, charting the planets has been made easier through computer programs such as Ganntrader 2. Other financial astrology programs

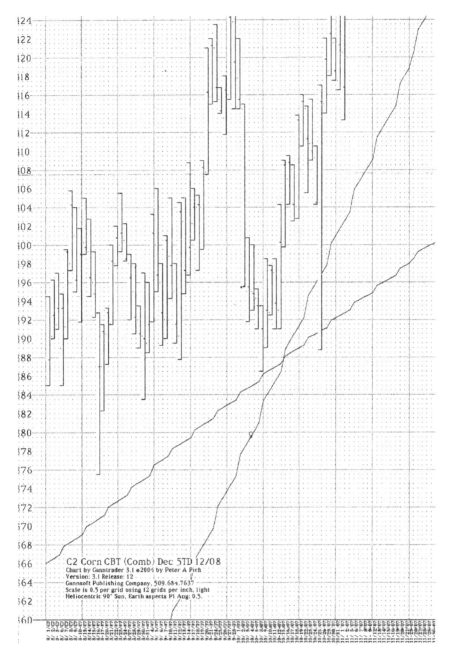

FIGURE 11.4 2008 Daily December Corn. This is a chart of the longitude of two planets. One plant moves faster than the other. Note that after the crossing of the two orbits the market accelerated to the upside.

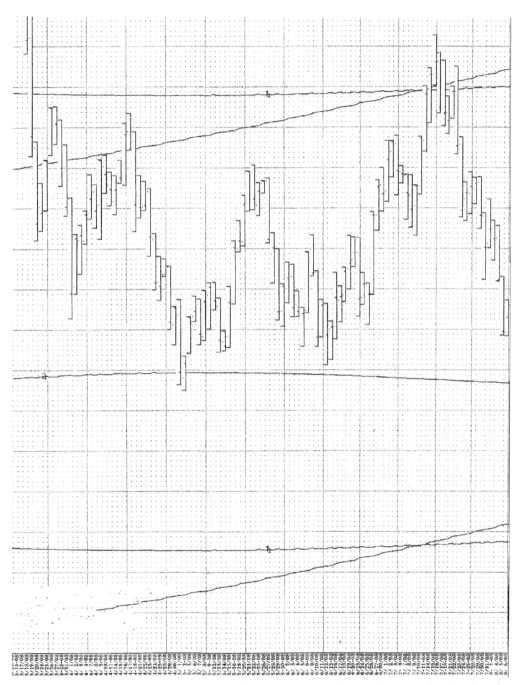

FIGURE 11.5 2008 Daily December Gold. This chart shows how two slower moving planets are controlling the range. The longitude of Uranus is providing support and the longitude of Saturn is providing resistance.

available today contain computerized ephemerides. In short, the data necessary to make a forecast are available today in easy-to-access form. However, there is still one point that needs to be addressed.

Although the data are readily available, forecasting is more of an art than a science. This is because interpretation of the astrological data requires deep study and practice as opposed to just reading the numbers from a book or computer. This study involves knowing the characteristics of the planets, planetary rulerships of the various markets, and the phenomena created by the planets.

In summary, in order to construct a market forecast using natural cycles, you must have a basic understanding of financial astrology. This basic understanding of astrology should include knowing how to read an ephemeris, learning the planetary rulerships, and knowing how to interpret planetary phenomena. After this basic knowledge is acquired, study and practice are required in order to learn how the information applies to the futures markets. Only after learning how to apply this information should the trader attempt to make a forecast and trade his interpretation of the natural dates.

Many of Gann's forecasts and trades were triggered by his understanding of natural cycles or financial astrology. The methods that he used included predicting tops and bottoms, changes in trend, and support and resistance. His understanding of natural cycles came from deep research and study of various methods of financial astrology. He was also a trader. While he used the forecasts as a guideline for his trading activity, he did adjust the forecasts to the current market conditions.

ANNIVERSARY DATES

Natural cycles are applied to fixed dates that occur throughout the year (Figure 11.6) in the case of sun and moon cycles, and at predictable intervals in regard to planetary conjunctions, squares, trines, and oppositions. When using these cycles to forecast tops, bottoms, or changes in trend, the trader relied on exact dates that were known in advance.

Anniversary date cycles use the same concept as the natural cycle, but are not known until a top or bottom is formed. The basic definition of the anniversary date is a one-year cycle from a major top or major bottom. For example, a major top on March 17, 2008, has a six-month anniversary date cycle due on September 17, 2008, and a one-year anniversary date cycle due on March 17, 2009. Each year on March 17, into the future, the anniversary of that major top will be due. The same holds for a major bottom anniversary date (Figure 11.7).

Minor Divisions of Time

Variations of the anniversary cycle occur when this cycle is divided into $1/4, 1/3, 1/2, 2/3$, and $3/4$ time periods (Figure 11.8). Since an anniversary cycle is approximately 365 days, a $1/4$ division is 90–91 calendar days, a $1/3$ division is 120–122 calendar days, a $1/2$ division

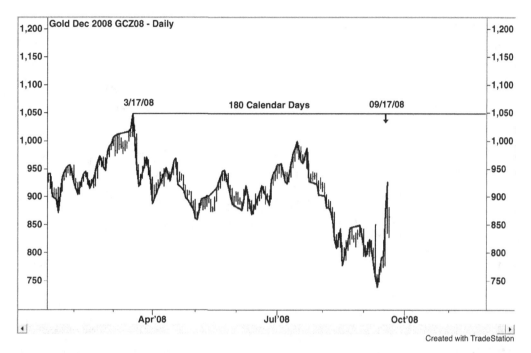

FIGURE 11.6 Anniversary Date Cycles. 2008 Daily December Gold made a major top on March 17, 2008. It is important to watch the gold market each March 17 into the future especially if this top ends up being the all-time high.
Copyright © TradeStation.

is 180–182 calendar days, a $^2/_3$ division is 240–244 calendar days, and a $^3/_4$ division is 270–274 calendar days. These divisions represent the most important anniversary date cycles.

Combining the Yearly Anniversary Date with the Minor Divisions

Another variation of the anniversary date is the combination of the one-year anniversary date and the division of time periods (Figure 11.9). For example, the current time period may be $1^1/_4$ anniversary cycles from a main top or main bottom. Another example is $2^1/_2$ anniversary cycles from a main top or bottom. It is important to maintain accurate records of these cycle dates as they extend out into the future. The purpose of studying these cycles is to find clusters of anniversary cycles in the future that can be used to forecast a top, bottom, or change in trend.

How to Apply Anniversary Dates to Trading

Following the construction of a properly drawn main trend indicator chart, the trader will have before her a chart filled with main tops and bottoms, plus the prices and dates at

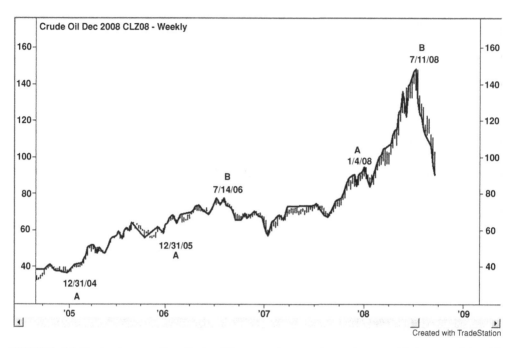

FIGURE 11.7 Anniversary Date Cycles. The more data you have, the more likely you will be able to find time clusters to forecast tops and bottoms.
Copyright © TradeStation.

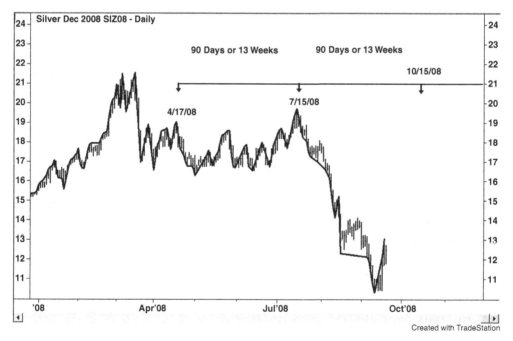

FIGURE 11.8 A 13-Week or 90-Day Cycle
Copyright © TradeStation.

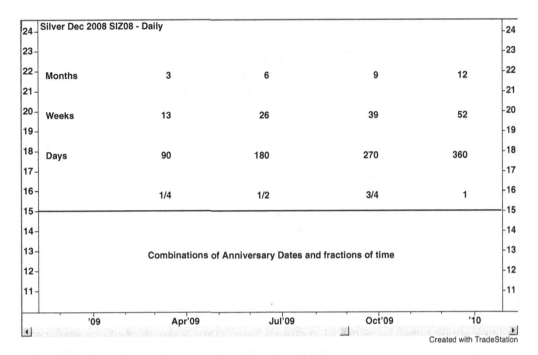

FIGURE 11.9 Anniversary Dates and Division of Time. Anniversary dates can be studied year-to-year or fractions of the year.
Copyright © TradeStation.

which these tops and bottoms occurred. These data should be recorded on a spreadsheet in order to have a permanent record of the date of each main top and main bottom.

Monthly Main Trend Chart. The more data, the better in the case of analyzing anniversary dates. This is because the trader is looking for important future cycles so that he can accurately forecast future tops, bottoms, and changes in trend. As mentioned earlier, the easiest way to maintain these records is to start with the main trend indicator chart and record all main trend tops and bottoms in a spreadsheet format. The best time period to follow initially is the monthly chart. The monthly main trend indicator chart usually provides the trader with a minimum of two major tops and bottoms during the life of an individual contract. Using the data from 10 to 20 years worth of monthly charts, he may be able to construct a valid forecast of future tops and bottoms, as indicated by clusters of main tops and main bottoms at or near the same calendar dates.

Weekly Main Trend Chart. The second important trend indicator to construct and analyze for important cycle dates is the weekly main trend indicator chart. This chart offers the trader more anniversary cycle dates for future forecasts. It also contains the contract highs and lows and any other main tops or bottoms that appear on the monthly main indicator chart. The dates that overlap are the most important to use for future forecasts. Once again the key is to note the clusters of main tops and main bottoms at or near the same calendar dates. Five to 10 years of weekly chart main tops and main bottoms will yield a large sample of these anniversary dates.

Daily Main Trend Chart. The third important trend indicator to construct and analyze for important cycle dates is the daily main trend indicator chart. This chart offers the trader even more cycle dates than the weekly main trend indicator chart and the intermediate trend indicator chart for future forecasts. It also contains the contract highs and lows and any other main tops or bottoms that appear on both the monthly and weekly charts. In addition, some of the main tops or bottoms that occur on the weekly chart but not on the monthly chart occur on the daily trend indicator chart.

Short-term traders should focus their attention on the cycles on the daily chart. If the trader charts this contract from the first trading day, then by the time the market reaches the active stage, a series of 90-day cycle dates should have been established. These dates are important in forecasting future tops and bottoms.

Prolonged Moves in Time

When learning how to construct the swing charts, starting the chart after a prolonged move in time is strongly recommended. Studying the short-term cycles of each market shows that a prolonged move from top-to-top, top-to-bottom, bottom-to-bottom, or bottom-to-top is often associated with a 90-day cycle. In other words, if the market is 90 calendar days from a main top and currently in a downtrend, then 90 days from this top the market is most likely to begin showing signs of bottoming. Reverse the signal from bottom-to-top.

In addition to forecasting the up and down swings, the trader may look for topping action when a market is 90 calendar days from a previous main top or 90 calendar days from a previous main bottom. The trader should note that this cycle is used to predict future tops and bottoms but not changes in trend.

Remember that a change in trend occurs *only* when the market crosses a main top or main bottom, not when the market forms a main top or main bottom. This means that although a main top or main bottom has been formed, this action combined with the cycle work will only be a clue that a change in trend may soon take place.

The Importance of the 90-Day Cycle

The basic function of the anniversary date is to identify the dates on which the market is likely to top or bottom in the future. The most common anniversary date cycle is the 90-day cycle. As the market approaches a 90-day top, the trader should watch for a signal top formation, as this will combine the best of time and pattern when forecasting the top. Conversely, as the market approaches a 90-day bottom, the trader should watch for a signal bottom formation, as this will combine the best of time and pattern when forecasting the bottom.

Combining the Three Main Trend Charts
to Forecast Tops and Bottoms

The combination of the three main trend charts makes this technique a valuable tool for forecasting future tops and bottoms. The ability to isolate the future month, week, or day of a major top or bottom is very important. For example, by studying 10 years of monthly data, the trader can determine with a high degree of accuracy in which month of the year a contract is likely to top or bottom. She will also be able to determine which week of the month the market is likely to top or bottom, as well as which day of the month and week the market is likely to top or bottom.

Depending on how aggressive the trader is, instead of using the monthly main trend indicator chart to forecast, he may use a monthly intermediate or monthly minor trend indicator chart. These charts will give him more cycle top and bottom dates to choose from and are more likely to post clusters of dates because of the many dates that can be matched up. This technique can also be applied to the weekly and daily charts.

Anniversary Dates Forecast Future Tops and Bottoms

Identifying anniversary dates helps in forecasting future tops and bottoms, not changes in trend. A change in trend only occurs when a swing top or swing bottom is crossed. Such a change may occur several days or weeks after a cycle top or cycle bottom has been formed. Intense study of how far in time after a cycle top or cycle bottom a change in trend occurs may help the trader determine more precisely when to expect a valid change in trend in the future. The way to do this is to gather data on change in trend dates and forecast them into the future in the same way that is used to forecast future swing tops and swing bottoms. After doing this, look for clusters of anniversary dates showing when these changes in trend have occurred based on the past history. By doing this the trader will be able to accurately predict future changes in trend.

Besides using combinations of swing charts to link time with pattern, another way to predict future trend changes is to combine anniversary dates, especially the 90-day cycle, with the signal top or signal bottom. As stated in Chapter 7, following a prolonged move in time, watch for a signal top or signal bottom to indicate an impending change in trend.

Recall that the definition of the signal top and signal bottom includes the phrase "following a prolonged move in price and time." The 90-day cycle can help the trader pinpoint the signal top and signal bottom. Since many cycle tops and bottoms occur in conjunction with the 90-day cycle, it can be called a *prolonged move in time.* Look for signal tops and signal bottoms when a 90-day cycle is due.

Although the 90-day cycle has been discussed most frequently, the 180-day, 270-day, and 1-year cycles can also be used.

In summary, the goal of using anniversary dates for forecasting is to identify with a high degree of accuracy which month, week, and day the cycle top or bottom will occur. It is therefore important to obtain as much information as possible regarding past tops and bottoms, since this information is useful in predicting future tops and bottoms.

Thus, the trader should look at the main trend chart with the largest period of time. Combinations of monthly, weekly, and daily main swing charts should help identify more precisely a future top or bottom.

SEASONALITY

The one-year anniversary date chart can also be called a *seasonal chart* (Figure 11.10). This chart differs from the popular seasonal technique used by many analysts that identifies the time periods in which the market is likely to rally or break based on the historically largest dollar moves throughout the year.

Constructing a Simple Yearly Forecast of Tops and Bottoms Using the Monthly Chart

A simple forecast of tops and bottoms involves the placing of previous main tops and bottoms on blank chart paper at the time of their occurrence. The data can come from a monthly, weekly, or daily main trend chart. This is another reason why strict records of this information should be kept.

In order to construct a simple yearly forecast of tops and bottoms, the analyst needs a sheet of blank chart paper, a green pen, a red pen, a ruler, and a database of main tops

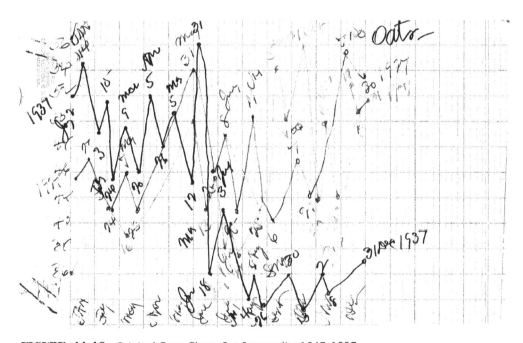

FIGURE 11.10 Original Gann Chart: Oat Seasonality 1847–1937

and bottoms, complete with price and time identified. The piece of chart paper should be long enough so that the trader can forecast an entire year on it.

The first step is to place the time periods forecast along the bottom of the chart. List the months along the bottom of the monthly chart, the weekending date along the bottom of the weekly chart, and calendar days along the bottom of the daily chart.

Price is irrelevant on this simple forecast chart, but setting prices along the left side of the chart inside the all-time price range or at least the 10-year range could be helpful. Price will be necessary when building a more complex forecast chart.

After placing the time periods on the chart, the analyst can use the database to find the main swing tops and bottoms for that particular market.

The second step is to place arrows at the top of the monthly portion of the chart to identify the main tops. Use the red pen to draw the arrows and mark the time period on the chart during the month a main top took place. For example, if a main top occurred during January, place a red arrow at the top of the chart on the time period representing January. If the next main top occurred during March, place the arrow at the top of the chart during the time period representing March. Repeat this procedure for each year in the database.

Next, place arrows at the bottom of the monthly portion of the chart to identify main bottoms. Use the green pen to draw arrows and mark the time period on the chart during the month when a main bottom took place. For example, if a main bottom occurred during February, place a green arrow at the bottom of the chart on the time period representing February. If the next main bottom occurred during July, then place the arrow at the bottom of the chart during the time period representing July. Repeat this procedure for each year in the database.

The fourth step is to identify the months that contain clusters of tops and bottoms. This chart is designed to give the trader a general look at the market, because it contains the main tops and bottoms on the monthly chart. The objective of the chart is to identify which months the market has tended to make tops or bottoms.

Constructing a Simple Yearly Forecast of Tops and Bottoms Using the Weekly Chart

The first step in constructing this chart is to place the identified week-ending dates along the bottom of the chart.

Price is irrelevant on this simple forecast chart, but setting prices along the left side of the chart inside the all-time price range or at least the 10-year range could be helpful. Price will be necessary when building a more complex forecast chart.

After placing the time periods on the chart, the analyst can use the database to find the main swing tops and bottoms for that particular market.

The second step is to place arrows at the top of the weekly portion of the chart to identify the main tops. Use the red pen to draw the arrows and mark the time period on the chart during the week a main top took place. For example, if a main top occurred during the week ending January 4, place a red arrow at the top of the chart on the time period representing the week ending January 4. If the next main top occurred during the week ending March 10, place the arrow at the top of the chart during the time period representing the week ending March 10. Repeat this procedure for each year in the database.

Next, place arrows at the bottom of the weekly portion of the chart to identify main bottoms. Use the green pen to draw arrows and mark the time period on the chart during the week a main bottom took place. For example, if a main bottom occurred during the week ending February 10, place a green arrow at the bottom of the chart on the time period representing the week ending February 10. If the next main bottom occurred during the week ending July 16, place the arrow at the bottom of the chart during the time period representing the week ending July 16. Repeat this procedure for each year in the database.

The fourth step is to identify the weeks that contain clusters of tops and bottoms. This chart is designed to give the trader a more specific look at the market than the monthly chart, but not as detailed as the daily chart, because it only contains the main tops and bottoms on the weekly chart. The objective of the chart is to identify during which weeks the market has tended to make tops or bottoms.

Constructing a Simple Yearly Forecast of Tops and Bottoms Using the Daily Chart

The first step is to construct a chart of the entire calendar year.

Price is irrelevant on this simple forecast chart, but setting prices along the left side of the chart inside the all-time price range or at least the 10-year range could be helpful. Price will be necessary when building a more complex forecast chart.

After placing the time periods on the chart, the analyst can use the database to find the main swing tops and bottoms for that particular market.

The second step is to place arrows at the top of the daily portion of the chart to identify the main tops. Use the red pen to draw the arrows and mark the time periods on the chart on the day a main top took place. For example, if a main top occurred on March 5, place a red arrow at the top of the chart on the time period representing March 5. If the next main top occurred on April 10, place the arrow at the top of the chart during the time period representing April 10. Repeat this procedure for each year in the database.

Next, place arrows at the bottom of the daily portion of the chart to identify main bottoms. Use the green pen to draw arrows and mark the time period on the chart on the day a main bottom took place. For example, if a main bottom occurred on February 10, place a green arrow at the bottom of the chart on the time period representing February 10. If the next main bottom occurred on July 16, place the arrow at the bottom of the chart during the time period representing July 16. Repeat this procedure for each year in the database.

The fourth step is to identify the days that contain clusters of tops and bottoms. This chart is designed to give the trader a more specific look at the market than the monthly and weekly charts. The objective of the chart is to identify which day of the year the market has tended to make tops or bottoms.

Top and Bottom Forecasts and Price Levels

The previous section dealt with the tendency of the market to form main tops and bottoms at various time periods throughout the calendar year. This section discusses a technique that identifies price levels at which the market has tended to make tops and bottoms. As stated several times throughout this book, price and time analysis has to be emphasized. The trader must learn to use price and time together and not stress one over the other.

Main Tops and Bottoms with Price Levels

This technique is basically the same as the previous one, only instead of placing red arrows at the top of the chart to identify main tops, the analyst places an "X" on the chart on the date and at the price the main top occurred.

For example, the November soybeans made a main top in June 1988 at $10.46. On the price and time seasonal monthly chart, the analyst would place a red "X" on the time line representing June and on the price line representing $10.46. The technique is basically the same as the previous method for bottoms also, but instead of placing green arrows at the bottom of the chart to identify main bottoms, the analyst places an "X" on the chart during the month and at the price the main bottom occurred.

This procedure is repeated for the weekly chart. Here, the November soybean main top occurred the week ending June 24, 1988, at $10.46. On the price and time seasonal weekly chart, the analyst would place a red "X" on the time line representing the week ending June 24, 1988, and on the price line representing $10.46.

Repeat this procedure for the daily chart. Here, a November soybean main top occurred on June 23, 1988, at $10.46. On the price and time seasonal daily chart, the analyst would place a red "X" on the time line representing June 23, 1988, and on the price line representing $10.46 (Figure 11.11).

Value of the Price and Time Seasonal Chart

The value of the price and time seasonal chart is that the analyst will be able to see at which price level the market is likely to make tops and bottoms. This is important because sometimes a seasonal tendency fails. This usually happens when a market with a seasonal uptrend is trading at a historically high price level or when a market with a seasonal downtrend is trading at a historically low price level.

For example, the November soybeans have a seasonal tendency to trade lower starting June 23. This is usually a valid analysis if the market is trading at a high price level, but a poor one if trading at a low price level. Using seasonal price and time analysis, the trader will be able to see at which price levels or zones the market is likely to top

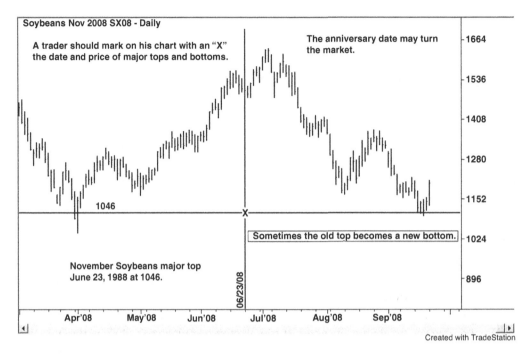

FIGURE 11.11 Daily Forecast Chart. Place a major high on the monthly, weekly, or daily chart on the date and at the price it took place; for example, November soybeans made a major high in June 1988 at 1046. This technique gives you price and time.
Copyright © TradeStation.

and break in confirmation of the seasonal trend, and at which price levels or zones the market is likely to fail by trading in the opposite direction.

Variations of the Seasonal Chart

The previous sections used main tops and main bottoms to identify possible future main tops and main bottoms. A variation of this technique is to use monthly tops and bottoms instead of main tops and bottoms.

Using this technique the analyst takes a specific calendar month and identifies the calendar days on which the market has made a monthly high or low. This is different from the monthly chart that identifies main tops and main bottoms, because a monthly high or low is not necessarily a monthly main top or bottom; for example, a main top or bottom that occurs prior to the start of the new month and continues in one direction throughout the month.

This technique helps to identify the tendency of a market to top at the beginning, in the middle, or at the end of a month.

Monthly Seasonal Chart. The chart sets the previous month to zero, and up-and-down moves are tracked (Figure 11.12). It shows the trader how far above the previous

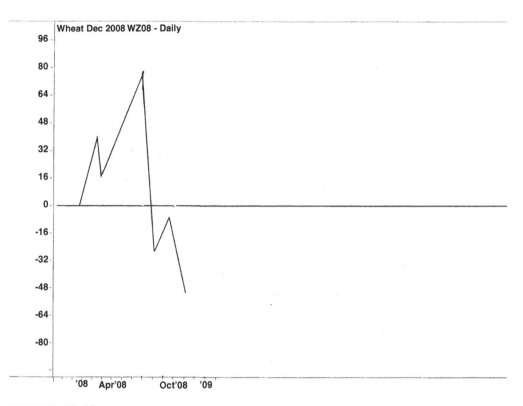

FIGURE 11.12 A 10-Year Seasonal Forecast

month's close the market is likely to rally, and how far below the previous month's close the market is likely to break.

Ten-Year Seasonal Chart. One of Gann's favorite charts was the 10-year seasonal chart. It shows the trader the seasonal tendency of a market based on a 10-year cycle. On this chart the analyst starts the new year at zero, then tracks the swings of the previous 10-year increments. For example, for a 2009 forecast, the analyst would draw the swings of the market for 1999, 1989, 1979, 1969, 1959, 1949 and each year that ends in 9. The outcome gives the trader an opportunity to see how the market trades during 10-year cycles (Figure 11.13). This chart can be used to forecast the direction of the market and time bottoms and tops.

SWING CHARTS

Basic Use

The swing or trend indicator charts were covered extensively earlier in Chapters 5 and 6. A properly constructed swing chart can provide the trader with valuable timing

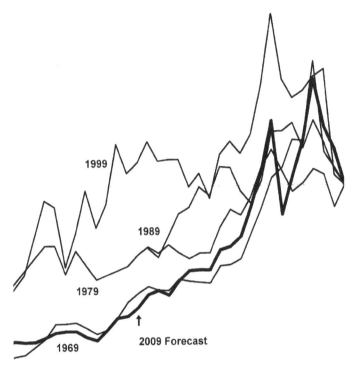

FIGURE 11.13 A Gann 10-Year Seasonal Chart to Forecast 2009. Gann would create a seasonal forecast by making a curve of the market based on 10-year patterns. To forecast 2009, use the charts from the years ending in 9: 1999, 1989, 1979, 1969, 1959, 1949.

information. This information can aid the trader in forecasting the duration of both rallies and corrections during an uptrend and breaks and corrections during a downtrend.

By definition the rallies in an uptrending market in terms of time should increase over the life of the uptrend. One of the first signs of an impending top is a rally that falls short of a previous upswing in terms of time. In addition, the rallies in terms of time should be greater than the corrections. Other signs of an impending top are a correction that lasts longer than the previous upswing, and a correction in terms of time that is greater than a previous correction in terms of time. Finally, the combination of a shorter-than-expected upswing in terms of time and a longer-than-expected correction in terms of time should be seen as a strong indication that the trend is getting ready to change.

The opposite is valid in a downtrending market. By definition the breaks in a downtrending market in terms of time should increase over the life of the downtrend. One of the first signs of an impending bottom is a break that falls short of a previous downswing in terms of time. In addition, the breaks in terms of time should be greater than the corrections. Other signs of an impending bottom are a correction that lasts longer than the previous downswing, and a correction in terms of time that is greater than a previous correction in terms of time. Finally, the combination of a shorter-than-expected

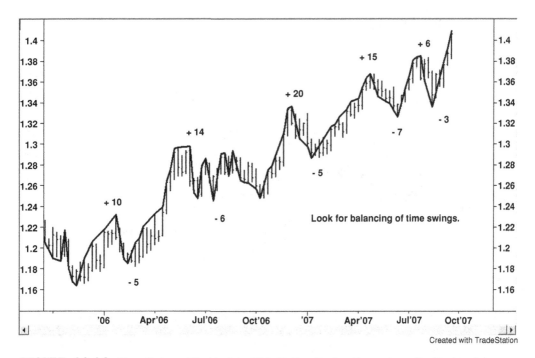

FIGURE 11.14 Time Swings, Weekly Euro/U.S. Dollar. During the major rally, the breaks range from 5 to 6 weeks.
Copyright © TradeStation.

downswing in terms of time and a longer-than-expected correction in terms of time should be seen as a strong indication that the trend is getting ready to change.

In Figure 11.14, the market is in a uptrend. A rally from November 5, 2005, to January 25, 2006, was 10 weeks. The correction was 5 weeks. The next rally was 14 weeks and the correction was 6 weeks. The next upswing was 20 weeks, followed by a 5-week decline.

The forecast is for another rally of 10 to 20 weeks followed by a 5- to 6-week decline. The actual rally was 15 weeks followed by a 7-week break. A break that fails to equal or exceed the previous break is a sign of a top. In addition, if the market doesn't have a minimum 10-week rally, then this is a sign the trend may be getting ready to turn down.

Setting Time Objectives and Stops with the Swing Chart

The swing chart can also be used to set time objectives and stops. This chart offers the trader an opportunity to go with the market rather than trying to beat it.

For example, during an uptrend, a trader could use the swing chart to forecast the duration of the next upswing. After establishing a long position in the direction of the trend, she should strongly consider liquidating the position when either a time objective or a time stop is reached.

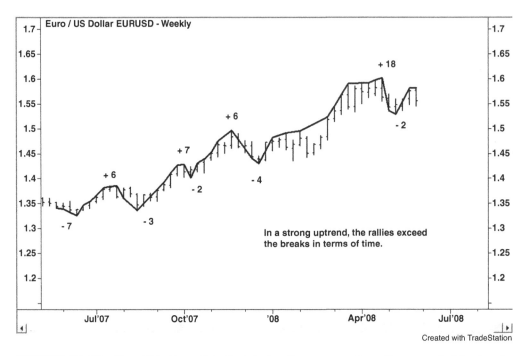

FIGURE 11.15 Time Objectives. Note that during the up move the rallies exceeded the breaks in terms of time. The first sign of an impending top would be a change in this pattern. Copyright © TradeStation.

A time objective is reached if the trader has a profit on a trade and the market has reached the date on which the market is expected to make a correction based on the swing chart (Figure 11.15). On this date, the trader should take the profit on the opening, on the close, or at a price predetermined by either a percentage retracement or Gann angle. The key is to liquidate the position on the day that the swing chart forecast the next top or bottom is due. This form of profit taking allows the trader to trade with the market according to time. Holding on to the position will indicate the trader wants to beat the market. In that case, the trader can accomplish his objective by staying in longer while looking for a strong move that exceeds the previous move in time. At the same time he assumes more risk, because if the swing reaches its objective exactly, he may give back some or all of his profits.

A time stop is reached if the trader has a loss on a trade and the market has reached the date on which the market is expected to make a correction based on the swing chart. On this date, the trader should take the loss on the opening, on the close, or at a price predetermined by either a percentage retracement or Gann angle. The key is to liquidate the position on the day that the swing chart forecast the next top or bottom is due. This form of stopping out of a losing trade allows the trader to trade with the market according to time. Holding the position will indicate the trader wants to beat the market. In that case, the trader can accomplish her objective by staying in longer than the swing suggests while looking for a strong move that exceeds the previous move in time. At the same time she assumes more risk, because if the swing comes to an end exactly, she may increase her loss by holding on to the position.

Chapters 5 and 6 should be carefully studied, as a properly constructed swing chart can yield valuable information on market timing. The duration of the upswings and downswings should be recorded and analyzed to help determine market strength and rhythm. Clues about when a market is going to form a top or bottom or change trend can be found in the swing chart. The keys to remember are that during an uptrend, the rallies in terms of time should equal or exceed the previous upswings and that during a downtrend the breaks in terms of time should equal or exceed the previous downswings. Finally, the duration of the swings can be used to take profits or stop out a loss.

SQUARE CHARTS

Squaring a Range

The chapter on Gann angles showed the analyst how important the range of a market is in determining support and resistance. This chapter also covered the price zones created by the Gann square. Another important aspect of the Gann square is timing, a feature we now address. The Gann square chart uses a range and important divisions of time inside the range to identify further tops and bottoms.

Constructing the Square Chart and Divisions in Time   The steps for constructing the Gann square for timing are the same as for the Gann square for pricing support and resistance.

Step 1: Find a main range. (A main range is created by a main top and a main bottom.)
Step 2: Divide the range vertically into time periods.

The major time periods are 25.50, and 75 percent of the range (Figure 11.16). These points represent $^1/_4, ^1/_2$, and $^3/_4$ retracements of time, respectively. For example, if the range is 50, then 25 percent of the square in time is the range times 0.25. In this example,

$$50 \times 0.25 = 12.5$$

The time period will be represented by the type of chart used, either monthly, weekly, or daily. In this case, 25 percent of time represents 12.5 months, weeks, or days.

Fifty percent of the square in time is the range times 0.50. In this example,

$$50 \times 0.50 = 25$$

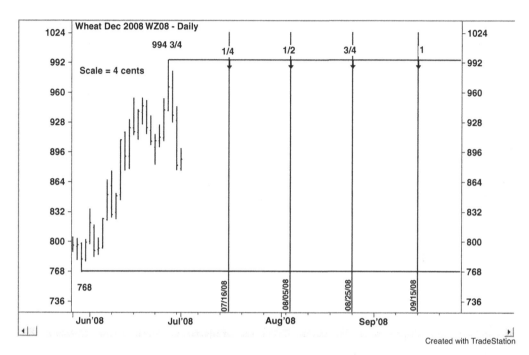

FIGURE 11.16 Squaring a Range. Main top = 994.75; main bottom = 768; range = 226.75. Scale = 4.00, 1 square of time = 56.69 days. $^1/_2$ square of time = 28.34 days. $^1/_4$ square of time = 14.17 days.
Copyright © TradeStation.

The time period will be represented by the type of chart used either monthly, weekly, or daily. In this case, the 50 percent of time represents 25 months, weeks, or days (Figure 11.17).

Seventy-five percent of the square in time is the range times 0.75. In this example,

$$50 \times 0.75 = 37.5$$

The time period is represented by the type of chart used either monthly, weekly, or daily (Figure 11.18).

Step 3: Identify these time periods on the chart.

It is important to mark these time periods on the chart, as they represent dates on which the market may have a top or bottom. Often the market exhibits high volatility on these dates.

These time periods remain intact as long as the market remains inside the range used to identify them. When the range is violated, the dates are no longer valid for tops and bottoms. Because these ranges are more likely to remain intact over a longer period of time, it is suggested that major ranges, such as the all-time range or the second- or third-largest range be used. In addition, they are more likely to signal major top or bottom formations. The contract range may also be used, as can

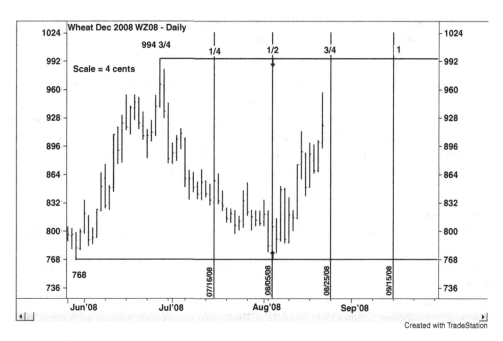

FIGURE 11.17 Squaring a Range, Time Divisions. Notice how the market turned up when time reached $^1/_2$ square.
Copyright © TradeStation.

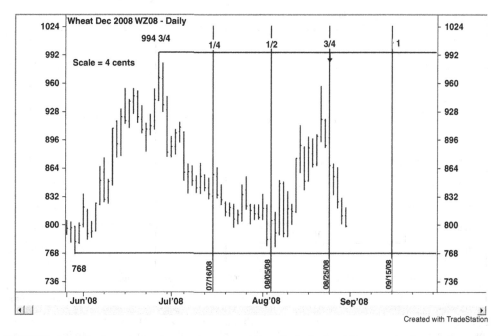

FIGURE 11.18 Squaring a Range, Important Time Periods. In this example the market turned down close to $^3/_4$ square.
Copyright © TradeStation.

the large ranges on the daily chart, but remember that these ranges are likely to be exceeded often throughout the life of the contract.

Other divisions of time that could be used to identify future tops or bottoms are the 33 percent and 67 percent time periods. These represent $1/3$ and $2/3$ retracements of time. A 33 percent retracement of time is found by taking the range times 0.33, and a 67 percent retracement of time is found by taking the range times 0.67. In our example, if the range is 50, then a 33 percent retracement of time is 16.5 months, weeks, or days. A 67 percent retracement of time in a range of 50 is 33.5 months, weeks, or days.

Time Clusters   As stated earlier in the chapter, the best time to anticipate tops or bottoms is when two or more timing dates land on the same time periods. The market is made up of several main ranges that combine to form the contract range or the all-time range. Because of this overlap, conditions exist at times when several "square dates" are due at the same time.

For example, there may be a time when $1/4$ of one square is due the same weeks as $1/2$ square of another range (Figure 11.19). These are important setups to watch for, as

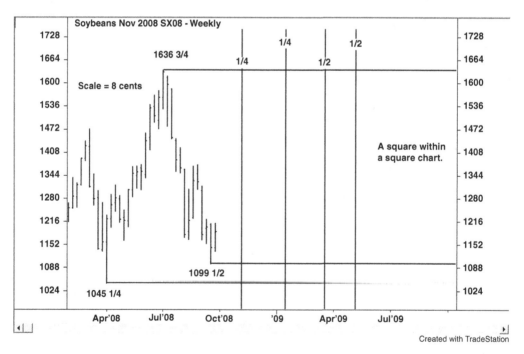

FIGURE 11.19   Squaring a Range, "Square within a Square." 2008 Weekly November Soybeans. Look for divisions of time from each square that develops inside of the major square to form potential change in trend time zones.
Copyright © TradeStation.

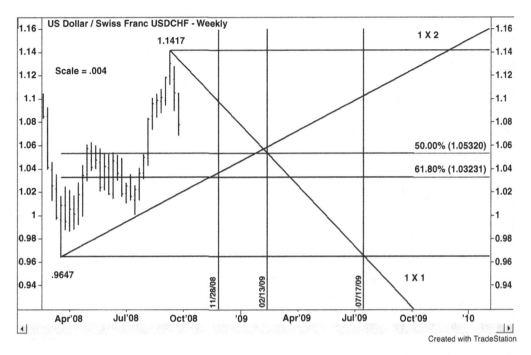

FIGURE 11.20 Square of a Range and Gann Angles. Weekly U.S. Dollar and Swiss Franc. Note how the Gann angles converge at the 50 percent price and time point. This convergent point or clusters of price and time can become important support or resistance.
Copyright © TradeStation.

they are often associated with the formation of major tops or bottoms. This is especially true if the market is trading at or near a historical top or bottom (Figure 11.20).

Squaring a High Price

One technique utilized by Gann was squaring a high price. Squaring a market by a high price yields additional time periods to watch for tops and bottoms. This is especially important on the weekly chart. In order to square a high, the analyst must know the main top and the scale used by a particular market. Once again, the all-time high, or the second- or third-highest high, is important to use to project future tops and bottoms. Unlike squaring a range, squaring a high price extends into infinity, as each high from the past is related mathematically to each high or low in the future (Figure 11.21).

For example, assume a major top in Microsoft at 53.97. Based on a scale of .50 points per month for Microsoft, a top or bottom can be projected every 107.94 months. The squaring of the high was determined by dividing the major high of 53.97 by .50 points per month. The result was a cycle of 107.94 months. Every 107.94 months, or approximately 9 years from the month ending December 31, 1999, traders should watch for future tops

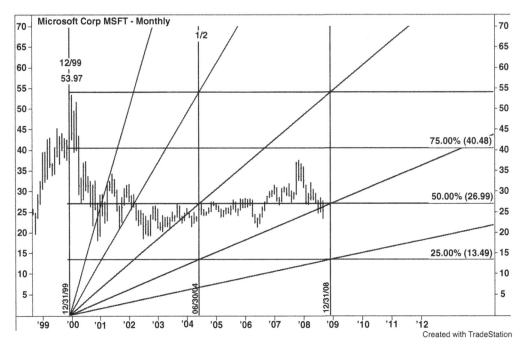

FIGURE 11.21 Squaring a High Price. Notice the amount trading activity on both sides of 50 percent of the all-time high at 26.99. This market will have to hold above the this price and the uptrending Gann angle the month ending December 21, 2008 or this stock will weaken further. Copyright © TradeStation.

and bottoms. Also look for future tops and bottoms at the important $^1/_4$ and $^1/_2$ time divisions.

Squaring a Low Price

Another technique utilized by Gann was squaring a low price. Squaring a market by a low price yields additional time periods to watch for tops and bottoms. This is especially important on the weekly chart. In order to square a low, the analyst must know the main bottom and the scale used by a particular market. Once again, the all-time low, or the second- or third-lowest low, is important to use to project future tops and bottoms. Unlike squaring a range, squaring a low price extends into infinity as each low from the past is related mathematically to each high or low in the future (Figure 11.22).

For example, Euro/U.S. Dollar made a major low of .8227 from October 26, 2000. Based on a scale of .008 pips per month for the Euro/U.S. Dollar, a top or bottom has been projected every 102.84 months since the main bottom formed the month ending October 31, 2000. This squaring of the low was determined by dividing the major low of .8227 by .008 pips per month. The result is a cycle of 102.84 months. Every 102.84

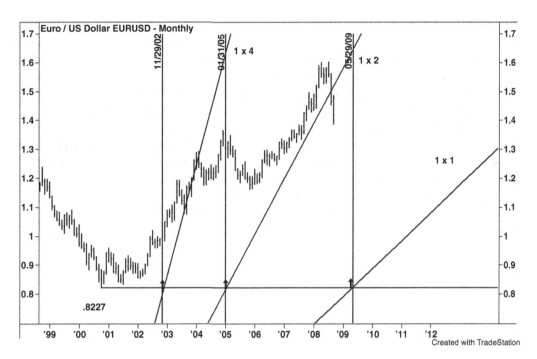

FIGURE 11.22 Zero Angle from a Low. The Gann angles from zero can be used as support or to identify the time period when a possible change in trend may take place.
Copyright © TradeStation.

months, or approximately $8\frac{1}{2}$ years from the month-ending October 31, 2000, traders should watch for future tops and bottoms.

This concludes our discussion of square charts. Possibly the three most important timing tools Gann used to forecast tops and bottoms were the square of the range, the square of the high, and the square of the low. These tools use prices to determine when tops and bottoms may be due. Study and practice are necessary in order to use this technique. Careful analysis should be done to determine the accuracy of this method. While exactness is aimed for, using a square can give a good indication of where the top or bottom is going to occur. Learn the characteristics of this timing device and of the market to which it is being applied in order to determine its usefulness in predicting tops and bottoms.

SUMMARY

It is important to note that markets are made of both price and time. The idea behind successful trading is to balance the two. Of the two, however, time is the more powerful. In order to time a top or a bottom, the trader should be aware of the various methods used to determine these tops and bottoms. Timing can come in the form of cycles that can be natural and adaptive. These cycles can be represented by natural phenomena, such as planetary movement, or they can be applied directly from past market action, such as the anniversary dates and time divisions. Timing can also be achieved by using an adaptive method that uses the actual price movement of the market to determine and forecast future tops and bottoms, such as the square of the price range, the square of the high, and the square of the low. In addition, the duration of the up and down swings can be used to forecast future tops and bottoms. Finally, it should be noted that a combination of the timing methods is strongly suggested. Experience shows that market tops and bottoms will most likely occur when clusters of time indicators come together simultaneously.

You have now been introduced to the basics of Gann analysis. The next chapter gives examples of how to apply these techniques to real markets.

CHAPTER 12

Combining Pattern, Price, and Time

The Euro/U.S. Dollar Forex Market

G ann was admired for his keen insight and accurate glimpses into the future; he nonetheless was—and is—dismissed by many as being too unconventional, too eccentric and abstruse. However, despite his detractors, his theories remain fundamentally solid and have been successfully adapted by several generations of traders. Perhaps the most significant of these theories, Gann Theory, is based on the premise that specific geometric patterns and angles have unique characteristics that can be used to predict price action. By combining these patterns with price and time, and by finding a vital balance between these three primary indicators, future market movement can be forecasted.

In this chapter the focus is on using Gann's three primary indicators: Pattern, Price, and Time to analyze the Euro/U.S. Dollar Forex market. One reason this market was chosen is because it did not exist when Gann was alive and is a perfect example of how his methodologies can be applied to all markets. Another reason for choosing the Euro/U.S. Dollar Forex market is because it is often described as volatile and unchartable. The reader will see in these examples that once one applies the proper technical analysis tools, one will begin to be able to derive important information and interpret the movements of this market regardless of how long a market has been trading. In addition, this example supports the claim that Gann analysis techniques can be applied successfully to all markets without the need for computers or complex equations—just a simple trend indicator.

THE INTERMEDIATE TREND INDICATOR

This is analysis of the Weekly Euro/U.S. Dollar Forex market. The purpose behind this analysis is to show the analyst/trader, how to read a swing chart and the type of information that can be derived from this chart.

Although a swing chart can be started anytime and anywhere on the chart, it works best when started at an extreme. The extreme can be a low or high or year or any other major time period. On November 15, 2005, the Weekly Euro/U.S. Dollar chart made a low at 1.1637. The intermediate or 2-Bar trend was down at the time with the last swing top at 1.2589 on September 2, 2005 (Figure 12.1). The analyst should always know the direction of the trend with which he is working. This is a personal preference issue as discussed in Chapter 5 based on the characteristics of the swing chart chosen for analysis. In this chart we can see where each top and bottom is identified with its price over or under the swing. Since this is an intermediate trend chart, 1.1637 has not yet been identified as a bottom because the market has only posted one week of a higher-high and a higher-low.

This chart can also be looked at in terms of price and time. In other words, instead of marking the top and bottom on the chart, the analyst can note the size of the swing (Figure 12.2) or the duration of the swing (Figure 12.3). From these charts, the trader can learn the characteristics of the market. During downtrending markets, for example, the breaks tend to be greater than the rallies in terms of price and time. During uptrending markets, the rallies tend to be greater than the breaks in terms of price and time. The trader should make note of the size and duration of the swings to look for clues that the market is topping or bottoming or the trend is getting ready to change. The size and duration of the swings can also be used to forecast the next swing. After a bottom is

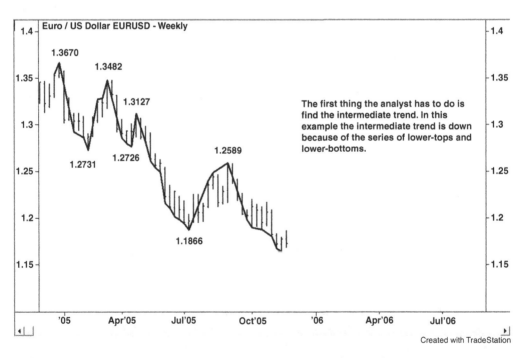

FIGURE 12.1 Weekly Euro/U.S. Dollar: Intermediate Trend Indicator Chart
Copyright © TradeStation.

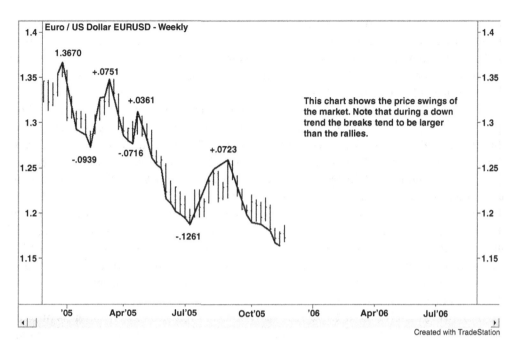

FIGURE 12.2 Weekly Euro/U.S. Dollar: Price Swing Chart
Copyright © TradeStation.

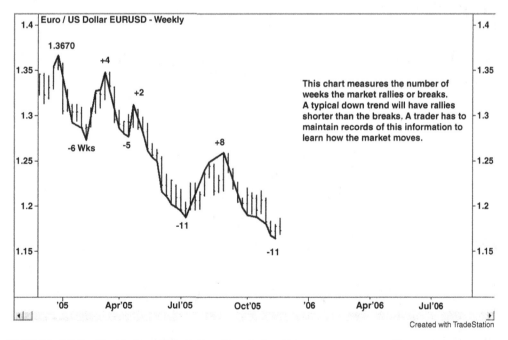

FIGURE 12.3 Weekly Euro/U.S. Dollar: Time Swing Chart
Copyright © TradeStation.

made, for example, the trader can add the previous upswings to that bottom to forecast where the next upswing is likely to be and when. The same information can be used to forecast potential bottoms. From a new swing top, subtract the size of the previous swings from the top and add the time to the date of the top to forecast the next down swing (Figure 12.4 and Figure 12.5).

With the upmove from 1.1637 to 1.2323, the market revealed its first clue that a bottom was being formed or that the trend was getting ready to turn higher because the duration (time) of the rally exceeded the previous rally. Once the analyst has observed this, he should begin to look for another clue, which would be a secondary higher bottom. This bottom is often referred to as the test of the main bottom. The Euro/U.S. Dollar made a secondary higher bottom on February 27, 2006, at 1.823. After this bottom is formed the analyst will once again determine the size and duration of the previous down move to determine if there were any clues that this will be a major bottom. The fact that the break from 1.2323 to 1.1823 was less than the previous break from 1.2589 to 1.1637 was a strong signal that the trend was getting ready to turn up (Figure 12.6). This action is known as overbalancing. In other words, the rally has exceeded or overbalanced the previous move in terms of price.

Following the bottom at 1.1823, the market went on a strong rally in terms of price and time and changed the trend to up on the swing chart when it crossed the previous swing top at 1.2323 (Figure 12.7).

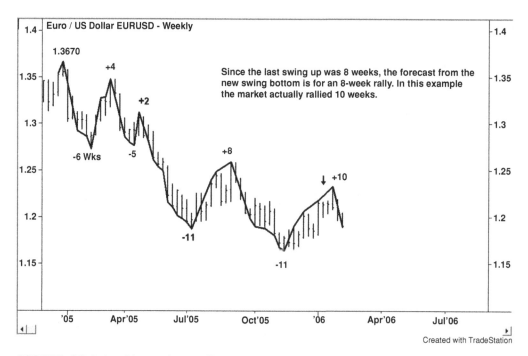

FIGURE 12.4 Weekly Euro/U.S. Dollar: Swing Time Forecast Chart
Copyright © TradeStation.

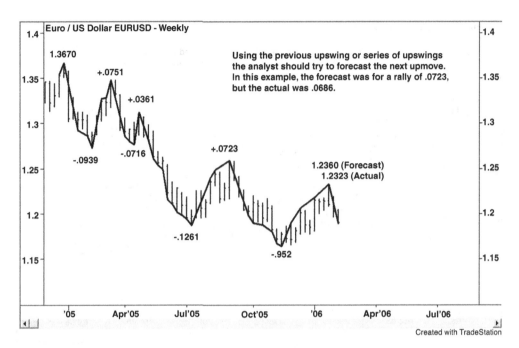

FIGURE 12.5 Weekly Euro/U.S. Dollar: Swing Price Forecast Chart
Copyright © TradeStation.

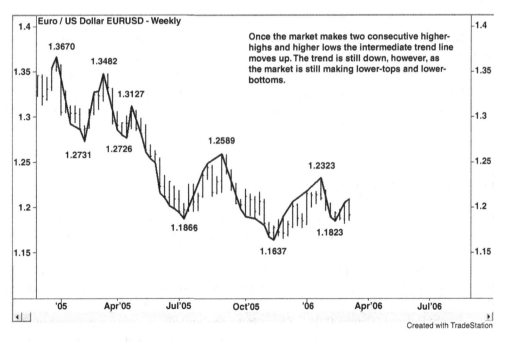

FIGURE 12.6 Weekly Euro/U.S. Dollar: Price Begins to Overbalance
Copyright © TradeStation.

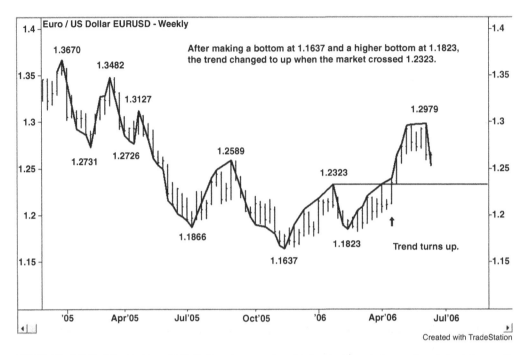

FIGURE 12.7 Weekly Euro/U.S. Dollar: A secondary higher-bottom is formed and the intermediate trend turns up.
Copyright © TradeStation.

When analyzing a market, it highly suggested that you start with a trend indicator. Study and experiment with various types of trend indicators to determine your preference as every trend indicator has its own characteristics. It is also important to keep records of the swings of markets especially in terms of price and time as these records will help you learn how and when a market may change trend (Figures 12.8–12.10). As the uptrend develops, continue to follow the techniques described above and in chapter ton trend indicators (Figure 12.11).

THE SIGNAL BOTTOM

After building and studying a swing chart, the analyst may notice that the swing chart has a tendency to give back some of the gains. This can be taken care of by applying a few of the exceptions to the swing chart rules.

We begin the analysis of the Weekly Euro/U.S. Dollar contract at an extremely low level (Figure 12.12). This Forex market made a major bottom at 1.1637 the week ending November 18, 2005. The date of the exact bottom was November 15, 2005. This bottom was a Signal Bottom (Figure 12.13). Following a prolonged move down in terms of price and time and after taking out the previous week's low, the market closed higher, above the opening and over 50 percent of the week's range. The follow-through rally the next

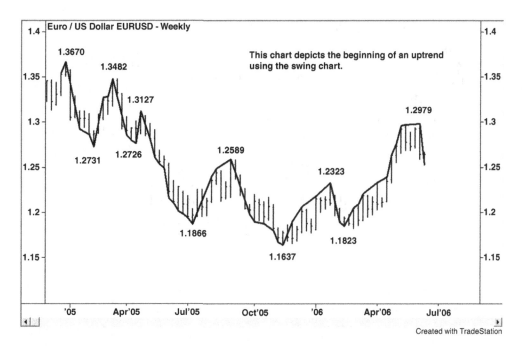

FIGURE 12.8 Weekly Euro/U.S. Dollar: Chart Depicting the Start of an Uptrend
Copyright © TradeStation.

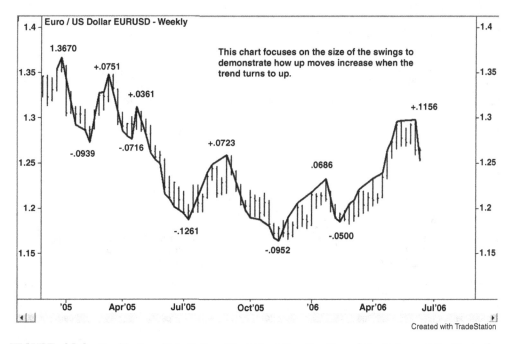

FIGURE 12.9 Weekly Euro/U.S. Dollar: Chart Depicting the Size of the Swings at the Start of an Uptrend
Copyright © TradeStation.

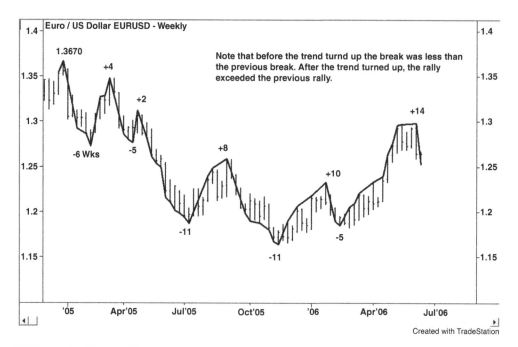

FIGURE 12.10 Weekly Euro/U.S. Dollar: Chart Depicting How Time Influences the Start of an Uptrend
Copyright © TradeStation.

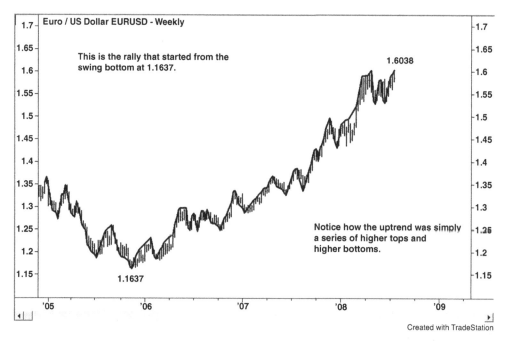

FIGURE 12.11 Weekly Euro/U.S. Dollar Chart
Copyright © TradeStation.

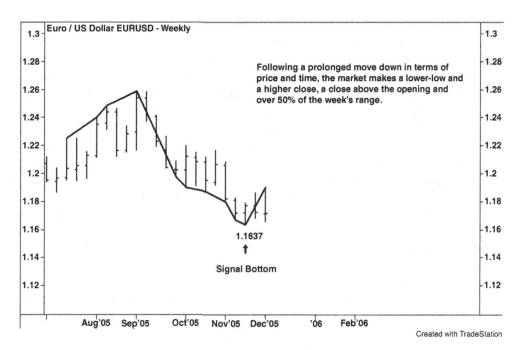

FIGURE 12.12 Weekly Euro/U.S. Dollar Chart: The Signal Bottom Formation. The market is in a prolonged down trend in terms of price and time.
Copyright © TradeStation.

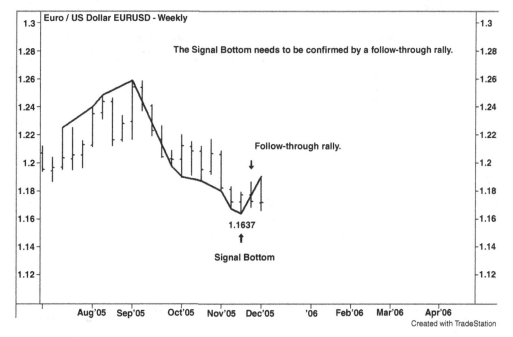

FIGURE 12.13 Weekly Euro/U.S. Dollar Chart: The Signal Bottom. The market needs to follow-through to the upside to confirm the Signal Bottom.
Copyright © TradeStation.

week confirmed the reversal bottom at 1.1637, however, the intermediate trend remained down as the market had not crossed a swing top.

Following this Signal Bottom, two courses of action were possible. First, traders who were short this market could have moved their stop down from above the last swing top at 1.2589 to lock in profits. This is because the Signal Bottom is an exception to the Trend Indicator Stop Rule. Those trading the pure trend indicator would have left their stops over the last swing top at 1.2589. Following a prolonged move down in price and time, the trader has to make a critical decision when the market posts a Signal Bottom. Moving a buy stop down to lock in profits means the trader may have to sell again at a lower price if he is stopped out and the downtrend resumes. Leaving the stop above the swing top may lead to the trader giving back much of his gains if the Signal Bottom turns the market higher eventually to a point where the trend changes to up. Discipline is the key in the decision process. If the trader has the discipline to re-enter the short-side after getting stopped out, then he should move the stop down to above the high of the Signal Bottom day (Figure 12.14).

The second course of action is designed for aggressive countertrend traders. This type of trader is willing to take the long side of the market in the hope of catching a bottom and the start of a possible change in trend. When attempting to enter the market, the trader simply places a buy stop above the high of the Signal Bottom day and enters the long side on the confirmation of the Signal Bottom with a protective stop under the

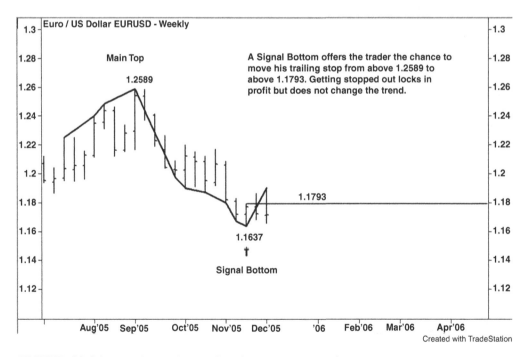

FIGURE 12.14 Weekly Euro/U.S. Dollar Chart: Proper Stop Placement
Copyright © TradeStation.

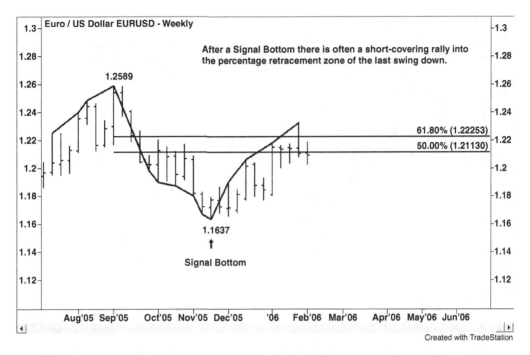

FIGURE 12.15 Weekly Euro/U.S. Dollar. After confirming the Signal Bottom the market may thrust higher into a resistance zone.
Copyright © TradeStation.

bottom. In order to have confidence when trading against the trend, the trader should know something about the size and duration of the market's swings. This can only come from study and experimentation.

Once the decision is made to trade against the trend, the trader should be aware that the market may thrust higher and run into resistance at a retracement point or a downtrending Gann angle. Another situation that is likely is the retracement of the first leg up and the test of the Signal Bottom. Many times after a successful test of the Signal Bottom, new buyers enter the market and a rally ensues that eventually changes the trend to up (Figure 12.15).

THE SIGNAL BOTTOM: THE FIRST LEG UP

One of the most commonly traded patterns is the Signal Bottom. While some traders use it to lock in profits on a swing chart, others use it as a countertrend entry signal. Sometimes after this signal is generated the market runs into resistance and resumes the downtrend (Figure 12.16). At other times the market completes the first leg up, reacts to resistance, and then starts a new leg up (Figure 12.17). The new leg up usually starts at a retracement point or a Gann angle or a combination of the two. The bottom that is

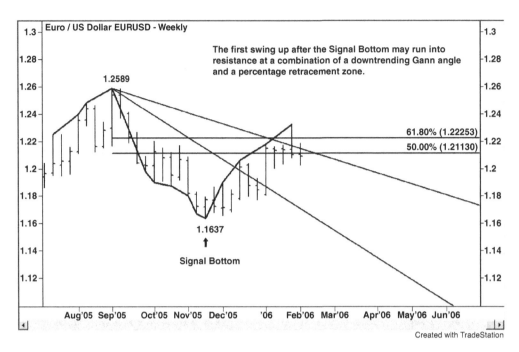

FIGURE 12.16 Weekly Euro/U.S. Dollar. The first leg up from a signal bottom often runs into resistance.
Copyright © TradeStation.

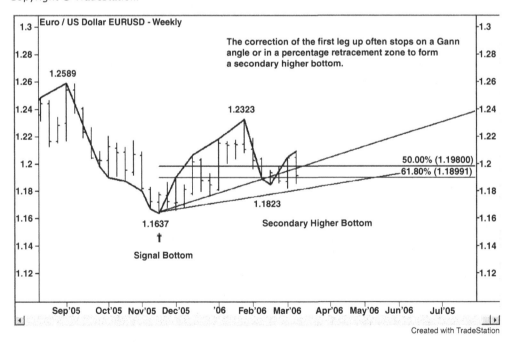

FIGURE 12.17 Weekly Euro/U.S. Dollar: The Secondary Higher Bottom
Copyright © TradeStation.

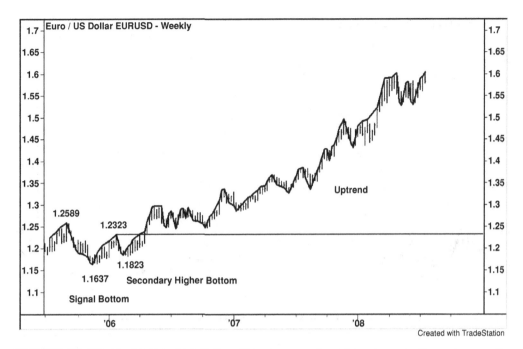

FIGURE 12.18 Weekly Euro/U.S. Dollar. After the secondary higher bottom, the trader uses the trend indicator to follow the swings.
Copyright © TradeStation.

formed after the correction is called a secondary higher bottom. The formation of this bottom is usually the first indication of an impending rally and often leads to the taking out of a previous swing top to turn the trend up.

After the formation of the secondary higher bottom, the trader should pick up the trend indicator chart and follow the swings of the market (Figure 12.18). In summary, the Signal Bottom can be used to lock in profits before the trend turns up or as an aggressive way to enter the market looking for a countertrend move. The key is to study and experiment with this type of entry and exit. Learn to determine the best price and time indicators to validate the signal as entering and exiting the market too often can lead to excessive losses.

GANN ANGLES

Another way to analyze the Weekly Euro/U.S. Dollar market is to use Gann angles. Gann angles will help the analyst find support and resistance as well as determine the strength of the trend.

The analysis of the Weekly Euro/U.S. Dollar chart begins by drawing Gann angles from a swing bottom. Rather than show Gann angles from every swing bottom, in order to keep the charts clear, Gann angles will be drawn from the intermediate bottom from

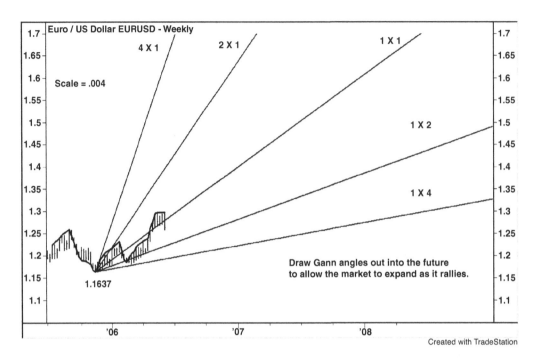

FIGURE 12.19 Weekly Euro/U.S. Dollar. Draw uptrending Gann angles from the intermediate main bottom at 1.1637 using a scale of .004.
Copyright © TradeStation.

1.1637 the week ending November 15, 2005, and from any every other relevant intermediate bottom. The scale for the Weekly Euro/U.S. Dollar chart is .004 (Figure 12.19). It is important to draw the angles out into the future and let the market find them instead of adding to them as the market trades. This way you will know ahead of time where the angles are (Figure 12.20).

In addition to showing support from a main bottom, Gann angles can also be used to determine a change in the trend. For example, during a prolonged move down when the market is making lower tops and lower bottoms, the market is usually following a Gann angle down. As the market starts to develop signs of a bottom on the trend indicator chart, it also begins to signal strength by breaking through or crossing over a downtrending Gann angle. This signal is not strong enough on its own to trigger a change in trend and should be used with other trend indicators to signal strength (Figure 12.21). After the market made the bottom at 1.1637 it rallied to overtake a downtrending Gann angle the week ending December 16, 2005.

As the rally develops, traders should keep track of penetrations or lost motion moves through the uptrending angle. This helps in the placement of stops. Throughout the rally from November 15, 2005, to September 1, 2007, the market had four lost motion trades. After penetrating the uptrending angle, the market regained the angle, and the trend resumed (Figure 12.22).

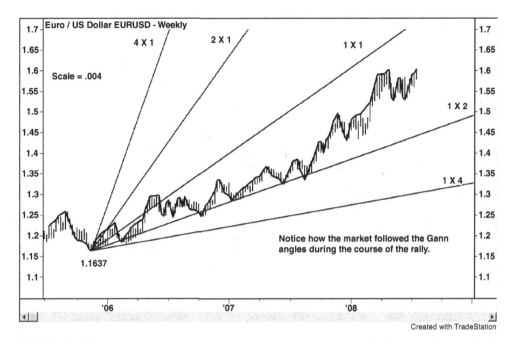

FIGURE 12.20 Weekly Euro/U.S. Dollar. Draw the angles out into the future as far as possible to allow the market to find them.
Copyright © TradeStation.

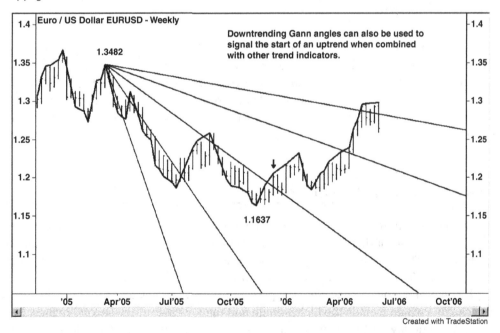

FIGURE 12.21 Weekly Euro/U.S. Dollar. Penetration of downtrending angle may indicate a change in trend.
Copyright © TradeStation.

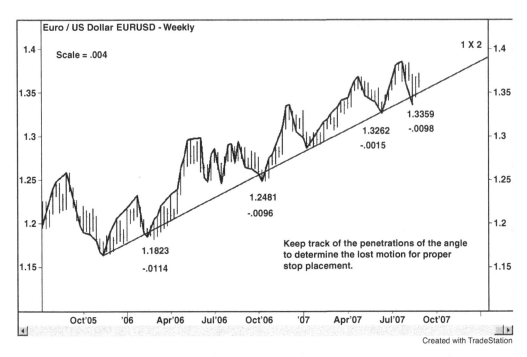

FIGURE 12.22 Weekly Euro/U.S. Dollar. Calculation of lost motion through an uptrending Gann angle.
Copyright © TradeStation.

The key to working with the Gann angles is to place them on the chart as soon as a swing bottom is formed and then draw them out into the future. This allows the trader to know ahead of time where the support or resistance may be formed. In addition the angles forecast where a market could trade on a particular date. Working with the trend indicator chart, the easiest strategy to follow is to trade in the direction of the trend and use the Gann angles for entry.

PERCENTAGE RETRACEMENT ZONES

Every time the market forms a top or bottom, Gann angles should be placed on the chart and every time the market forms a range, percentage retracement price should be placed on the chart. The most important percentage prices are the 50 percent price and the 61.8 percent price. These two prices form a support or resistance zone.

If you prefer, you can calculate the percentage retracement zones for only the major ranges. This would include the highest-high and the lowest-low, the second-highest high and the second-lowest low, and the third-highest high and the third-highest low.

The first major range on the Weekly Euro/U.S. Dollar chart is the December 2004 top at 1.3670 to the November 2005 bottom at 1.1637. This range creates a 50 percent and

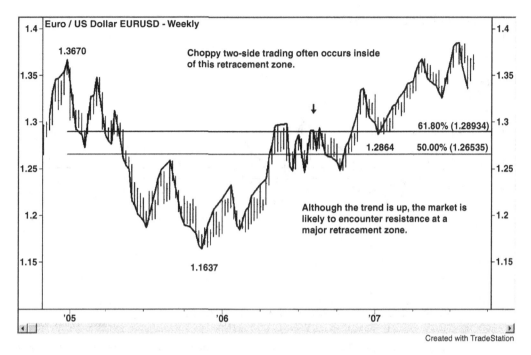

FIGURE 12.23 Weekly Euro/U.S. Dollar. At a minimum calculate the percentage retracement zone of the major range.
Copyright © TradeStation.

61.8 percent retracement zone at 1.2654 to 1.2893. Between the week ending May 5, 2006 and the week ending November 10, 2006, the market traded for several weeks on both sides of this zone. This choppy trading action represented the battle between the longs and the shorts. Typically the market will trade this way inside of major retracement zones. Therefore starting a swing chart at or inside of this zone often results in whipsaw-like trading. It is often better for the market to clear out of this zone before attempting to trade it (Figure 12.23).

In addition to maintaining the major retracement zone, an active trader may want to calculate the percentage retracement zones of each swing range. The trader can then try to buy pullbacks into the zone when the trend is up and sell rallies when the trend is down. Throughout the rally in the Weekly Euro/U.S. Dollar, the market made several moves into retracement zones that turned into intermediate bottoms (Figure 12.24 and Figure 12.25).

It is very important that you define yourself as a trader. In other words, define yourself as a trend or countertrend trader, find out if you are the type of trader who likes to buy strength and sell weakness, or one who prefers to buy dips or sell rallies. A percentage retracement trader is usually a trader who prefers to buy the breaks in the direction of the main trend. In order to take advantage of the percentage retracement trade, it is important to know the trend and define the range.

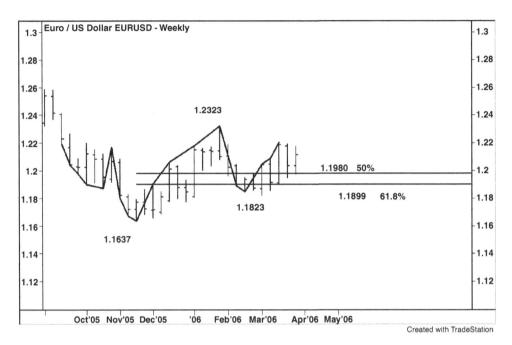

FIGURE 12.24 Weekly Euro/U.S. Dollar. Active traders should calculate the retracement zone of every swing range.
Copyright © TradeStation.

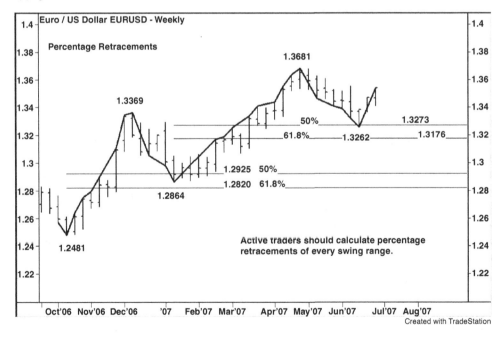

FIGURE 12.25 Weekly Euro/U.S. Dollar. Trend traders should use the percentage retracement zones to buy or sell according to the trend.
Copyright © TradeStation.

The next section looks at how the percentage retracement zones and the uptrending Gann angle offered several opportunities to trade the trend without buying strength. These two price indicators created value zones that encouraged buying. Earlier it was stated that one can buy on the Gann angle and in the retracement zones. This technique combines the two into one buy signal.

PERCENTAGE RETRACEMENT ZONES AND GANN ANGLE COMBINATIONS

Earlier in the book it was stated that Gann thought markets moved in horizontal, diagonal, and vertical lines. In this section we analyze the Weekly Euro/U.S. Dollar pair in terms of the horizontal and diagonal—in other words, the combination of percentage retracement zones and Gann angles.

The logic behind using these two price tools is that often a percentage retracement stops the market or a Gann angle stops the market. Therefore the two of them combined may form a stronger support or resistance area.

The first area of interest is the swing from the 1.1637 bottom to the 1.2323 top. This range creates a retracement zone of 1.1980 to 1.1899. The trader wants to identify when the Gann angle will travel through this zone to set up a possible countertrend buy. In Chapter 9 an equation showed how to calculate the date an angle will cross a certain price. In this example, the uptrending 1 × 2 Gann angle crosses 1.1899 the week ending February 17, 2006, and 1.1980 the week ending March 7, 2006 (Figure 12.26).

Throughout the life of the uptrend continue to look for areas where the Gann angle crosses the percentage retracement zone. This setup allows you to buy at a price that is likely to attract interest. Remember it is not the angle that turns the market but the size of the buying in that area of interest (Figure 12.27).

Gann angles can provide support and resistance by themselves as well as determining the trend; however, when combined with horizontal retracement areas like percentage retracement zones, they can create powerful buy or sell zones. The key is keeping the Gann angles and the percentage retracements up-to-date. The next section will show how time may have had an influence on the turns in the market.

TIME INDICATORS

Without really mentioning it, time has already been introduced during the analysis of this market. In the section on the trend indicator chart, the topic of time swings was covered. Gann angles are a combination of price and time. In this section squaring price and time will be discussed as to how they apply to the Weekly Euro/U.S. Dollar market.

The first square for timing is the square of the weekly range. The first square is created by subtracting the top at 1.3670 from the week ending December 31, 2004, from the bottom at 1.1637 the week ending November 18, 2005. This creates a range of .2033

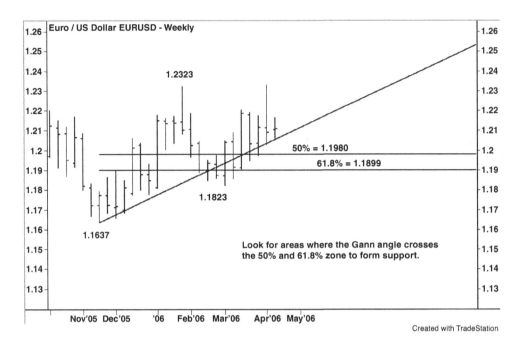

FIGURE 12.26 Weekly Euro/U.S. Dollar: Gann Angle Crossing Percentage Retracement Zone. The combination of these two price indicators can turn a market.
Copyright © TradeStation.

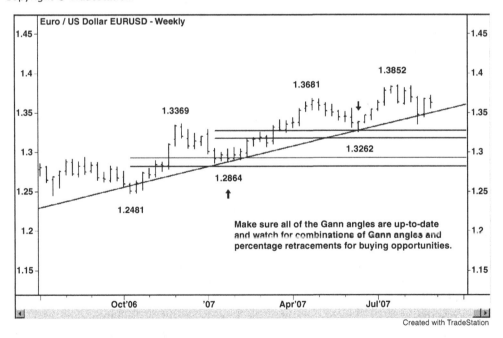

FIGURE 12.27 Weekly Euro/U.S. Dollar. During an uptrend continue to watch for areas where the uptrending Gann angle crosses the percentage retracement zone.
Copyright © TradeStation.

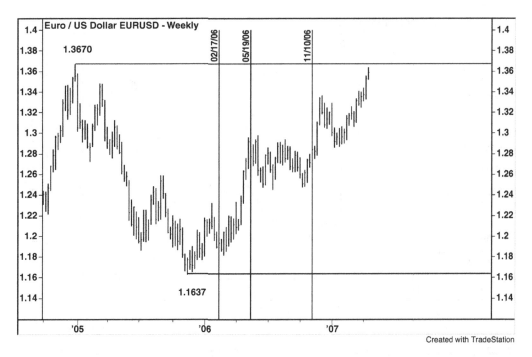

FIGURE 12.28 Weekly Euro/U.S. Dollar: Square of the Range
Copyright © TradeStation.

(Figure 12.28). This square suggested possible changes in trend the weeks ending February 17, 2006, May 19, 2006, and November 10, 2006. This square remained valid until the market traded through the top in April 2007.

The square to create for timing is the Square of the Low. The low price is the main bottom on November 15, 2005, at 1.1637. This low squares time the week ending July 28, 2006, the week ending April 13, 2007, and the week ending August 29, 2008. All came close to short-term tops, but nothing produced a change in the trend (Figure 12.29). The August 29, 2008, date came after the weekly trend had turned down on the swing chart and at the same time the market accelerated through uptrending Gann angle support (Figure 12.30).

THE FORECAST

Looking at the Weekly Euro/U.S. Dollar chart one can see that since the main top was made in July 2008 at 1.6038 the market has felt selling pressure. The swing chart turned down on the weekly chart the week ending August 8, 2008. The major uptrending angle from the 1.1637 bottom was also broken, which gave further indication that the main trend had turned down.

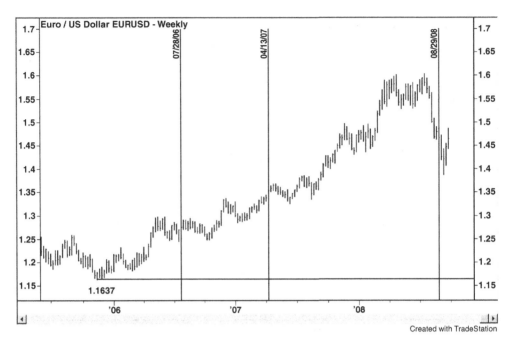

FIGURE 12.29 Weekly Euro/U.S. Dollar: Square of the Low
Copyright © TradeStation.

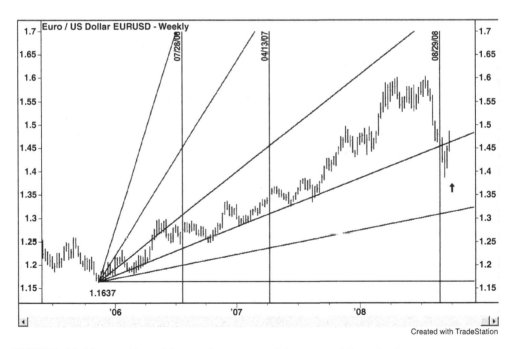

FIGURE 12.30 Weekly Euro/U.S. Dollar: Square of the Low and Gann Angles
Copyright © TradeStation.

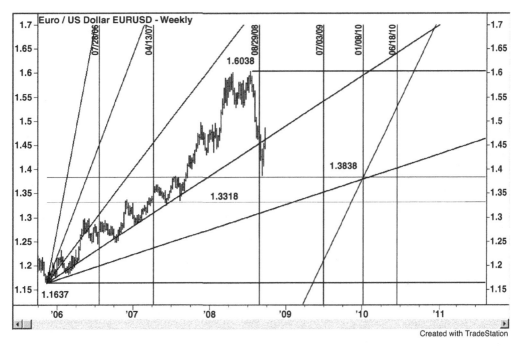

FIGURE 12.31 Weekly Euro/U.S. Dollar Forecast
Copyright © TradeStation.

As of September 2008, the trend was still down; however, the market was finding support at 50 percent of the 1.1637 to 1.6038 range at 1.3838. Trading action indicates the start of a possible short-covering rally, which should trigger a retracement of the first break from the top. Based on the range of 1.6038 to 1.3881, look for a minimum retracement to 1.4960 to 1.5214. If the forecasted rally stops at 1.4960 to 1.5214, then look for another break to 1.3057 to 1.2803.

The key date to watch in the future is the week ending January 8, 2010, when price and time form a major cluster at approximately 1.3838 (Figure 12.31).

CONCLUSION

As you can see from this analysis, as an analyst or trader you do not need to have fancy equations or oscillators. You can see that it is still possible to analyze a market using simple open, high, low, and close data. Once you understand the basic tools you need to analyze a market then the rest is up to study and experimentation. Remember the markets move diagonally, horizontally, and vertically. Learn how to use the tools to determine when these three factors converge. Always know the trend and keep looking for price and time balancing points to help you improve your analysis and trading.

About the Author

James A. Hyerczyk is a registered Commodity Trading Advisor (CTA) with the National Futures Association located in Palos Park, Illinois. Mr. Hyerczyk has been actively involved in the futures markets since 1982. He has worked in various capacities within the futures industry from technical analyst to commodity trading advisor.

Using W. D. Gann Theory as his core methodology, Mr. Hyerczyk incorporates combinations of pattern, price, and time to develop his daily, weekly, and monthly analysis. His firm, J.A.H. Research and Trading publishes a daily, weekly, and monthly advisory service on the Futures, Forex, ETF, and Equities markets. Information on his newsletter as well as the TradeStation code used in this book is available at www.patternpricetime.com. He also manages an educational, research, and consulting service.

Mr. Hyerczyk has provided technical analysis for The Hightower Report, eSignal, FuturesSource, CQG, and numerous financial market web sites including ForexHound.com, FuturesHound.com, Traderslog.com, and TradingMarkets.com. Mr. Hyerczyk has presented seminars for Bloomberg, Reuters, and *Futures Magazine* in the United States, Malaysia, and Guatemala as well as private seminars in Budapest and Moscow. He also facilitated a technical analysis class at the Chicago Mercantile Exchange.

His published works include articles for *Futures Magazine*, *Trader's World*, *SFO Magazine*, *Forex Journal*, and *Commodity Perspectives* (Commodity Research Bureau). The first edition of *Pattern, Price & Time* (Wiley, 1998) is available in English, Russian, German, Japanese, and Chinese.

Mr. Hyerczyk is a member of the Markets Technicians Association and holds a Master's degree in Financial Markets and Trading from the Illinois Institute of Technology.

Index

A

Active angles, 38
Active degrees, 38
Analysis paralysis, 155
Angle charts, 43, 46. *See also* Gann angle charts
Angles, 29. *See also* specific types
Anniversary dates, 31–32, 210–216
Astrology. *See* Financial astrology
Average true range, 122

B

Balanced swing charts, 129–133
Balance points, 42
Bear market, 81, 159
Bottoms, 69, 87
    false, 138
    forecasting, 139, 215–219, 236
    multiples of, 149–150
    using swing charts to predict, 222
Break, prolonged, 128–129
Breakouts, 121, 132
Bull market, 80, 158, 189
Buy points, 95–97
Buy stops, 78, 97–98

C

Calendar days chart, 52, 54
Candlestick trading, 2, 141
Celestial phenomena, 203–206

Charts and charting. *See also* specific types
    basics, 45–68
    consistency in, 55
    construction, 50–56
    long-term, 51
    objective of, 80
    software programs, 56–57
    types of, 57–66
Closing, market, 140
Closing price reversal bottom, 137
Closing price reversal top, 134
Commodities, 23, 134
Continuation method, 52
Correction, 69, 72, 79, 83, 222
Countertrend trading, 136, 139, 140
Cycles, 32

D

Daily charts, 30, 48, 60, 208, 209, 220
    constructing yearly forecast using, 218–219
    and trend trading strategies, 116, 117–118
Daily intermediate trend indicator, 78, 79
Daily main trend chart, 214
Data, 55–56, 66
Day trading, 55, 148
Diagonal charts, 62
Diagonal support and resistance, 143, 198
Division of tops, 149–150
Double bottoms, 125–127, 162, 163
Double-bottom top, 138